IT IS BLISS HERE

IT IS BLISS HERE

LETTERS HOME 1939–1945

MYLES HILDYARD

BLOOMSBURY

First published 2005

Copyright © 2005 by Myles Hildyard
Introduction copyright © 2005 by Antony Beevor

The moral right of the authors has been asserted

Bloomsbury Publishing Plc, 36 Soho Square, London W1D 3QY

A CIP catalogue record for this book
is available from the British Library

ISBN 0 7475 7802 8
ISBN 13 9780747578024

1 2 3 4 5 6 7 8 9 10

Typeset by Hewer Text UK Ltd, Edinburgh
Printed by Clays Ltd, St Ives Plc

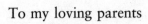

To my loving parents

Acknowledgements

My gratitude to my fellow officers in the Sherwood Rangers will be obvious from these letters. The men who meant most to me are dead.

For encouraging and helping with the publishing of this selection of my war letters I would like to thank my friend Andrew Threipland. The book would not have happened without him. At Flintham, Sue Clayton typed the enormous bundle of manuscript letters; in Scotland, Hilary Neville Towel edited the letters with skill, speed and knowledge, Caroline Smith put the result into computer-accessible form and Gill Williams, Andrew's assistant, kept finding the useful papers. Caroline Dawnay, my agent, showed faith with the project for little reward; my publisher Mike Jones of Bloomsbury showed patience and judgement. Those two professionals demonstrated the proper meaning of that word. My friends David Rowbotham and Robert Harrison at Flintham make my life here possible.

Flintham Hall, Nottinghamshire, April 2005.

Introduction by Antony Beevor

Myles Hildyard has always been an unconventional hero in my eyes. I first heard of him many years ago when staying with relatives in Nottinghamshire who were neighbours. I greatly liked what I heard about him. Nottinghamshire has never exactly been a cosmopolitan county and Myles was a true original. He was, in a way, the local equivalent of Nancy Mitford's Lord Merlin. He lived at Flintham, perhaps the most gloriously romantic Victorian house in England, and was unfazed by the rigid mores of the post-war period.

In the war, he had served in the local yeomanry regiment, the Sherwood Rangers, and won the MC. Long in advance of the decriminalisation of homosexuality in the Army, he used to bring his male partner to regimental dances. It is a striking tribute to Myles's character and popularity that this should have been accepted in those unenlightened days and not become a subject for scandal.

These wartime letters to his parents and his brother Toby constitute an unusual and frank memoir for the period. They begin just before the outbreak of war, when Myles was recruited to the Nottinghamshire (Sherwood Rangers) Yeomanry – to give it its full title – by the adjutant, Gerald Grosvenor, later the Duke of Westminster. The Sherwood Rangers, as part of the Territorial

Army, was one of the last unmechanised cavalry regiments. So Myles's letters provide an intriguing glimpse of a vanished military world, with riding masters, high-backed saddles, the clink of spurs and charging with drawn sabres at dummy opponents made out of sacks stuffed with straw.

What an unmartial nation we were in 1939! One marvels at the amateurish night exercises, largely dictated by the stabling and hospitality offered by grand houses in the area. Surprisingly little had changed in Britain's class system since the deployment of yeomanry in the troubles during the decade after Waterloo. Yet although an officer still enjoyed a life of privilege, with soldier servants and mess staff, no subaltern could really afford to be a prat. Good regiments had their own way of dealing with the arrogant and the stupid, shunting the hopeless cases away to where they could do no harm. Myles Hildyard, with his enquiring mind, was the opposite of a prat. In fact he soon proved himself to be an outstanding officer, but as a green young subaltern he realised that he too needed an air of authority so he grew a moustache in an attempt to look older to his soldiers.

This thoroughly engaging account takes us on an intriguing journey, both literal and personal. From the stables of Nottingham-shire, the regiment was shipped over to France. This was during the Phoney War, but they were not bound for Lord Gort's British Expeditionary Force on the Belgian frontier. The Sherwood Rangers were heading for Palestine to join the British cavalry division. The whole regiment, chargers and all, travelled down France by slow troop train to Marseilles. And there, the young yeomanry subalterns began their *éducation peu sentimentale* in some squalid dive, gawping in amazement at a woman having sex with a donkey.

The regiment was finally loaded on to a troopship, with the horses in improvised stabling in the hold, rather like the cavalry division on its way to the Crimea nearly a century before. And on reaching Haifa, they disembarked, having lost fewer chargers than usual during the voyage, and rode to their camp.

Myles is fascinated by all he sees and he proves an excellent observer as the squadrons on patrol wind their way over the rocky landscape of the Judaean hills. In many passages, his account is more like a delightful travel book of the Middle East than a war memoir, but that was an accurate reflection of those well-read British officers whose curiosity extended well beyond the limits of night-clubs and polo fields.

Outside of Haifa and Tel Aviv, Palestine had hardly changed since the Crusades. Yet life in camp for a young subaltern remained one of minor privilege and petty humiliation. Unlike most young cavalry officers, Myles never stopped reading and thinking. He was afraid of becoming a dilettante, but his philosophy was simple and humane. 'I believe in the happiness of individuals and the practising of simple virtues.'

He and his fellow officers were cut off from the real war of Blitzkrieg and bombing. The greatest danger seems to have been little more than a brick thrown by rioters when they were ordered to deploy in Jaffa as a form of mounted police. Not long afterwards, the regiment, along with the rest of the cavalry division, heard that they were to lose their horses. Most of the yeomanry regiments converted to tank or armoured car units, but the Sherwood Rangers were ordered to retrain as an artillery regiment. In February 1941, Myles was sent to Crete with two batteries from his regiment. They were to be coastal gunners, guarding the sea approaches to Canea and the port of Suda Bay. Life for the next couple of months was rather idyllic. It consisted of training and exploring the island, which appealed to the remains of a classical education from his idle years at Eton.

On 20 May 1941, the German invasion of Crete began. It was the first airborne invasion of a major island in history, and although the allied soldiers and officers set to the destruction of the German paratroopers with a will, their commanders in the key western sector were confused. General Freyberg, a brave but unintelligent man, had convinced himself that the real attack would come by sea. The Sherwood Rangers were ordered to keep their guns pointing out at the horizon while the battle was being lost at Maleme airfield, over to their left and just within range. Suddenly, after a week of fighting and constant air attacks during daylight, they were told that the island was to be evacuated. They were to disable their guns and march south over the White Mountains to the fishing village of Sphakia where the Royal Navy from Alexandria would attempt to evacuate as many men as possible.

This retreat, with some brave and disciplined groups mixed in among a demoralised and often shameful rabble, is famous from the pages of Evelyn Waugh's brilliant but bitter novel *Officers and Gentlemen.* Just as the retreat began, Waugh had arrived with Colonel Robert Laycock, the dashing leader of a commando brigade sent as reinforcements. It was a bitter fate to be delivered straight into the midst of a military disaster. Layforce, as it was called, was given the task of providing a rearguard for the retreat, against the harrying attacks of the German 5th Mountain Division, which had been air-landed at Maleme.

In the darkness of the night in the White Mountains, Myles suddenly heard Laycock's voice and recognised it immediately. He knew the Laycock family from Nottinghamshire, and one of Bob Laycock's brothers served with the Sherwood Rangers. There, in the Cretan wilderness, Laycock and Hildyard chatted about mutual friends in Nottinghamshire, then carried on in their different directions. Laycock bumped into Colonel Guy Salisbury-Jones, an old friend from the Household Division. After their chat, Salisbury-Jones turned to his companion, Monty Woodhouse, who later became the leading Special Operations Officer on Crete and then in Greece. 'Funny thing,' he said. 'Last time I saw him he was riding up the Mall at the head of a Sovereign's escort of the Household Cavalry.' Woodhouse agreed that it was indeed a curious thing.

Myles was to encounter Laycock again during the last hours of the evacuation on the night of 31 May. General Freyberg had issued orders that first priority was to be given to front-line units who had borne the brunt of the battle. Layforce, as the last to arrive, could embark only after all 'other fighting forces'. Not surprisingly, with thousands of soldiers packed into the ravines around Sphakia, news soon got round that this was to be the last night of the evacuation. Anyone left behind would become a prisoner of war. A cordon of troops with fixed bayonets held back the mob of stragglers. Myles and a group from the Sherwood Rangers were waved through as they had been 'fighting forces', but then he heard a voice he knew well from Eton. This officer claimed to be an embarkation officer and demanded that he too should be allowed to pass.

Myles and his men proceeded to the queues on the beach. 'We form up about 11 p.m., and with some difficulty and jostling get into our position. But unfortunately about then the rearguard begins to arrive and pass through us (Layforce – Bob just cut in).' Laycock had rounded up as many of his men as he could find and pushed in ahead of the Australians, Royal Marines and the Sherwood Rangers, despite the order that Layforce, as rearguard, was to hold the perimeter. It is most improbable that Myles and his companions were doomed to imprisonment because of this queue-barging by less than a hundred men, but the surrender on the island produced an intense and understandable bitterness among those left behind. An unnecessary defeat is probably the hardest defeat of all to stomach. And for Myles and the others left behind on the island, once the Royal Navy from Alexandria could not risk any more ships in the evacuation, their fate was indeed hard to bear. Exhausted, dehydrated and malnourished, they were forced to march north again – back across the 'via Dolorosa' of the White Mountains to improvised prison camps on the north coast.

In 1990 when I was researching my book on the battle of Crete, Myles lent me the diary he had kept. We talked a lot about the battle, especially the order to keep the guns pointing at the sea while the battle was being decided at Maleme, but there was no doubt that for Myles and others to whom I spoke that slog back up the mountain roads was the cruellest journey of their lives.

A strange coincidence also emerged from this meeting with Myles when he began to describe his escape from Crete. Myles and a great friend from the Sherwood Rangers, Michael Parish, managed to slip out of the badly guarded prison camp, and seek shelter, like many other prisoners, with Cretan families in mountain villages. Myles's portrait of the Cretans is utterly convincing, with their bravery and kindness as well as their total inability to keep a secret. Their instinctive resistance to the parachute invasion, using old guns and even kitchen knives, had outraged German commanders, who carried out punitive executions against selected villages. Myles and other prisoners had to go higher into the mountains to escape the sweeps, living in shepherd huts and suffering from dysentery.

Using bribery and persuasion, they eventually managed to get places on a boat leaving the island. Myles's cheque, drawn on the local branch of the Westminster Bank in Newark, was accepted by the boat-owner (who clearly believed that an Englishman's word was his bond). Its arrival back in Nottinghamshire via an incredibly circuitous route prompted the manager to ring Myles's parents to enquire whether it should be honoured. This telephone call provided the first indication that Myles had survived the battle of Crete. His mother fainted on hearing the news.

Myles and Michael Parish planned to hop from island to island across the Aegean to the Turkish coast. They stopped off on the small deserted island of Polyaigos. This was where the steam yacht *Kalanthe*, commandeered by the British Legation in Athens, had been sunk by Messerschmitt 110s in April during the evacuation of Greece. Most of the passengers and crew had been on dry land and witnessed the strafing and bombing in front of their eyes. The yacht had been used to evacuate senior officials and officers, including Harold Caccia, the First Secretary, as well as his family. There had also been members of the British Military Mission to Greece and Yak Force, Peter Fleming's band of semi-irregulars responsible for demolition. One of Fleming's group was Oliver Barstow, Nancy Caccia's brother. He had manned the Lewis guns when the German aircraft attacked and was killed. He went down with the vessel.

Just before Myles and Michael Parish reached the island in August, fishermen had recovered the two bodies from the wreck. Myles and Michael Parish buried the bodies, without knowing who they were. Fifty years later, it was possible to bring Myles together with the Caccias and over dinner they concluded that Myles had indeed buried Nancy Caccia's brother, Oliver Barstow.

The trans-Aegean escape continued, but on Milos Michael Parish fell from a cliff and was badly injured. Myles managed, through energetic persuasion, to persuade other boat-owners to take them on, and finally, on 3 September, the second anniversary of the outbreak of war, they reached the Turkish coast.

Myles, awarded an MC for this remarkable escape, returned to his regiment, by then preparing for the desert war. The Sherwood Rangers had now been transformed into an armoured regiment with Sherman tanks. But first of all, Myles was allowed some leave in Cairo. He soon found himself fêted for his exploit and taken up by some of the great hostesses, including Momo Marriott, the daughter of Otto Kahn. He met Princess Aly Khan and Randolph Churchill, 'who is the most unpopular man in the M[iddle] E[ast] and very unattractive'. Myles's descriptions provide a marvellous slice of Cairo's social life. He also became friends with another controversial character, Mary Newall, the leader of a volunteer ambulance detachment, who became the mistress of Sir Walter Monckton, the head of British propaganda in Cairo and the man who had drafted Edward VIII's instrument of abdication. This dramatic character, who designed her own uniform, was known as 'pistol-packing Mary Newall', because she permanently carried a large revolver in a leather holster. Myles spent some leave travelling round Syria with her and once again his letters display a voracious interest in all he saw.

In May 1942, Myles became an intelligence officer, and he proved extremely competent. The only near-blunder occurred when he located some Italian wafers in a captured bag of what looked like emergency rations. Fortunately, he asked an Italian prisoner to translate what it said on the package before he handed it over to the cookhouse. It turned out to be gelignite. On a rather more serious note, his comments on the hard battles that summer during the retreat to El Alamein and Monty's transformation of the Eighth Army are well worth reading. In a letter home, he describes Monty perfectly. 'He is a very odd little man with a terrific histrionic sense, and a great soldier.'

The Sherwood Rangers, under an excellent commanding officer, transformed themselves from brave amateurs into an effective armoured force. But like the best of cavalry regiments, individuality and even eccentricity remained protected characteristics. One of

Myles's brother officers was Keith Douglas, the outstanding poet of the desert war and probably the greatest British poet of the Second World War. Douglas, who had little interest in county life, was at first slightly exasperated to find himself in a cavalry regiment where talk in the mess tended to be about hunting and shooting. When the Battle of Alamein started, Douglas deserted his post as an instructor in camouflage, stole a lorry and drove back to his regiment to join the fighting. He should have been court-martialled, but the Sherwood Rangers approved. His book *From Alamein to Zem-Zem* is one of the great classics of warfare.

The fighting was hard, even before they reached the Mareth line, and the casualty rate for officers terrifyingly high. Douglas was one of the casualties, wounded this time, not killed. His death would come in Normandy a little over a year later. Although an outsider, both socially and temperamentally, Douglas came to admire the sacrifice of his fellow officers in the regiment. 'How then can I live among this gentle/obsolescent breed of heroes and not weep?' he wrote in his poem entitled 'Sportsmen'. Myles, when introduced to Vivien Leigh in Tunis during her morale-raising visit to the troops, was taken for a poet, so perhaps she had already heard of Douglas.

After the conquest of Sicily, and then action in Italy, the regiment was withdrawn for retraining back in Britain. Myles was put to work planning for D-Day. But he also had time to mix in rarefied literary circles, when taken up by Harold Nicolson and James Lees-Milne.

On D-Day, the Sherwood Rangers launched two squadrons of swimming tanks at Gold Beach. They fought inland and liberated Bayeux that evening. Casualties remained high. Keith Douglas was killed three days later near the village of St Pierre, and a shell struck regimental headquarters at Tilly-sur-Seulles on 11 June, killing Bob Laycock's brother and two other officers. Myles, meanwhile, enjoyed the comparative safety of 8th Armoured Brigade headquarters where he continued his work as an intelligence officer. The brigade was part of the 50th (Northumbrian) Division, and as in most periods of war, there were far more hours of inaction and waiting than of fighting. This was especially true then since Montgomery's two armies had become enmeshed in the Norman bocage, a nightmare for attackers, with sunken roads and hedges which concealed enemy anti-tank guns.

During this time, Myles fell in love with 'Jimmy', a good-looking young officer in the 11th Hussars, fighting on the same sector. It seems to have been a pretty chaste infatuation. On 15 July, he describes how he has a picnic with Jimmy just after the hugely destructive battle of Caen. 'Not sure how Jimmy would have reacted if I had tried to stage big seduction scene, but didn't anyway. Civil affairs colonel says 6,000 killed in Caen.' Their trysts seemed to consist mainly of 'slipping away' to do things like read Logan Pearsall Smith's *Trivia* together. The description of this romance, both touching and clear-sighted, is a wonderful corrective to the preposterous notion that such things never happened in the British Army. My father-in-law tells the story of the debate on the Wolfenden Report in the House of Lords. Apparently, Field Marshal Viscount Montgomery of Alamein rose to state categorically that he was quite convinced that no homosexuality had ever occurred among any of the hundreds of thousands of men under his command during the war. This statement produced a moment of astonished silence followed by suppressed snorts of disbelief and then an uproar of laughter.

Myles, like almost everyone, was carried away on the wave of optimism which followed the collapse of the German armies in France, till the rapid advance into Belgium and southern Holland was brought to a sudden halt in the autumn. It proved to be a winter of cruel disappointments, especially for the Dutch, who had almost nothing to eat. For British officers, however, their thoughts were turning to the post-war world – what it would be like and what they might be fit for. In March and April, the advance into Germany accelerated dramatically, but there were still casualties, all the more terrible for coming so close to the end. Jimmy's troop in the 11th Hussars was ambushed and almost wiped out by a German assault gun the day after he handed it over to another subaltern. But life as a conqueror, even a rather junior one, had its advantages. Officers and soldiers alike were 'liberating' whatever took their fancy.

'Everybody is after loot,' Myles wrote to his brother, 'the gentry for Mercedes Benz, shotguns and drink, the chaps for anything they can lay their hands on.' Myles even finds that, when he admires a picture in a house in Brussels, the owner presents it to him. It seems typical of Myles that he managed to acquire as interpreter and cook Count Hugo von Schönborn, a contemporary artist connected to the imperial Austrian family.

Wars, as Myles found, tend to end 'not with a bang but a whimper'. The surrender of Hamburg, which Myles played a part in negotiating thanks to the linguistic services of Graf von Schönborn, was one of the last major events for the British Second Army before the surrender to Montgomery on Lüneberg Heath. With the 11th Hussars once again in the lead, the British Army entered Hamburg. The Germans could not have been more co-operative. They were terrified of Marshal Rokossovsky's armies trying to force their way through to seize Schleswig-Holstein and Denmark as well as the main Hanseatic ports.

Myles had hoped to spend VE Day 'lying in the sun and looking up into a tree', but his beloved Jimmy was in hospital with a cracked skull. Myles drove a great distance to see him. That night the British made German villagers build large bonfires with the Nazi flag on top to celebrate, and it sounded as if a new offensive had started, with every weapon and flare to hand fired off into the night sky. Not surprisingly, amid such drunken revelry, a few farms burned to the ground and prize hangovers were suffered. But no war produces happiness, even for the victors. Myles found his love for Jimmy was very one-sided. And the hedonism of Berlin, where he went to visit his friends in the 11th Hussars, proved distinctly ersatz.

'The position seems to be,' he writes, 'that no one meets any Germans but prostitutes and black marketeers.' Allied troops could make small fortunes bartering food and cigarettes for Leica cameras, money or jewellery. But most of Myles's young officer friends longed to return home and get married. It was not a case of 'bugles calling from sad shires', but hunting horns evoking the Englishness of the chase and the hunt ball.

For Myles, of course, the return home and future friendships

10

were unlikely to be so simple. 'What is true for most people is not true for me,' he remarks in a letter to his brother, without a trace of arrogance or self-pity as he analyses his feelings about other people. 'The trouble for me is that I react so seldom and that I am spoilt and want so much from people. Consequently I am always in danger of being lonely and bored. Which is why I love Flintham, where I am happy alone.' Then he adds with an ironic after-thought: 'But I am sure the only answer is to get married.' It is this honesty and perspicacity that make Myles Hildyard such a prodigiously interesting person and this collection of letters such a pleasure to read.

Foreword

My original idea was to choose extracts from the letters of all three brothers to our parents. Toby and I were much of an age; he joined the RAF. John was six years younger and at home most of the time, till he joined the navy. Many of Toby's letters home were lost en route; he told me he wrote twice a week. I stored most of my early letters from my parents in Cairo, never returned there after Alamein and they were lost. The letters I received from them between November 1940 and April 1941 were lost after the Battle of Crete. Toby and I wrote to one another throughout the war and we both sent these letters on to Flintham. John's were few but his news about Flintham was all important to me. Our letters found their way into a chest of drawers in the attics and I rescued them very late in my life. I owe my parents a considerable debt for keeping them.

I have kept the selection almost entirely to my own letters, using short excerpts from others only occasionally. A good deal of my incessant thinking about Flintham has been removed, as well as references to friends and family, acknowledgements of letters and parcels I'd received, and many other domestic details. Indeed, more text has been omitted than remains. At certain times, such as my escape from Crete and the invasion of France, I have supplemented my necessarily spasmodic letters with condensed extracts from my diary. The Cretan diary was originally one continuous piece of writing; I have added dates in this version to make the chronology of our escape more transparent. Other small amendments – such as the addition of italics, and the consistent styling of dates, addresses and titles – have been made for reasons of clarity. My only intention here is to give a flavour of the war as I experienced it. To that end, this selection is as accurate as I could wish.

Naturally, I minimised the dangers and discomforts of war in my letters to loved ones. I was not too interested in war, but it will be obvious that I enjoyed myself. I lived a more interesting and social life than before or afterwards. In my war there were few responsibilities, good friends, some very great friends, little need for money, interesting surroundings, sunshine, the sea.

I was indeed lucky in the autumn of 1938 when I told Gerald Grosvenor at a party I would join up. When I told my parents and they asked what I had joined, I didn't know. It turned out I had joined the local Yeomanry, the Sherwood Rangers, one of the few remaining cavalry regiments. I don't care much for horses but it was a brilliant choice, and in 1939 I was glad enough to escape taking my Bar finals.

I started the war in A Squadron in Newark, sleeping in the Ram Hotel. The troopers slept in Hole's Brewery. We mobilised before war was declared and the very first night there was a false alarm, all over England I think. We had to get the men up and we marched them out of the town and back again. Patrick McCraith tells me he was in Mansfield with B Squadron and on Sunday 3 September the Vicar of Mansfield, Hughes, who was also Regimental Padre, was handed a message in the pulpit in a very full church, all B Squadron and their wives. He stopped his sermon to read it and then said, 'War has been declared. I am afraid it will be a long war and a lot of you won't come home.' Many of the wives wept.

I had a car and used to drive home at night without getting permission; there was strict blackout and only side lights were permitted. Eventually I was hauled up and ticked off by the Adjutant, Gerald Grosvenor (later Duke of Westminster), the man who collared me at this party, and of whom I stood in great awe. Regimental Headquarters were in Newark. I don't remember if we had a mess, and it is too late now to ask my fellow officers, all dead I think.

Miles Hildyard

September 1939, Brookside, Welham Road, Norton, Malton

I am billeted alone in a sort of bungalow villa on the edge of the town and couldn't be luckier – a ground-floor bedroom with a low window and sofa in it, looking out on to a lawn with a rock pool, Chinese bridge and artful well head, a bathroom and a charming Mrs B who gives me a very good breakfast and if I refuse a cup of tea, brings it along.

My men are about a mile further out and in a loft. I think even they were a little shaken when they first saw it. Considering how long we were at Newark one might have expected a little more preparation, but we've spent all our time so far making the most elementary improvements, and still there's nowhere to wash. Luckily it's been a fine day and so everyone is cheerful. They are in a racing stable which has produced twenty-something St Leger winners, a very odd place partly in a stone pit, all wonderfully dilapidated.

We have a few horses arriving tomorrow but mostly not till Friday, so we shall have time to get ready. Once they come the men will have very little spare time. It's marvellous how quickly 60 men can do things. I managed to steal all the regimental spades and barrows and we dug out a big yard covered in grass down to its old stone bottom in two hours.

I shall have to buy a bicycle – there are none left to hire. The Squadrons are so far apart that I haven't seen Michael [Parish], but I don't think he's here anyway. But Billy [Brooksbank] and Oswald [Normanby] must be around somewhere.

30 September 1939, Settrington House, Yorkshire

So far my removal here [to B Squadron] hasn't turned out half badly. Settrington is about four miles outside Malton, a little village of a few houses along a stream. I am in the Rectory, the rest of the officers are in the House, a big square stone place which belonged to Lord Middleton till this year when it was bought by some people called Storey who have done a great deal to it. All I've seen is very ritzy, very big bedrooms, but I imagine not many as the officers have to share. The Rectory is almost as large, and has in it one troop of soldiers and a lot of evacuees and school mistresses beside myself! The Rector's name is Burnett, and they were at Belton before. I don't see anything of them except for Mrs Burnett who appears now and again to say how dreadfully uncomfortable I must be, which I am not in the least. She is very concerned, too, about the feeding of the troops and wants to open a canteen of her own. She has daughters but I can't distinguish between them and the school mistresses, which is difficult because some girls are always inviting the troops in and being rather a nuisance and I don't like to tick them off in case they are my host's family.

I have a new servant on trial [Yates], quite old and uninteresting but apparently the only clean man in my troop. The troops are almost all miners, from Welbeck and that way, cheerful and quite different to A Squadron who were farmers and townspeople. They sing very well, mostly hymns. When I was with A Squadron our first lot of horses arrived and my troops got a pretty rotten lot. We went out on our horses this morning for the first time. A lot more arrive tomorrow and I hope the Bournes' will find their way here, as I told Angela to label them as my chargers. We had several bad-looking

18

falls this morning but luckily they did no harm. I suspect we shall be put through it riding.

[Flash] Kellett isn't such a dragon really, he has a ferocious manner and is very strict, but off parade he's quite pleasant and there's nothing he hasn't done and no place he's not been to. I shall certainly learn much more than I would have in A Squadron because we have a tutorial every day and I have an hour with the Squadron Sergeant Major as well, while Reggie Bush never told us anything. No idea yet what use is going to be made of us. There are an enormous lot of troops here (we are repeatedly warned to give away no information if we value our skins). Kellett thinks we should go to Greece.

When I was with A Squadron we got our first lot of horses, which were Mr Argles' collection and my troops got a pretty rotten lot. Today there arrived Shephard of Elston's consignment, and everybody is raging about them and turning most of them out. I got the Bournes' two, of which one is tiresome and anyway probably wouldn't carry me, the other, a black one, will I think do me very well. I didn't enjoy myself at all riding without stirrups.

6 October 1939, Settrington

We had a night scheme yesterday, and I had the right-hand outpost flank. We never saw any enemy but we held two crossroads and held up everybody who came along. It was pitch dark and they thought it was the end. Today we had a lecture, very boring, to all the Brigade officers, from regiments, and I and Patrick McCraith alone went on horses, pirouetting through the greasy streets of Malton with our servants behind us. I'm the hell of a horseman. Yesterday I was practising turning a horse and dug my spurs into it which are 'regimental', specially bought in London, with great rowels on them. It stood up on end, I came off, and it flew away. This is no unusual occurrence, but this horse never halted again, it leapt a fence on a bank above the road and came down on its nose with my sword all over the street.

Before the Bournes' horse arrived I was always being put on to the most awful horses which other people couldn't control, and now the Bournes' horse has gone lame, but I've got plenty of horses in my troop to choose from. The last lot came from Ipswich way and were much better, though I had one which sat down and rolled madly when you got on and another you couldn't get near its head. Major Kellett took photographs of Shephard's lot to the War Office and made a row, which I should think will be passed on.

I think my men are complete sods and my NCOs useless and I'll be glad if they are all sent home. I never saw such a lot and regret my old troop very much. Apparently it's the worst troop, and it's No. 1 troop, so on parades I have to do everything in front with nobody to copy. C Squadron is thought the best squadron, but I think it's because they're very well drilled. Left to think for themselves they certainly couldn't do a thing. I'm very jealous of Patrick McCraith who has been very gloomy and done all the things I feel like, falling asleep after lunch and complaining a lot, so Kellett has sent him home for a fortnight!

I'm so glad Toby is in the War Office. Certainly we shan't be here so short a time as the threatened six weeks. My moustache is coming along nicely but I don't think it's very pretty. However it's part of my scheme of frightfulness towards my troop.

Michael Parish is just back but I've had no chance of getting hold of him. I'm really enjoying myself, I hope you're trying not to worry. I still think we shall probably all be ruined so don't economise too much on the new farm house – of which I'd love some news. [The old one had been pulled down by the RAF on the requisitioned land.]

I hear meat ration is to be 1s 6d a week and think you'd better keep a few secret calves to fatten in the icehouse. One can't help assuring oneself that the war can't go on very long. I must say I'm getting a bit sick of it, though really we should only be thankful we're not in a trench. I bet this is as muddy though as anywhere.

24 October 1939, Settrington

We have been doing cadre classes for officers twice a week which I rather hate, mainly because we go to C Squadron's training ground and they provide the horses, which are always the ones they hate too much to take out themselves in the morning. Today we did sticking our swords into sacks. I have made up my mind never to stick it into anything more interesting. The last course we had, I strained my back pulling at a woolly bear with a mouth like iron, doing a charge with drawn swords. I never could ride properly with one hand and I was always covertly trying to collect my reins with my sword hand. However, my back seemed to turn more into ordinary lumbago and I've started a new cure for it, which is sprinkling sulphur in my socks. I got this from an old farmer Michael Parish took me to see last Sunday. His wife is some relation of Michael's, and they've lived in this farm 300 years.

On Friday we went out on a scheme, riding to Wykeham Abbey, where we arrived and fed the horses in the dark. The men slept by their horses. We on the contrary had dinner with Lord Downe and his American wife and slept in comparative luxury above the stables, having turned down Lord D's bedrooms. I had to get up at 5 a.m. and water and feed the horses again in the dark. The scheme initially was Kellett's to see how the 'administration' – food etc., worked, but it was of course adopted by the Regiment and we were supposed to fight the other two squadrons on our way back. This was a pretty good flop as most of our men got lost and had no idea there even was an enemy. Michael also charged a section of mine and almost killed one man. Yesterday we jumped without reins or stirrups and it wasn't at all difficult or didn't seem to be. I went out alone in the afternoon and jumped a ditch and soon after noticed I was covered in blood, so I felt myself all over and eventually I traced it to my horse's nose bleeding!

5 November 1939, Settrington

I wonder if you are having a Guy Fawkes? I hope so. Particularly as I left John a large box of old papers to burn.

We have a charming day before us tomorrow. Before breakfast while it is still dark we exercise the horses. Then we clean and load up. We lead the horses into Malton in time for a train leaving at midnight, with all the joys of boxing horses in the dark. We arrive next morning about 5 a.m., still in the dark, disentrain and walk to our new billets. We were going to a village called Riby. Head-quarters of the Regiment is at Brocklesby Park and the rest of the Brigade is cursing the Colonel [Lord Yarborough] who they think has manoeuvred the whole thing. Brocklesby Park, Habrough, Lincs will be my address till you hear another. Apparently there is no electric light in that part of Lincolnshire, it certainly doesn't sound madly comfortable, but I've no idea yet which troop goes where.

I'm sorry to leave here in a way, because it's very pretty country and I know people around, but any change breaks the monotony of it. How long we are likely to stay at Riby no one has the least idea. C Squadron, with Michael Parish, is far worse off than we. They haven't yet found billets for officers, I'm afraid they may be miles from us. Anyway, look up Brocklesby on the map, it may be within 100 miles of Retford or Doncaster! [My father's courts; he was a judge.]

9 November 1939, Riby Grange, Grimsby

In the end we marched out at 2 a.m. on Tuesday morning and walked the horses into Malton. Luckily it was a fine night. Boxing horses is a pretty awful game and not improved by a blackout. We arrived at Brocklesby at lunch-time and unpacked the horse train which was waiting and rode the horses out to our new quarters, riding on their blankets, which is torture, as they slip and bareback is bad enough.

My troop and another is in the stables of Riby Hall, some miles from Brocklesby. Riby Hall was the Pretymans', they sold ten years ago and the house was pulled down, so it is like Clumber [former seat of the Dukes of Newcastle in North Notts], a great heap of brick and plaster. There is a wonderful lime avenue leading to it and a fine park, though all the oak has been cut. Behind the site of the hall surrounded by fir trees are the stables and a few offices, which were being used as a pig farm. We had to get the horses under cover before dark, and I put five in the laundry!

There is no electric light in these parts; they have acetylene which is very dangerous. If you turn it off too far it comes on again, or the engine doesn't work properly and it goes right out and then comes on again! I am putting shower baths in my laundry, which looks as if they expect us to stay, for the army is surprisingly mean. The more I'm away from the militia the better I'm pleased, and I like it very much here. But they talk of a division of cavalry going to Palestine, and ours is the only division.

16 January 1940, Marseilles, France

A note to tell you I'm well and I'll write again. We had a good crossing in the sunshine, with a destroyer ploughing ahead and planes above. I slept part of the time. It got dark soon after we arrived, and unloading off the ship and on to the train about a mile away was not made easier by an air raid alarm which put all the lights out. We arrived at our destination Sunday night but stayed in the train till Monday morning which was beautifully warm and sunny, after very cold days all the time. The train ran along by the road but we saw the Palace of the Popes across it in the sun.

Our final destination is some dozen miles from Marseilles in a chateau built about 50 years ago, with quite 49 years' dilapidations behind it. The room next to mine is unsafe. The food is unbeliev-able. We sleep ten in a bedroom. None of the doors shut. There is one bathroom, used also by Indians and Frenchmen, but the water is generally cut off. However the thing is to go in and bathe luxuriously at a hotel and dine in the town. Everything is fortunately very cheap and though it means getting a taxi from a village three miles away, which isn't easy as all taxis distrust us very much on account of past contestations, our taxi yesterday, which waited for us all evening, came to only 12/-. [We went to some sort of 'exhibition' where a woman had sex with a donkey. I was shocked by Sidney Morse going up on stage to have a closer look.]

The chateau is on a slope looking across to a long range of very big mountains not at all far away. It is backed by woods and in front of it is a terrace falling about 50 feet sheer white stone and creepers to a dry semi-circular pool surrounded by a hedge of pollarded plane trees with a central avenue towards the mountains.

The first night after we crossed we got off after dinner and got up at three to water. The next night everything looked better. But at about nine my black Kate and a friend in the same carriage decided to lie down. Kellett and about a dozen men were with her when they all started the hell of a shindig, kicked out the light, Kellett and most of the men. When this quieted and we were hanging on outside panting, we were horrified to see another old ride of mine calmly walk out of the door of the next carriage which had been deserted by its guards. We weren't at a platform, and the silly animal just dropped and hung over the side. When it was cut down it fell on a gas jet, scrambled to its feet, missed a goods train just coming in and made off. It was caught, none the worse, and had to be led a mile along the rails to a goods siding while the train was shunted.

About midnight we got to bed. At one o'clock a man managed to stop the train by waving a torch with a red handkerchief and reported a horse with colic. It was suffering agonies and of course couldn't be walked around. Patrick sat on its head for two hours till we reached a town, when it died. I think travelling in the boxes must have been the nearest thing to hell imaginable – there wasn't a lamp to each carriage and anyway all the paraffin ran out after the first night and to sit on a heap of straw with four plunging animals on each side of you in an endlessly long swinging train must have been even worse than being in a truck of 50 hommes, 8 chevaux, where the beer we gave them actually froze.

24

20 January 1940, Marseilles

I can't describe what it's like here with a wind like a saw coming straight off the Alps. We have been bitterly undeceived after our first day, it has never since been really warm. We get up at six o'clock which annoys us as no other squadron in the Brigade gets up before nine – the joke being that we are all the same invariably finished later than any one else. We work fairly solidly till 1.30. After that there is nothing much but stables about four o'clock. But stables are no joy when every single pipe is frozen or burst and we have to walk the horses in search of a trickle and provide the cookhouse by a chain of dirty horse buckets down a hill. The food has improved just a little, it is still bad. The chateau is still frigid, but I moved into a bedroom vacated by some Indian officers, with lots of sun and a huge fire all day, and only three of us in it. I can't sit and write or read because there is only one stable lantern per room, and they only give us 'supper' in the evening, which effectively empties the place.

We have now exhausted all the amusement places of Marseilles and are quite willing to leave, in the hope of finding it warmer further south. About half the officers and men are voiceless, we all cough, the hospital only takes men with high temperatures, the hotel is full of sick officers. But *everyone* is being put on the boat. The convoy officers – Australians – say it has been very rough.

30 January 1940, Haifa, Palestine

It was very rough the first day out of Marseilles. We were a convoy of six liners, some of them built as troop ships, and I think three had horses on them. Ours was commanded by Yarborough and was quite a good Bibby Line boat, though meant for Indians, with no hot water. The horses walked in 11 miles and up ramps into the ship, whose holds were all baled off for them. So tight they couldn't fall down, and three holds deep. The bottom holds, and I had one to look after, were very smelly and hot at moments.

25

We had quite good cabins and I shared one with Michael. With it being rough and smelly I felt really ill. Flash Kellett was in command on another boat with three funnels and he had 15 horses die the first night, though none of our regiment. We only lost two altogether.

The next day, and till we arrived here, was calm and sunny but I lay on my bed and only got up to go to the horses, and the other day I didn't get up at all. There's a sort of flu cum laryngitis which everyone caught at Marseilles and I got a mild form of that. The Colonel had it on the boat too and the doctor, and I was looked after by the black ship's doctor. All the deck hands and stewards were black sort of Malayans and used to burst into one's room at all hours without knocking, looking like unemployed miners, very dirty with turned up coat collars. It made me frantic and I frightened our steward till he would only come at all when Michael told him to. Michael was very good with them. This sort of flu is mainly an extremely painful cough and a temperature of 102. But I hadn't much of a cough, my temperature was only 101, but I was very upset inside and felt up to nothing, even reading.

We arrived here very early yesterday morning. We expected to disembark almost straightaway and reveille was four o'clock, but they made us wait anchored by the mole. It was raining and terrifically windy. After lunch they sent out a launch for me. I was driven in an ambulance to the army hospital, sitting in front. The town by the sea [Haifa] is all the most ultra modern architecture. Most people wear Arab muffler things round their heads, some of them coloured robes as well. Behind is an older town on a hill. We drove about five miles, with hills on one side, all very rocky and in parts very bright green, rather Irish. I'm in the hospital now, so I haven't seen much! But I'm told that our boat had to go into the bay again it was so windy and they aren't ashore yet! We go somewhere for three weeks' rest, but I've forgotten the name, I hope someone here knows.

10 February 1940, Haifa

I've been here a week, and am quite well again. Eric Sanders and I left the hospital by car, and we lunched with the Yorkshire Hussars on the way. At first we drove down the coast right against the sea, later we kept rather more inland. All the way through rich-looking arable land, with strong foothills on our left. I gather this good agricultural land along the coast has mostly been bought up by the Jews. We passed some Arab villages, all on the hill slopes and none on the flat ground, a collection of one-storey stone boxes, small and square and not particularly old when you looked into them. In one place the hills did pull themselves together a little and produce some overhanging crags full of caves, but no one peeping out of them.

There were plenty of Arabs on the roads, bearded gentlemen sitting on large mattresses on very small donkeys, followed by a procession of injured-looking camels tied head to tail. I am determined to have a camel, I like their outlook. Other Arabs just sit about on the side of the road and watch their donkeys eating. They wear the right clothes and obviously ought to be encouraged. The women even carry very large water pots balanced on their heads. Saturday is the Sabbath and there were plenty of Jews about too. Girls in very short shorts, young men in lounge suits, enjoying an outing into the country. We passed several small Jewish towns, and finally Tel Aviv which is I should think their ideal – very modern buildings, very smart shops, all well lit up at night, quite uninteresting and guaranteed up to date.

Our car carried us to Brigade Headquarters, in the middle of a large camp. The idea was it should carry me on to my camp, but Eric wanted to come too on a visit and so I had to wait for him to pass the time of day with everybody there. This took time and I found a rather nice young man (who turned out to be Haig's son) from whom I learnt that Mikey Crichton-Stuart was in the camp, forming a pioneer regiment of mixed Jews and Arabs. So I walked off miles to find him, and he'd gone to Haifa for the weekend. By the time I'd got back it was dark, and internal security regulations ordered me to proceed in two cars with an armed guard in each and a machine gun tied on the back. The Brigadier had been issued on arrival a few days before with four cars, but three had been smashed up – one had simply been removed the night before, driven past the guard with a shout of 'Officers!' and left in an unmendable state in a ditch on the road to Jerusalem. It was smeared with hair and blood and Brigade Intelligence had spent all day checking up on the hospital. When I arrived the news had just come in that it was camel's hair! So as there weren't two cars, I had to stay the night, and dine with the Brigadier, whose name is Miller.

The Brigade Major very kindly insisted on my not sleeping in the tent provided, which would certainly have killed me as I'd no blankets with me and it's quite cold at night. Next day I came over here. Here is the Scots Greys' camp. The Greys are away building a camp for us in the hills, and we change over on Thursday. I share a room with Michael Parish, which is an intervention of Providence as it was arranged before we came, in a rather shabby one-storeyed house. The men live in wooden huts, with real beds, and have never been so comfortable, nor are likely to be again.

Kellett went off for a week to watch some brigands rounded up and he thinks there will be an Arab outbreak in the summer, because they have so many arms and have been so harshly treated, but all the locals say everything is over. I was very pleased to see some actually riding camels today. You have to keep swinging back and forward, though Mikey says it's more comfortable than a horse. My dear Kate, Mrs Bourne's hunter, has taken to tiggering mildly which gives me indigestion. She is incapable of walking. She is vastly admired and looks beautiful, which is surprising as she was in a very poor state at Riby and could hardly stand up on the train. She has a particularly engaging habit which is without the least warning when you're walking along to flop down on her knees ready to roll. The first time I was asleep and it gave me a nasty surprise.

I've got a new groom out of the reservists. It's an extraordinary thing but over half my 19 reservists were servants in the army before – either first servants or grooms. Yates my first servant is doing quite well and Michael has stopped him gasping all the time which makes all the difference. Every afternoon all subalterns and all servants parade in the so-called football ground and do shun and slope arms. This makes us mad, being hot, tiring and unnecessary, and torture holding a rifle in some absurd position while the Sergeant Major adjusts some half-witted servant. We work all the time, at absolutely nothing, but I believe we shall work infinitely harder at our new place. It is apparently such an extra boring and uncomfortable place that it is vital to exhaust the men or they will shoot the officers. My men are of course quite out of control already and have adopted an owl noise which runs up and down the line unmindful of my crimson indignation.

Our luggage hasn't arrived yet which is rather boring, particularly as I packed various military paraphernalia I ought not to have done. We went to a terrible film last night, *Huckleberry Finn*, avoid it. But we've seen some quite good ones. Either in English or French, with a vertical slip at the side in every other language, Arabic, Hebrew, German etc., appearing some pages behind the script. Talking German is almost a necessity in the shops, which seems a little strange in this war. We can get the news much better than at Flintham and it is repeated next day in the local paper, so we learn what is going on, though without enormous interest. I wait very impatiently for more important news, of Flintham. What are you doing? Not I hope lamenting the young heir's absence among cannibals, all is well at the moment.

14 February 1940, Haifa: Letter to Toby

Our Loggia has a marble floor, with purple bougainvillea from roof to balustrade, and we look down through leafy palms on marble steps, falling in shade towards the sea, while all around the orange groves bask in the sun. Bearded Arabs, dignified and ridiculous on diminutive asses, lead past strings of camels loaded with fruit. Not all this fertile coastline is used for fruit growing, but whereas

Allenby's soldiers landing not far south must have faced a desert plain no different from that which met Crusaders' eyes, today its whole extent is watered and well tilled. Night comes on quick and early, all at once the air turns cold and the sky reflecting for a moment the sun's lost warmth, throws a blue back cloth behind the moon, which hangs ready made for some Passion Play Bethlehem scene. And in the Arab villages which crown the low hills with high mud courtyard walls and heavy doors, and a tall tower and a few tall palms, mothers sit motionless with downcast eyes, their arms round silent children, and with them in the room a cow and its new born calf, a donkey and some chickens. It is the first story we ever learnt, come to life . . .

Toby! Is that how it is, do you think?
or is it – up at 5.45
      and forty stupid men to chase
      and someone always chasing after oneself
      and no peace and a hot ride
      and horses –
            shying at camels
            falling down
            rolling in the sand
            needing attention
     and watering for hours
      with the sun murdering the back of one's neck
      and sand in one's shoes
   and everybody ill
     with pneumonia
     and influenza
     and Gippy Tummy
     and worms
         Having to take morphia to forget
    Is that how it is? Toby?
Well actually, a bit of both. But quite fun.

19 February 1940, Latrun

We are now under canvas. I have a rather small tent to myself, which is quite comfortable and cosy with my camp bed – lame in one leg since Michael sat down on it too heavily – a bedside table and a writing table with chintz covers, a low cupboard with drawers, a deck chair, washing tripod, and, most important of all, my high-pressure lamp which gives out a vast amount of light and heat but causes too a vast amount of trouble. During dinner tonight it has burnt through the roof of the tent, so I suppose Yates has been busy. We are covering it with a patch and hook and hoping to disguise the damage.

We are called at 5.30, and since the first morning when I lay in bed with the sun streaming in and thought it was fun and that lots of people have saved up money to do the same, I haven't found much time to appreciate it. We are just starting a very severe training programme, which looks like leaving us very little spare time indeed. And apart from my ordinary objections to over much army, it will be a pity if one can't get around and see something of the country. About half a mile from us is the village where Christ revealed himself to Cleopas and another man (St John Didymus) on Easter Day. We are on a slight hill and on the other side of us, again on the side of a hill, is a large Trappist monastery built less than 40 years ago rather in the Austrian style, white and buttressed, with a red roof. So far as we can make out there are 32 monks there, of whom only two can speak to one. On the gate it says it is the Trappist Monastery of the Sept Douleurs, and Michael and I, rather overwhelmed by military troubles, thought of presenting ourselves as two more.

Since beginning this I have broken off first for a lecture on how to lecture to NCOs, and then for a lecture on how to instruct in the Hotchkiss gun. I am now lacerated and bleeding, having failed to come to any terms at all with the horrible machine. There's few things I dislike more than lying about on the ground with an oily gun and trying to remember names for the bits of it and what to do with one's hands. I evolved a theory during last Sunday's sermon

31

that the Romans of the Fall were probably not a crowd of depraved and decadent theatre goers, but merely civilised people like myself with no passion for catapults and even, with the barbarian at the gates, a considerable lack of interest in the lower forms of humanity.

We had a rather marvellous ride here, leaving behind us the orange groves for fields of barley, and the plain for the faintly rising stonier slopes which lead us to the barren hills now immediately behind us. With the horses two abreast and a gap between squadron and troops, the Regiment stretched several miles and one could see it winding ahead just as the Crusaders must have seen their horsemen. We climbed a hill and passed through one most exciting Arab village, a maze of high walls and narrow alleys and grilled windows sometimes blue colour washed, like a page out of the *Arabian Nights*. Fortunately there were plenty of Arabs sitting at corners to point out the way or I might well be chasing round the place now. Further on I picked a bunch of wild pink cyclamen growing in the rocks and soon after these hills the new camp came in sight. But first we had to cross a main road – to Jerusalem – and as I got to it there passed an armoured car or two and then a limousine with a Union Jack on its bonnet, so I halted my troop to let them pass.

The next thing I heard was my name and out of another flag-bearing car behind me there debouched a bevy of old gentlemen in red hats and young ones in coloured trousers. I approached with great bonhomie and looked down from Kate's great height on the GOC Palestine and other military notables who had just been seeing off Mr Eden from the airport. I had to get off and assist in a review as other troops came past, an honour granted to no one else but which I could have done without. One general in attendance had a black patch over his eye like a pirate [Carton de Wiart], the gentlemen in coloured trousers were ADCs [aide-de-camps] from odd regiments known as the Cherry Pickers [the 11th Hussars]. Eden was here looking at the Australians who are reported to be settling in very well

We have with us the Yorkshire Dragoons whose mess is along-

32

side ours but so far we've seen absolutely nothing of them, as we hold them in great contempt and no doubt they think the same of us. We imagined this [Latrun] to be a permanent camp; there are a good number of fine wooden huts and the place must have cost a good deal. But I believe we are moving again in a few weeks, and a lot of work will have been wasted.

3 March 1940, Jaffa

I had come home and changed into trousers and was standing around timing my departure for the stables to the last second as usual when Michael came past at 60 mph on a motor bicycle and roared straight along the verandah. I followed to expostulate at anyone daring to set out for the stables later than myself and found it to be a genuine alarm, which was annoying as I had to put on my boots again. Then when I got down to the horses I'd left my map behind and had to go back. However all passed off well and I boldly led the whole regiment into Jaffa. Where we are now.

Within 20 minutes of arriving we rode off into the town and I was sent to a big roundabout with two troops to help the police. There were no police there, actually. The roundabout had a fountain in the middle and a garden round it where I put my horses and sent patrols out down the six streets which met there. It soon got dark and cold. We were supposed to be enforcing the Tel Aviv curfew (Jaffa is all Arab and has no curfew this time) and all the police did in my quarter was to dash round in armoured cars collecting prisoners. When they actually stopped by my side I had to arrest anyone passing, otherwise I just told people to go home and they were all nice Kensington High Street harmless people. When eventually it was time to go and very cold I had lost a man and took an hour to find him. I got to bed at twelve.

Then yesterday we were called out again. I was again advance troop to the Regiment and led the way sword in hand on my prancing Kate. (Kate is hair-raising in towns as she prances incessantly and the streets here are like glass.) When we got to the beginning of the main street I was told things were very nasty and I must charge if necessary. There were some stones lying in the streets. But nobody about. We went to my roundabout of the day before and that was Regimental Headquarters all day. We had to be stricter actually because of the Brigadier who dashed about smashing car windows, socking harmless people on the jaw and swearing at us for not being rough enough. He actually ordered A Squadron to fire. We all think this very stupid and bad policy and though it's true one crowd did give the police and A Squadron a bad time with stones, most of the town were well behaved and it was silly enough locking everybody in the streets up for the night without hitting them over the head as well. A Squadron charged 12 times using their swords, but we did nothing.

Now I'm back sitting on my camp bed. The curfew goes on Tuesday, today is Sunday and I expect we'll stay here all week. It's a pity the English papers are so late out here as I don't know how much is in them about our White Paper etc., most people out here seem anti-Jew but I think the Arabs have about 900,000 square miles outside Palestine and I'm pro-Jew. They have of course developed the country as the Arabs don't attempt to do. I gather that only the first Jews to come through, with plenty of money invested in the electric light etc., are doing at all well.

6 March 1940, Palestine

The curfew has now been lifted and the police expected great trouble, so we were out at 3 a.m. and again at night yesterday, but nothing happened and I wasn't in the unfortunate squadron which had to stay out all night. The day before yesterday was complete curfew all day and we were out all the time doing nothing but – when the Brigadier wasn't about – trying to be kind, helping people to get food and giving quite illegal passes. We opened a café for our men and sent for the best barber in the town and had him cut our hair in the cinema on our roundabout. Coming back from a patrol I met a stream of cars on a main street and signalled them to

34

stop (to examine passes) and when they swept on I gave the front one an almighty swipe across the bonnet with my heavy stick and prepared for the next one, which came on with much hooting and in it was the GOC [General Officer Commanding] Palestine proceeding north surrounded by red-hatted generals, red flags and followed by yellow police cars.

Yesterday I spent much time arranging for the men to go to the cinema round the corner, with Arabs who couldn't speak English or German, and I wrote on a piece of paper 'all Notts Yeo return to billets' and thought I had made them understand that I wanted this on the screen if I ordered it. With much ceremony and after much talk I was conducted to the manager's office where I handed over my piece of paper. They stamped it and with smiles of deep understanding gave it me back! So then I wrote it myself on a piece of film. Of course just before the men were due to go we were ordered out, but we're going tonight to see Eddie Cantor in *Ali Baba Goes to Town*. I don't know whether it would be more exciting to see my handwriting on the silver screen than annoying to be called out. Also I'm sure it will be upside down, but in the quarter of an hour I had I couldn't explain this to my Arab friends.

12 March 1940, Latrun

We are back among the rocks and I wish we weren't. Our last night in Jaffa I got an hour off and walked out into the town, which was fascinating in the light of a few bare electric light bulbs, much more so I expect than by day. The main streets were full of people and Arab music issued from all the shops, but it was always the same music as it came from expensive radios. However it produced the right atmosphere. There was a square in the middle of the town with a sort of campanile in the middle and in the centre of a row of shop arches a bigger one through which one could see a most beautiful-looking courtyard. I tried to walk in and was stopped, and found it was the cloister of a big mosque. I expect the mosques are all Turkish, they have many low round domes and a tall praying

35

tower and because they are beautifully built in stone in a very old-fashioned style, probably look much older than they really are. The town runs steeply uphill from the sea, and at night standing on the shore and looking at the faint outline of buildings piled up above one with here and there a lighted arcade and a few lights throwing a spotlight on a doorway or overhanging window it was hopelessly unreal, like a rather unoriginal bit of stage scenery. I have always loved the sort of gentle sunlight which makes me think of old varnish rather than the bright sun, but one realises here very well how much one owes in England to cloud and shadow.

Riding back it was quite lovely and for the first time I admired the country. The earth, soaked during the night, was dark and purple or bright green with barley and as we approached the hills the sun lit up an Arab village piled up like Carcassone on a hilltop, and the clouds broke up the usual monotony of the view with shadows. It rained all along the high road and came down in buckets as we arrived at our bivouac halfway home. This was no distance from Jaffa and in sight of our camp but the Colonel was anxious we should spend a night in the open and a scheme had been arranged for the next day. He was unlucky in striking the first rain for months, but not in the least deterred by it.

The famous scheme was an attack by us on the other half of the Regiment which has been here all the time. One squadron of our lot made a feint in front while the rest of us made our way round a flank through the hills, led by me studying my map like mad. It is excessively difficult in a country of interminable rocky hills and no roads but little tracks like rabbit runs, invisible of course where they actually cross rocks, and I was much complimented on finding the way. It cost my troop four shoes and innumerable cuts. The battle was a complete fiasco and we never saw the enemy nor did anyone else.

I have been made Messing Officer which means my leaving my troop and squadron and becoming a solitary soul in the Regiment. I am very sorry to leave B, particularly as my troop is now running so well that I'm pretty sure they won't give it a new officer, but leave the sergeant in charge. My new job has certain advantages, self-sufficiency and no riding, and perhaps leading to better things, but as a job I'm sure I'll hate it and anyway I regard it as a comedown to spend one's day adding up figures. Not that I don't need the experience but the Regiment is likely to pay dearly for it.

17–19 March 1940, Latrun

Our luggage has finally arrived. It is definitely known to have gone halfway to America but whether because the captain was given the wrong sealed orders or just forgot what Post Q stood for, I don't know. Mine was intact but a great many trunks in all the regiments had been burst open and field glasses, coats and other things stolen, so naturally everybody is furious.

I don't think the war is going very well, do you, but it doesn't seem to be a very serious war, so you're really no worse off than if I'd chosen to be resident magistrate at Mwanza, and I shall come back brick red all in good time. You will be relieved to hear that the War Office has announced we mustn't marry natives nor visitors to the country! Everybody's wives are arriving but it's still illegal. It must be an odd life for them; at present they are mostly at Rechovot and see their husbands twice a week in the afternoon. But we move again immediately after Easter halfway up the coast, and this time entirely under canvas, not even a wooden mess or offices. My new position as Messing Officer is still a little undefined as my squadron is anxious to have me stay with it but I don't think it's possible. I have just ordered hot cross buns and cochinealed eggs for 800, also beer which may be irreligious, I don't know.

Easter Monday, 25 March 1940, Latrun

I have actually girt up my loins and gone to Jerusalem.

Michael, Stan Christopherson and I went there after lunch on Easter Sunday, with Henry our Arab taximan. It's uphill all the way through the Judean hills and a lovely road through gorges and along hillsides looking down precipitously on stony valleys, the road in the past a renowned engineering feat and quite the most terrifying switchback I've ever been in. We were among houses and arguing whether it was an Arab village or a Jewish settlement before we realised we had reached Jerusalem. Our road brought us into the modern town and nothing could be more disappointing, the usual concrete. We went to the famous King David Hotel, the doors were flung open by Ethiopians clad in scarlet. There we collected Michael's friend Araminta MacMichael, the High Commissioner's daughter, and another girl and took to the road again, for Jericho. I may say I had intended to go to church but that went by the board, and I had done it twice here at camp so I had at least no conscience.

The road to Jericho is new and you can see the old road, a track winding up and down, crossing wadis and looking definitely the worse for wear since the Good Samaritan took it. You pass his Inn too. You go downhill to Jericho over mountains which look even more sterile than those towards Jaffa and then they change into very odd mountains – the Judean desert. They aren't rocky and at present they are fairly green and they are rounded and lie in folds, like a pile of soft velvet or a cushion that's been sat on. After a time in these you pass a notice saying Sea Level but you go on down. Here you would turn north for Jericho and the great attraction of orange groves in blossom, but we went on to Kellin on the Dead Sea. Kellin is a police station, a restaurant, four-storey slum tenements and a hotel, just in front of the lake. But the view down the lake from the hotel is the best thing I've seen since Canada, particularly as nobody warned me.

We returned long after the road is supposed to be closed to all traffic and as none of us had any arms the High Commissioner's daughter might easily have been abducted. The Jericho road approaches Jerusalem from the side of the old city, passing below the Mount of Olives and right against the Garden of Gethsemane, and as we topped the last hill the domes and minarets stood up black against the fading light, the first insinuation of something exciting. We drove up to Government House, which is on a hill by itself some way outside the town looking over it. It was built about nine years ago I think, and could hardly be bettered. Inside everything is Moorish, with white vaulting and round arches, and very well furnished. We spent the evening there and stayed at the King David.

Today I insisted on having no guide or guidebook and we had a marvellous day. All the time we've been here there have been parties to Jerusalem for the men, taken sightseeing by the parson. Though impressed, officers who went with them came back very disappointed by the tawdry Roman Catholicism they found instead of gardens and holy places. Today we went into the old city which is surrounded by a very high wall, mostly built by the Turks in the 16th century though in parts very much earlier. Inside is mostly markets, either very narrow streets or arcades. I found and recognised the via Dolorosa, and we eventually found our way to the Dome of the Rock. It was past the hour allowed for sightseeing, but we got special permission. This is definitely the most beautiful place in Jerusalem. It is a very big open piece of ground taking up one end of the old city, looking out on to the Garden of Gethsemane and the Mount of Olives across a small valley. In the valley are the tombs of Absalom and others. That of Solomon is inside the area, near the Golden Gate, which is a big gate in the wall, bricked up. They say if Allenby had opened it there would have been no more troubles. The area round the Dome of the Rock is the highest and in the middle is the Dome itself. The bottom part of the Dome is marble, most of it covered with very beautiful mosaic tiles placed there by Suleiman the Magnificent. Inside it is rather dark, and very splendid.

Outside, on the lower platform on one side is another mosque, Al Aksa, rebuilt by Saladin, you can't go in. Below and beyond all this area are what are known as King Solomon's stables, a colossal underground place with fifteen rows of piers. The Templars kept their horses there. All the Muslims were charming, remarkably ungrasping and everything was in superb contrast with Christian efforts at grandeur. The Church of the Holy Sepulchre is in the so-called Christian quarter, hidden away among markets. It has an unbelievable number of nooks and crannies. I didn't realise but the Crucifixion site is inside it, unless you take sides with General Gordon who found another place outside the wall. You go upstairs

39

inside the church and find two appalling chapels side by side. One is the Greek Church's and contains the site of the cross, the cracked rock etc. all covered in marble, more or less under the altar. The RC chapel which contains nothing but proximity, has an image of the Virgin in a glass case strewn with Victorian jewellery, worth I was assured £1,000,000. I couldn't see anything to make me believe this.

We have great hopes of our next place, Karkur. The only known fly in the ointment being no huts and a great shortage of tents. Two and a half officers to sleep in a bell tent. This will be ghastly. We all have enough furniture to make ourselves uncomfortably crowded. I expect we shall sleep out of doors and keep our clothes in the tent.

31 March 1940, Karkur

In my last letter we were then just going to move, which we did last Thursday and had a good deal of excitement. As I was in charge of the food and it was fairly complicated, with an advance party leaving Latrun early in the week, the main body riding later and bivouacking on the way and the rear body following, I went by lorry so as to be more mobile. The first two squadrons were watered in a village and then to avoid a crush moved on a mile and I gave them lunch. Everything had gone very well, we were supplying a hot lunch, two courses, and I was pleased with myself. Beyond the village you went down a hill. At the bottom on one side of the road was a small grove of blue gum or eucalyptus trees, where we had the officers' mess, the men's mess, and the water troughs. The other side of the road was wired. Then the road went up hill again. As I got to the top of the hill I saw an extraordinary sight, horses tearing up the road towards me, riderless but fully saddled, even with rifles on them.

There had been a stampede, which cost £5,000! The horses of the last two squadrons which had watered had gone back into the village while the men ate and the remainder watered. Suddenly, no one knows why, they had rushed down the hill, and the horses along the road had stampeded with them. When they came to the bottom where they could leave the road for the wood, they did so with a vengeance. Officers sitting comfortably at a long table covered in food heard and saw a wild rush of horses coming at them, and they and the men mostly got behind the very thin trees. Four horses jumped the officers' table without touching it, and a wave of 200 horses went through the wood knocking down every-thing and everyone they met. In front of the officers' mess Major Bennet's horse hit a truck and was killed outright, four others came down and had to be shot. The £5,000 is almost all saddlery etc., broken and lost. Ninety-six still haven't rejoined us!

Michael Parish was on the track where they turned off away from me, holding his horse, which joined in and left him. He brought in 16 by himself and a lot more were brought back from villages around during the day. Brooks was attending a man in the wood whose leg had been broken earlier on; he lay on him while two waves of horses passed over them. One officer was kicked on the head and about 12 men taken to hospital. Search parties were sent out for the horses, and the Regiment moved on. Two squadrons of course were perfectly alright, including my own. My lunch was rather neglected.

We dined in the open, and at dinner talked about the story that horses always stampede again the second night, and what should we do if they did. We were sleeping along the wire fence of an orange grove, with a wide stretch of grass between us and the horse lines. At midnight I was awakened by thundering hooves. Pretty well asleep I was out of bed and halfway through the wire before I knew what I was doing. Our horses had stampeded again. But halfway across the grass towards us they turned off towards the Dragoons, knocking down a tent one of their officers had brought, breaking a man's thigh in it and setting it alight with an almighty wallop. They went straight through their cookhouse and set that alight. I disentangled myself from the wire, well lacerated, and got dressed to go and see how my troop was. I found Michael still fast asleep. The stampede had again started in his squadron. The men were sleeping by their horses and had lucky escapes, a lot being jumped over but not many hurt. We again lost a lot of horses and had a business in the dark getting the lines down again and straightening out.

We were very cross when we reached here, Karkur, near Hederah on your map. I'm glad to say our tents are a long way from the horses and we have one each. On the other hand Yates drove a large snake out of mine, two others have been killed in other tents, one that kills in four minutes, also large scorpions, and appalling centipedes. The men have been issued with mosquito nets, but not us, the sand flies are said to be very bad and give you fever. There are woods around and the hills a few miles off, very like Latrun, and the unfortunate Dragoons are right among the rocks again. C Squadron and Michael have been sent for some weeks to the empty barracks at Hederah to calm down, they are very lucky really.

Today Michael P, Pat McCraith, Derek Warwick, Michael Riviere and Stephen Mitchell were asked if they'd like to apply for transfer to the Trans Jordan Frontier Force. Of these Michael is the only one at all keen. You can imagine how poor a view I take of Michael going, so I said I'd try and go too. I asked the Adjutant and he said my name hadn't been put forward as they needed me here, which was a compliment, but if I wanted he'd ask the Colonel. Which is as far as it's got. I don't think Michael would go if I didn't, but I should be lost here without him. We think it would mean being alone in a desert with about 50 men, possibly all Arabs, and we think we'd wear Arab headdresses like Lawrence. We'd be on our own entirely. Of course my new job has advantages that way, though not to that extent. The greatest danger is the question of how long we'd have to sign on for. But our brigadier formed the force, and I'm going to try and see him tomorrow.

2 April 1940, Karkur

My new job is Messing Officer for the men, not the officers, and though I didn't like it at first it's really a very good one. I was told definitely and apologetically by the Colonel that he wouldn't let me go to Trans Jordan. Far from having a bowler hat hanging over me I am apparently so vital that they can't spare me. In fact I was the only one to fulfil the conditions – not over 26 and unmarried – who was not given the opportunity. But only Michael is keen to go beside myself. He has been very much encouraged by the Brigadier with whom he has his meals at present. The Brigadier commanded the force and says he'll send Michael for two days to see how he likes it. Otherwise we learn nothing either of how the life would be or for how long. Anyway Michael says he definitely won't go if I don't, so that seems to settle it. I'm sorry I shan't be able to wear a red cloak.

12 April 1940, Acre, Palestine

I'm sitting in my tent on a hot afternoon as now we have a siesta from 2 to 4 p.m., rather maddened by flies which perpetually sting one's legs through one's stockings. Except for riding we wear shorts, and topees and mosquito nets have been issued to the men and are there for us when we want them. The weather doesn't really get much hotter actually.

The Regiment has been shooting at a very fine new range against the Cheshire Yeomanry near Acre. My troop went first and I've taken a good deal of trouble arranging this so that I could go with them, and then at the last moment I couldn't because of a court martial. The court martial had been impending since Good Friday when I arrested two of my mess orderlies for fighting their mess-tent corporal and as I charged them with this and insubordination to myself they had to be court martialled. It was very long and very tedious as I was only a witness and had to wait outside. However it went well for me as the second charge was very difficult to prove and if the defending officer had been luckier or cleverer he might have made me look a fool, but he missed his chance. I got to Acre for tea, taking my tent and Yates with me.

From Haifa you drive round the bay and Acre stands out into the

43

sea behind a great wall with domes and minarets above the houses, just as I'd imagined the towns do in Dalmatia. The camp is further on, right on the edge of the sea, with every conceivable luxury. The Cheshires who came out in the first flight before us have been there ever since and know nothing about roughing it. All the men are in big barrack rooms and even sitting rooms, there is a mahogany dining table and electric fans, a swimming pool and a proper cinema. It was a marvellous holiday for the men.

We dined that night with the Cheshires, and shot at 6.30 next morning. I shot quite appallingly and got bottom score for the whole two troops. I don't know why exactly. Michael Riviere who is a very good shot and won something at Bisley was next to me and began well but tailed off and we both had red flags fluttering at us frequently, meaning a miss. We were quite shattered by the shooting in a gas mask, which became hopelessly entangled in our glasses and I couldn't see a thing, not even my sights.

I kept at Latrun meaning to send you a target I shot the only time we fired there and got 19 out of 20 – four bulls and an inner, but now I can't find it, which is a pity.

22 April 1940, Karkur

A man in my troop died very suddenly and I had to go to the funeral, in the military cemetery quite near our last camp. My troop produced the firing party but they were very hurt because there was no band (there is none in Palestine), no deceased's horse – any old horse would apparently have done – and no gun carriage. Also no other officers but me. They mind these things very much, though to me it seemed a very good simple ceremony. Robinson, our new padre (awful word but parson sounds odd too) from Welbeck, seems good at taking services and I think improves a little on acquaintance.

My position as Messing Officer hangs in the balance, as I am being rather pressed to choose between it and my troop. With Michael away with his squadron I have had great fun taking them in rations and having meals with him, but they come back tomorrow and I don't much want to do nothing else but cook. On the other hand it has its advantages. The other day a patrol went out and the Colonel sent back a signal 'Practice turn out regiment patrol attacked by Grand Mufti and 50,000 men'. Wilfred Bennet who is n.b.g. took this seriously and everybody turned out in a great flap! Everybody that is but the Messing Officer, who had just enough sense to see it might be a practice and who stood around in shorts cheering on his friends as they dashed about in tin hats and then, when the whole regiment was mounted on parade, meandered up to Major Bennet and reported that the cook's lorries were ready too.

I have been very lame ever since the whole squadron went bathing on horseback and I mysteriously blackened a toe, but it's better though still odd. I hope no news is good news, as I expect you often do.

7 May 1940, Karkur

I think we take infinitely less notice of the war here than you do, having for one thing only a small local paper with no headlines and a wireless which says waa . . . rp, but we think the whole Norwegian show very poor.

Anyway if our territorials weren't trained, why weren't they? And if they knew they weren't why send them to be massacred, and then admit it? I am at present ADC to General Kontonzow and on leave in Moscow, having gone through a lot of trouble at the battle of Austerlitz. Last night I lost 43,000 roubles at cards which has caused my family trouble too. I am in fact immersed in Tolstoy's *War and Peace* and a little afraid we are in for another Napoleonic war. I have just finished Clive Bell's *Civilization*, a fascinating book and most interesting as it definitely appears I am about the only highly civilised person I know. From it arises a slight question whether after the war, instead of retiring to Trent Hills Farm and watching the roof fall in, I oughtn't to keep in closer touch with Michael Parish who is going to be dictator, and make things a little more civilised all along the line, but Clive Bell doesn't think you can be highly civilised and work, so that's lucky.

Later. Today we got up at 3 a.m. and fought a most successful battle. We were Nazis landing off iron-ore ships and trying to capture a food dump, and Kellett's scheme was to put some men on a train and send them off to get out at the station where the dump was. So I left at 4 a.m. to get a train from the starting point. I had most of the time with me a most friendly umpire, named Dugdale, who was Baldwin's private secretary and would be Chief Government Whip if he were in England now. He was once in the Greys and with his help and good luck my troop had colossal success, wiped out one troop, separated another from its base, seized the station, captured the enemy headquarters, placed a machine gun on the road and shot up two more enemy troops as they withdrew in the station. We were much congratulated and Dugdale said if he had a troop as good as that he'd be pleased and proud, and he's a Squadron Leader. I did lose almost all my men, not by death but while riding through very thick woods they just drifted away or I sent them back with messages and they got lost.

15 May 1940, Karkur

Over Whitsun, leave was granted as at Easter and half the men allowed away Friday and Saturday and half Sunday and Monday. Michael and I had planned to go to Syria later in the week to avoid a crowd; but we have just been allowed 72 hours' leave in every two months, and it suddenly struck me that we should be wasting our Whitsun leave and using up our 72 hours. I asked Kellett and he said that was exactly how it would be and why didn't I take the whole weekend off. This was too good to discuss further and like all army concessions obviously had to be acted on promptly. I departed hurriedly for Syria before anyone thought better of it, in Michael's car with some others who had only one night and would take the car back for Michael to come up in on Sunday.

46

The frontier isn't far north of Acre, you cross it right on the sea. You pass Tyre on the end of a peninsula jutting out into the sea, and drive through Sidon with an old castle and a harbour full of sailing ships. Round Beirut the mountains come down near the sea, instead of being bare and stony they are bright green with trees, the valleys rich in olives and orchards, the houses civilised with high red roofs. Just outside the town you pass through a pine forest of tall trees with flat umbrella tops, very imposing with their high bare trunks, and then the suburbs are hazy with avenues of jacaranda trees in bloom. It's a nice town, with lots of flowery walls and the houses pleasant and French.

The thing I most wanted to do was to go and see the ruins of Baalbec, one of the wonders of the world, but we didn't have time to visit them on this trip. We did drive most of the way across the mountains which separate Beirut from the level plateau where Baalbec lies some way to the north, but just short of the last and biggest pass we turned south and made a big circle through the mountains back to the coast. The highest mountains here were about 6,000 feet, further north they rise to over 9,000. It was a wonderful drive, on a very twisting road, with the scenery changing from valley to valley. In one, the nearest range was a rich reddish colour with plenty of pines and we came to a charming village like you might find on the Riviera, very unlike our Arab villages here, with a mill and water gushing out of a stone arch to drive it.

Syria, or the part I saw, is very like the Riviera. The mountains are the Lebanon. The famous cedars are not very plentiful, we saw none but there are some further north towards Tripoli where people go to ski. I really should know but don't how long the French have had Syria, I think 100 years. Michael says since the last war, anyway the impression one gets is of a much older civilization than one finds here, or at least a longer period of peace and prosperity.

Beirut has a lot of French people but more Syrians, good looking and more like the Egyptians I should think than the Arabs here. Some are rich and smart and wear their red hats and European clothes, in the country they all wear very full trousers like Turks.

47

The night life in Beirut is very gay and Michael, who enjoys most things to the utmost, was madly happy. The frontier is closed from 5 p.m. to 8 a.m. and we only just made it, particularly as in the middle of Beirut Michael stopped, rushed up to a woman in the street, begged her in appalling French to help him buy some silk and as usual at colossal speed carried all before him and bore off a bale of material which probably came from Nottingham, to send to a girl in Eaton Square whose loving letters written methodically every week are shown to everyone who cares to read them and answered I'm afraid very perfunctorily. This girl is doing secretary to the Lord Chamberlain at St James, dealing with prisoners of war, and might come in handy one day.

We are very depressed by the news. This morning I was as usual woken by Michael's wireless and having heard of the invasion of Belgium and Holland last night, was a little put back to hear the announcer say in his usual bored way, 'This morning's items include several new members of the cabinet, another successful RAF attack, the surrender of the Dutch, Mr Menzies . . .' as if the surrender of the Dutch were nothing at all. But by the time you get this that will all be old history. I do hope, though, that you are still concentrating on the better things in life and not worrying uselessly about what was certain to be horrible.

I think the reason I got such a good leave was that the famous battle was a try-out at the end of squadron training and our success would prove to the Brigadier that Kellett would make a good colonel. He was also delighted to hear the Squadron Leader of the regiment against which we fought, given severe rockets. One can't feel very certain what the future holds but I love you very much and hope you keep well.

27 May 1940, Karkur

Today the Colonel asked me whether I'd like to be a platoon commander in the Somaliland Camel Corps. This was in the orderly room, to be answered immediately; first I had to ask where Somaliland was, then I refused. Pat was sent for and told straight out that his name would be put in, he is shattered but I don't suppose anything will come of it. I didn't tell you that Wilfred Bennet has gone so Flash Kellett becomes second in command and Basil Ringrose sent to B as Squadron Leader with Pat as second in command of B. Flash remains very friendly to me.

We have a big scheme on Friday against another regiment and that finishes regimental training which has been most boring and unimproving. There has never been an enemy and nothing has ever gone right. Things are looking very black in Moscow and if we didn't know the trouble that is in store for Napoleon we'd be very worried. I think *War and Peace* is quite the best novel I've read.

You say the trouble with the democracies has been their wrong values. I had a discussion with our budding dictator Michael [Parish], whose values I consider contemptible, but I always find my mind so uninformed and full of various considerations that I have no strong opinion about anything. Certainly everyone has been money grabbing and smug, but would we be any better off now if we'd been more Christian? Everything seems to be a compromise.

I am very annoyed to hear you listen to the wireless a lot, I seriously think that is nerve wearing and you shouldn't do it. God knows the war is desperately important to us all; the BBC is a fraud and a fifth columnist in the home. Far better to go to church or make booby traps for parachutists disguised as Friesians. How are our pineapples? Remember to wear the orchids in future and not sell them. How are my white ones? Is my honeysuckle by the drinking place doing anything? Your letters are a very great joy, I'm afraid you and Flintham are all that matter to me.

14 June 1940, Karkur: Letter to Toby

My dearest Toby, your very sweet letter of no date by air mail arrived today, and has horrified me by the idea that you had – when writing – only a month's more training ahead. Nothing worries me

49

so much as the thought of your flying. I've been very bad about writing, but I've hoped you'd see my letters to Flintham, and news is scanty. The heat or the company makes one unintelligent, we spend a lot of our spare time bathing or sleeping, and then particularly in a khamsin one's tent is unbearable and the mess not quiet enough, and we have a blackout now and no lights in tents after dark.

My work as Messing Officer is about done as we have just gone on to field-service rationing and are supplied with so many rations per man instead of buying our own. It is infinitely worse food of course. We have just about run through our training. I'm not sure whether we start at the beginning again or what. And of course Mussolini has complicated things a little and we have to practise alarms and excursions. It is all so unreasonable and pointless that if you aren't in the middle of it, it seems impossible. And very frightening. Frightening that this is how the world is.

There is only one thing of which I feel convinced, which is that nothing is certain. Religion, history, criticism, morals, conventions, none of them are absolute, one can at very best point to the opinions one admires most. The opinions I hold are opposed to those of Michael Parish. I believe in the happiness of individuals and the practising of simple virtues, others prefer empires and will fight for Tungsten. The one thing I simply cannot understand is that anyone should think it worthwhile to spoil the lives of so many Germans in order to build up an empire which will make future generations no happier. I don't believe that any movement like Germany's can retain its force with brutality, even in success, more than a few years. Still, we undoubtedly had to fight, having settled in a cul-de-sac, for our liberty and honour.

I expect the sort of people you live with are pretty much like these here – many of them quite broad minded and commercially intelligent but no mental energy or depth. Michael Riviere I like very much, he is typical young Oxford intelligentsia though he kept a racehorse. We don't live in a world of arms and so we aren't perfect soldiers – half for instance have wives here. And for my part I know I could never be a proper soldier. I could never feel any enthusiasm. On the contrary I walk about thinking exactly the same

50

things I used to think by the lake at Flintham. Which is being out of touch with reality, but then I don't like present day reality and since I can't retire to a cave and wait for it to pass over, I ignore it whenever it is humanly possible.

I suppose people thought themselves to be living in an age of progress, well beyond the barbarity of war. They have been proved wrong and I believe one would always have to reckon with sudden bursts of brute force. Don't you think, though, that we may over-rate the horrors of Nazism? Success is only attained by ruthlessness. I believe that if this war should end in a compromise and leave Germany the leading power in Europe, we should after a very few years see her aspire to civilisation and culture. And a European federation on those lines might not be a bad thing. An immediate victory by the allies, without wakening the dull English, would almost have been a pity; an overwhelming victory would be both surprising and embarrassing. I am sitting alone naked on a long sandy beach. Just round the corner is a rocky pool where the elite bathe, but the elite are becoming a little too numerous and I have wandered off to write.

I am reading Havelock Ellis, *The Dance of Life*, which is the sort of book I like. Before that I was reading Balzac's *Droll Stories* on the lines of Rabelais, Daudet's *Sapho* and Prévost's *Manon Lescaut*, all of which lose I expect very much in translating into English, for they are not up to much. I have almost finished *War and Peace*, it's a marvellous book. I wonder if *War and Peace* is even better in the original. Like Proust it is a wonderful translation. Do you read much? You know, I never remember anything I read. Books are to me food. But considering how many I have read they have not brought me to make up my mind on any subject whatsoever.

I am in danger of being a dilettante. The earning of money never seems worth the uncongenial effort. But half my affections make me think I could make myself a farmer, and out of that possibly something more, a JP perhaps. Flintham is material for my feeling for family, for beauty, continuity, instinct to improve, and I believe that is life as God intended it. The grandeur which I loved as a child now is an obstacle. If I had money I should pull Flintham down, so

51

that the impressiveness of the house should not make a garden of the rest. But what about children and their education? (Everything in this view of living necessitates children, and nature a wife.) Well really, what did I learn at Eton? Where are my Eton friends? I learnt to be lazy, everything else I'd have learnt as well at home and at a grammar school, probably better. Of course if Eton survives and I had money I would send my sons there, but it is a good place for those who have uncivilised parents. If you have civilised parents you want a more practical education. And I'd be a civilised parent, if I could learn to be talkative.

It's very nice having Flintham to think about, isn't it? Flintham and you are so much a part of me that I feel no more separated here than if I was in my tower room. I think if anything happened to you I should turn to stone, so please be wide awake. Then when it is all over we will build you a house on the ploughed up part of the home farm field looking across the park and back towards Belvoir. We will have an underground grotto under the road for the dogs to use safely. Till we meet there to plan it God keep you safe and bless you.

15 July 1940, Haifa

When I last wrote we were expecting to move fairly soon to a new and very nice camp, right in the north. The regiment already there however kept a squadron on the Trans Jordan frontier and we tossed up which of our squadrons should take over from them and mine got it. We sent a reconnaissance party to inspect the place and they came back very wan. It was a complete outpost of Empire on the side of a wild hill, surrounded by barbed wire and guns permanently manned, with just enough water for the horses but none to wash in so that a mobile bathing lorry had to call once a week. A hot wind raged incessantly and had torn the tents to pieces, all the officers slept in one tent, and they shared the men's food. Everything about it sounded terrible, and it would mean leaving the sea and bathing. It seemed too much after our expectations of luxury.

The next thing that happened was walking back to my tent from the cinema I was hailed and asked if I could speak French, and told to report to the Colonel. France had just collapsed and the great question here was the future of Syria. One of our officers had been in Syria on sick leave and reported the French army very bellicose and pro-English. During that night Flash Kellett was sent off as a temporary colonel with a party of men to the Syrian border. Flash made a camp to receive French soldiers who should cross the border. He started the camp in great spirits, seeing himself a second Lawrence of Arabia, and he was given power to increase his rank so as always to be senior to anyone who should come over. In fact a varied but not very numerous selection came over – several hundred Czechs under a colonel who looked the worst kind of criminal, some Spaniards who had murdered their officers before leaving Spain, and a French officer leaving Syria so as to get arms. They soon stopped coming in any numbers and the whole thing was very disappointing.

A day or two later we suddenly heard that we were to lose our horses and the very next afternoon I rode on Kate leading two squadrons to the nearest remount depot, pausing on the way to have the photographs taken which I enclose. Poor Kate, I left her tied to a line, the rest of the horses were run loose into kraals and that night they stampeded again!

We are now to man coastal guns, and I went out on a tug, pulling targets like they do in the Solent. It was the first day I was ill and I felt simply dreadful and we made an awful muck of it and sank all the targets before the guns got a chance. The guns are charming, very Crimean. Do you know, when the men heard about the horses going they cheered, and have been as happy as can be ever since? So perhaps mechanisation wasn't such a cruel blow as one imagined.

We are always being asked to volunteer for strange things, and losing men for odd specialist jobs. Today we have a new one, guerrillas. They obviously envisage the break up of the Division. It doesn't look as though they ever expected anything to happen here, I should have thought there was always a risk of it at least. We are all going off in batches on Egyptian courses. I shall go probably for a fortnight and as we are due for ten days' leave, Michael and I might go and see a pyramid. Otherwise I should think Egypt would be foul and hot. I can't believe that a summer has gone by at Flintham without me to take note of it.

29 July 1940, Haifa: Letter to Toby

I have been ill, flu probably, and have had a nice rest, but feel even more at a loose end than before. I could get sick leave but there's nothing to do with it. Michael, who was ill with the same, went to Jerusalem to stay with the High Commissioner but he's lucky knowing them. As you'll have heard we very suddenly lost our horses, we presume because there was a scare that the Egyptians might rat on us and we'd need gunners there. However, I suppose we turned out not to be much needed and we do absolutely nothing at the moment but sit about and enjoy ourselves bathing and going out in Haifa.

Michael came back from Government House very cheerful about the war. One has no ideas about it practically and the paper simply reports the BBC which, since our raids, we know to be a liar, and so it is difficult to take an intelligent interest in what is going on. I don't think we shall be beaten and therefore we might conceivably win, but I can't imagine what'll happen to Europe then, and there are so many looming Russias and Japans, none of whom have any of the nice old instincts about sitting quiet and respecting your neighbour but are full of modern ideas about grabbing what you can. So I really believe the only thing will be for us to carry on and be utterly tough, having in any case made ourselves thoroughly hated by the blockade. Michael was quite right about Laval, wasn't he, but that France should sit down is too futile. Oh I do wish I was at Flintham with you, and even more I wish I knew what you are doing, and that we could be together.

I don't mind not being warlike. I think I'm merely lonely and bored. Are you? Michael collects parties of pretty awful girls, whom he treats like nothing on earth and they coo round him, while I'm taking lessons in the super casual manner combined with extreme exaggeration. Michael now wants me to buy a motor cycle. His car is always on the point of being sold because it costs so much, and today it came back from a garage with a big bill but minus my cigarette case which I left in the pocket, so I'm as sick as mud and livid.

4 September 1940, Port Tewfik, Egypt

We are at the south end of the canal. It ends at Suez and then there is a spit jutting out into the Red Sea with Port Tewfik on it and Michael and I are living at the very end of that doing a fortnight's course. We are living in what was the Quarantine Station, now occupied by a battery of gunners and a lot of Egyptians. The view out to sea is quite lovely with a great range of bare sandy mountains on the west side of it and further off to the east the distant hills of Sinai. But we have a dreadful room which only gives on to the little central courtyard, covered over with glass! The noise is like an underground station with hundreds of boots rushing up and down stone stairs and Egyptians yammering, but when I put my bed out on the verandah, I was driven in by the commandant.

We like the place very much for a fortnight but are hardly surprised to hear that three men have gone mad since they've been here. There's a jetty in front of the house where I bathe when I wake up. I haven't seen a shark though they come into the bay. Port Tewfik is all residential, with trees and grass-lined streets and gardens and villas. Almost all the people are French, in the Canal Company. That is a thing which surprised me very much, that Egypt seems to be more French than English.

We went to Cairo last weekend, two hours by diesel train from here, and stayed at the Continental Savoy, the only big hotel still functioning. Rooms are only 6/- a night to officers but everything else in Cairo is ruinous. It's not a very striking town but pleasant, the Gezira Club on an island in the Nile is just like Ranelagh, trees and grass and three polo grounds and a swimming pool, we slept under a tree after the best and cheapest lunch we've had, and talked to the intelligence officer of the Black Watch who was at Eton with me and was just back from Somaliland. Everyone has a great contempt for the Italians, and the Black Watch held up two divisions and made them run.

You will be glad to hear we went to the pyramids. We drove out of Cairo and came to a long suburban sort of road and there at the end of it a couple of slagheaps like you see from Welbeck park. You arrive at the famous Mena House hotel and there you sit with the greatest of the pyramids towering up above you, golden coloured and enormous. This is the pyramid of Cheops. They are quite high up, just where the desert begins, Mena House being still in the green delta. All these photographs of people on camels at the pyramids are taken on a tame beast kept for the purpose. There are three big pyramids here and some little ones. Down in the sand and looking towards Cairo is the Sphinx. It is in a sort of pit where the sand has been cleared out round it, and seems quite small compared with the pyramids. It is covered in stone slabs but is actually carved out of solid rock. Its face is flat with a very good profile.

We bathed in the swimming pool at Mena House and went out at night and didn't get to bed till six in the morning. I got up again quite early to go to the Muski bazaar, which was fascinating. Michael has a 16-year-old girl called Solange at the plage here for whom he has, for him, an amazingly virtuous affection and I went to the best scent shop in the Muski to buy a bottle for her. I sat in a chair while the proprietor rubbed my hand, my arm, my sleeve and shoulder and so round and back again with every kind of scent. I eventually bought a diminutive phial of lily of the valley.

I was weighed in Cairo and was 11 stone 10 which I can hardly believe though I am less fat. Michael has sold his car and bought a motor cycle while I was in Jerusalem and it's being painted army colours so we can take it anywhere, but we don't know now whether we are being separated or what.

8 September 1940, Palestine

We were recalled from Egypt precipitately and left expecting the high jump, only to find on arriving that nothing was going on in our little world at all. But while we were working not very hard on our gunnery course the Regiment had silently ceased to be gunners, and been put on guard duties over an enormous area, with the promise however of becoming knights again, though not of the Kate kind, as soon as the necessary should arrive. I am now with my battery guarding Lydda Airport. The men are on guard all day but Michael Riviere and I have nothing except a watch in a tower during the night, rather an interesting place and if you could only get into the same place in the Trent Hills [aerodrome close to Flintham] we could converse at midnight as easy as anything. When the Regiment reforms as above, I have been offered and accepted with joy the job of intelligence officer, which I have always coveted.

I agree with your George Townshend. I put everything down to the weakness of man individually. Looking at one's friends who are the sort of people who expect to direct government, one realises that though they are not bad, in a short life full of youth and inexperience and unavoidable ignorance and personal interests and old age and tiredness and the need to earn, faced with the overwhelming complexities of civilization, even the most brilliant and well intentioned are not up to what we need, while the majority are just children really. So many of the more intellectual people are lazy and escapist, parsons and dons. Of the tougher people, soldiers or businessmen or self-seeking politicians, none of them are anything like great enough to take in all man's needs and desires and work them into the world as we have found it. We lack leadership because in peace time a leader would need to have the experience of a hundred experts and a persuasiveness of a prophet. I think Townshend is right saying evolution will be slow, and he can't bank on the God of the Testaments alone. I don't believe in trying to deny man's nature, which may be to be holy but is also to have fun and do work and eat sufficient, and neither Christ nor the church can tell you how to find that.

15 September 1940, Palestine: Letter to Toby

Dearest Toby

Our posts have been very odd and vague references to the boring time you must be having in a convalescent home suggested nothing to me (I thought you were billeted there) till suddenly other letters reached me in Egypt reporting your progress and I realised you'd had a crash. Later, hearing Cranwell had been bombed, I thought maybe you'd got hurt in that, since then the early June letters have arrived and news of the actual accident. I am afraid being a selfish fish I merely hope it hasn't damaged your brain in any way and thank God you are not only alive but restricted to solid ground which I imagine must put back your training.

Mummy tells me they have both made their wills and I will make mine and enclose it in this. She says they haven't tried to apportion furniture etc., between us, which would be most difficult, but I've decided you shall take all the china and everything which is difficult to dust. For my other plans for entirely disorganising the house see my letter to them. How can I arrange to live at Flintham and farm and at the same time direct local town planning, agricultural improvements and embellishments and general welfare?

Elizabeth le Marchant, Denis's wife, arrived the other day from Cyprus [a detachment from Sherwood Rangers Yeomanry had gone to Cyprus in June] on her way home and said that it had been the best six weeks of their lives. Isn't it futile that people with plenty of money like that should have to wait for a war to discover it is possible to have fun outside Lincolnshire? I am living in an airport control tower cum meteorological station surrounded by machines making chirpy noises. I have to take a four-hour watch sometime during the night and I am learning that great poem 'The Pobble' as I take my constitutional round the wire fence. I am also quite keen on drawing and have illustrated a poem for Michael Riviere.

I have just written to Banham and congratulated him on getting married, basing the supposition on a reference of John's so I hope he isn't living in sin or anything. I've sent them a little book with

58

quite good photographs of Palestine. We aren't allowed out of here except to take the men bathing otherwise I'd take some photographs of Arab clothes. The futile Egyptians wear long, absolutely straight night gowns, but the Arabs wear an amazing amount of clothes. Although they appear to live in great squalor they are very decent, and shocked by nakedness. [When Michael and I were bathing in front of Jaffa a deputation came down on to the beach and stood between our wet naked selves and our clothes to protest.] Their women are a bundle of black garments though sometimes you see a gaily dressed one.

Michael and I got into trouble the first night in this house because we had the light on and windows open dressing for dinner and were walking about naked, and an irate man came down to our boundary wall, which is also heavily shaded by trees, and said we should be ashamed of ourselves and there were ladies in his house (miles off) and we should be blacked out. So we said, 'Oh, toddle off and shut up and who are you anyway?' And he said, 'I'm Lieutenant Hicks, and I'll complain to the General tomorrow', which he did and we had to rush off to apologise. But we managed it very well, and when he arrived back from his office he found us sitting on the floor winding his very blonde wife's wool and drinking his drinks.

We have lost 11 officers since war began, sent away on different jobs, and as we subalterns are now numerically superior, the other day we had great fun and demanded a mess meeting and played hell. Because up to now all our pay has gone in mess bills.

18 September 1940, Palestine: Letter to My Mother

I should think if I wished you very many happy returns of 18th October and sent you all my love for it, now it might reach you in time. Yesterday we had another mail and I got my fifth *Country Life* in ten days but no letters. Then, just as I was going to bed, they brought me the best collection I've had. A most entertaining letter from Dallas Pratt [a friend from Cambridge days] in America, a long description from Mrs Brewis of her visit to Flintham, a delightful letter from John, a typed letter forwarded from Malta from Stewards in the Strand to say they could now provide me with a special kind of torch ordered a year ago as being on my list of army necessaries.

Dallas says: 'Your friend Hugh has just written me a long and ominous letter which I have been too frightened to answer. He asks me to do some constructive feeling and thinking for America to strengthen the reasons for our existence, to evaluate and love the liberties of free men, to maintain and increase our faith in the democratic way of life etc. etc. so I know I am in for it . . . we are doing our best for the relief and practically every woman I know is knitting socks for you soldier boys and spending a lot of time raising money, making bandages etc. – I suppose you will say this is to salve a guilty conscience.'

I am very much struck with one of the meteorologists here aged 20 who left Germany aged 12 and was educated in England and was to have become English when he was 21, I've never met anyone cleverer. He doesn't eat meat, smoke, drink or dance but reads one intensive page of astronomy per day and other difficult subjects like navigation and wireless, but is also charming and I'm getting him to work out Michael's latest idea of burning European crops by scattering lenses in the fields.

I have just discovered that Michael Mosley has arrived out here. Presumably he will go straight to the Western Desert but I hope very much to see him when I am in Cairo. Michael Parish at the last moment has been sent to the island where Denis is, they think only for six weeks. I have left my battery and joined RHQ as intelligence officer and live in a bungalow with running water in my bedroom. Michael has much improved the lens idea and it is going to be sent round to the great ones here and in England. But he reminded me that the man who thought of the tin hat, after two years' fruitless attempt to arouse interest, had to throw himself out of the gallery of the House of Commons and break a leg before anybody would take any notice.

Not much excitement over the Italians. We feel an invasion of England is much less probable which cheers us up very much.

60

27 September 1940, Palestine

Listen, for Heaven's sake try and get hold of a big envelope containing a thin book and a letter I sent to Banham, because on a bad guess I've written to him assuming he's married again. Or do you think it's alright? I didn't lay it on.

I have no news. Japan has just come into the war but if they can't deal with China in all this time I don't see why it should be a major embarrassment. I sit in a comfortable office and make précis of very interesting reports on the Flanders and Somaliland campaigns.

2 October 1940, Palestine: Letter to Toby

I am a casualty in billets with a carbuncle! But instead of a carbuncle being a sort of wart as I always thought, it is an appalling sort of hole reducing one to complete crippledom.

The last big convoy brought three new officers and Michael Mosley to Egypt and Billy Brooksbank to Palestine. If my leg gets better in time I am off to Cairo at the end of this week on an intelligence course. This is said to be the best of all courses and about the only one it pays you to do well in, though it is a little late in the day to get a good job out of it now.

This place is swarming with nurses. The idea is that they were taken up to a steady old horse and if it shied violently they were allowed out to Palestine! There are 500 all in white with scarlet bits and sunshades and all out for a lark. Opposite me there are a whole lot of Poles who sing, very well but hymnfully at night. I hear Poles and nurses come past talking French like nothing.

10–21 October 1940, Cairo

Before coming down here for my course I spent a night in Haifa with Billy Brooksbank who was there also on a course. I saw Billy Maclean who sent you all his love. Billy Brooksbank was the same

61

as ever and I was very happy to be with him again. I don't think he brought much news out from England, except discussing politics. He has a strange idea that all the power is falling into the hands of the Air Raid Wardens. This sounds too absurd but I shall expect you to keep a family air wardenship warm for me. His Pixie Pease married someone else, who was killed within two months, but Billy has now found someone else. I had the usual rather foul journey down, and brought my bicycle and Yates. The latter was forbidden and I had to get him two consecutive stretches of ten days' leave, but it was mainly to give him a holiday. We are billeted in quite a good hotel with all expenses paid, but lose our allowances as a result, and of course one doesn't want always to feed in the same place. The course is very interesting and all sorts of important people lecture to us, including Wavell yesterday. I played tennis today for the first time since I've been out here and not badly considering, and I needed the exercise.

On Saturday night after dinner Aleco and I drove out to see the Tombs of the Khalifs by moonlight in a gharry – a two-horse carriage. We drove out of Cairo into the desert, between hills of sand and rock and came to an amazing town. Its houses with quite normal façades were in fact only shells in whose courts families are buried, the whole place inhabited only by stray dogs and in the centre of it some great mosques standing alone – the tombs of the Circassian Mamelukes who ruled Egypt from the 14th to the 16th century. On the same side of the town and right on the outskirts is the Citadel, built by Saladin with the aid of Crusader prisoners on the only hill in the Delta. The stones came from the pyramids. Cairo then had been founded about 200 years. It was Saladin who introduced the system of Mamelukes – white slave boys brought to Egypt and trained as the sultan's bodyguard who eventually got all the power, so that the Caliphs were only puppet rulers and the Mamelukes lived by terror. They weren't a dynasty, but each chose a boy in his bodyguard to succeed him. In 1811 Mohammed Ali invited all the Mamelukes to dinner and murdered all but one who leapt off the battlements on horseback.

I am sorry to hear you get alarms in the village and the milk is so low. About letting the farm, I don't think the war will be over for some years, do you, and the farm could be much better let. I am still agriculturally minded, but my idea would be if possible an extensive study of agriculture when I got back. After that I should like to farm myself and then take an interest in the farming world generally. But it's no use trying to plan anything now and a good tenant would take much off your hands. Against this, I'm afraid of the government taking over all let farms. I wish sometime you would work out the cost of the upkeep on Flintham, so that I should know how to regard my chances of living there some day. I can't see why Flintham should be so expensive to live in, but people always say those sort of houses are.

31 October 1940, Palestine

I am wondering what mail and parcels went down on the *Empress of Britain*. You can imagine the misery here – the news came over the wireless and we had no other intimation. On board were Lord and Lady Yarborough, several wives and many friends. Lord Yarborough telegraphed next day that Dandy Wallace's wife was missing and yesterday we heard that the other wives were all right. We heard today that Mrs Wallace was dead, she was a charming person.

You can imagine I was sorry to come back from Cairo where I enjoyed myself enormously. Flash Kellett came for two nights on his way back from a visit to Cyprus. Rather typically he had the boat wait five hours for him, and when he arrived at Port Said ordered the Admiral's barge to take him off before everybody else in time to catch the Cairo train which he did with éclat. I took him out to dinner and he came up to scratch and offered me a captaincy and staff job, to which I didn't say yes and didn't say no.

My last day I went to Sakkara with Christopher Sykes, who is, I believe, the greatest authority on Persia in England. We drove down the Nile and had a picnic lunch in a palm grove by an alabaster sphinx, one of the few remains of the city of Memphis, once the capital. Near by is a colossal statue of Ramases II, lying on his back like a train engine. You walk round it on a gallery. Sakkara is the nearest edge of the desert and was the cemetery of Memphis. The most noticeable thing is the Step Pyramid, the first built and supposed to be the oldest stone building in the world. We mounted donkeys and trotted off to see the tomb of Ti, secretary to one of the kings. He was buried underground, and above are several rooms entirely covered with bas reliefs, largely coloured, and the most delightful imaginable. He is shown presiding over work on his farms, and hunting, fishing, sailing etc. and they are the only beautiful things I have yet seen in Egypt. The last room has a slit in the wall opposite the door and if you put a light in you see a life-size statue walled up in a further chamber, looking at you.

Have you had any airmen to stay yet? It sounds a grand idea and I hope you are being très grand seigneur, and putting a room and the wine cellar entirely at their disposal. I envy them very much.

25 November 1940, Palestine

I have been banished to an outlying battery, to replace two officers away on courses, the Battery Commander and only officer left being Trotter, not at all a friend of mine. I was horrified, but in fact rather enjoy it. We are guarding what will be the biggest aerodrome in the East. The only accommodation for officers is a hut with two rooms, but one of these we use as a mess and I sleep in a very large tent. Trotter is perfectly amicable. My predecessors took it in turns to talk to him, as he doesn't read. He is quite a good soldier and disciplinarian and very idle, so the battery is contented.

Our hours are 9–10, 11–12, the latter generally a lecture by me. It seems hotter out here, I sleep after lunch, read a lot, and go for a walk at sunset. I have just finished the first volume of the *Seven Pillars of Wisdom* (published in two volumes) and am enjoying it immensely and very glad I didn't read it earlier. Everything that has happened so far has been in Arabia, which I know nothing of, but from now on it will be in Palestine and Syria. Here we are in a wide plain, to the west, high ground between us and the strip of desert and sea, to the east the Judean hills.

Yesterday I went out all day on a picnic with Flash Kellett and a lot of others. I rode in Flash's car and had to provide information about the places we went through. We took the Jerusalem road as far as the hills and then turned south through fine open rocky valleys, to Beit Jibrun, which lies surrounded by the most superb olive groves, dusty green with weird knotted boles, all enormously old. Behind the village is the site of the earlier, Biblical town of Mareshah, birthplace of Micah and Eleazer. On the way we passed the ancient Zorah, birthplace of Samson, and soon after the mound where Bethshemesh stood. Below us was the most marvellous view, the village of Zakariyah and the valley of Elah, and winding through it the wadi from which David picked a smooth round pebble to slay Goliath.

We drove on to a huge mound some miles further, Lachish, where we lunched. Here an archaeologist had been killed in the troubles and his house burnt. I picked narcissi – jonquils as they call them – under the walls, and explored the ruined house, museum and buildings. Beds still stood in the rooms, broken lamps and stuff on the floors, and I found some very exciting pottery and enamelled glass on a windowsill. The terrace was overhung with weeping willows and pepper trees, charming. We climbed the mound, on which the excavating trolleys still stood on rails. Only a small part had been excavated, and it is a mystery to me how there comes to be so much earth over the ruins on these high places.

Lachish was a very ancient Amorite fortress, an outpost on the road to Egypt. It was besieged by Senacherib after defeating the Egyptians, and he received here tribute from Hezekiah for the freedom of Jerusalem. However he then demanded the surrender of Jerusalem, but in the moment of Zion's despair the Assyrians were attacked by disease, and retired. As you know. From Lachish we drove up to Hebron, the highest point in Palestine, with a view over to the sea and the hills of Moab in Trans Jordan, and the wildest, where you still can only go in convoy and armed. Hebron is one of the oldest inhabited cities in the world, the home and burial place of Abraham, who lies in the cave of Machpelah with Sarah and Isaac and Rebecca and Jacob and Leah, under a mosque. This was built by the Crusaders on the remains of Justinian's church. The patriarchs are of course worshipped by the Muslims quite as much as by the Jews. The town was David's capital and the birthplace of Absalom.

We drove straight on to the Pools of Solomon. Here is a castle built by Suleiman the Magnificent and three great reservoirs, one below the other down a valley. These are called Solomon's because in *Ecclesiastes* he says, 'I made me pools of water'. Pontius Pilate repaired them to supply Jerusalem, and they are so used now. They are cut out of the rock at the bottom, solid stone above, up to 200 yards long each by half as wide, and fringed with trees and rosemary in flower. This time of year seems a second spring here, with the scyllas and croci and jonquils.

It is 11 p.m., time for me to turn out the guard.

26 December 1940, Palestine

I have just passed a man on a bicycle, a Trans Jordan Frontier Force man wearing his black astrakhan Cossack hat with a scarlet plume, and sitting happy as can be on the handle bars, a white turkey. I feel this must be an augury of some kind. I have just finished Stendhal's *Rouge et Noir* which I read with intense enjoyment. I could hardly put it down, and the French was so easy I could read it almost like English.

Did you listen to the carols from Bethlehem on Christmas Eve? If so, you heard me. I think it is broadcast every year, generally they sing in a little courtyard surrounded by high walls against the church. We arranged for a lot of the men to go up, but the District Commissioner forbade anyone to attend the evening services at Bethlehem and we had to cancel. However Micky Riviere and I went up to Jerusalem in the evening and on to Bethlehem with Flash Kellett and two others. We found the carols were being sung in a

66

tiny chapel of St George in a corner of the courtyard, but we were turned out as not having been invited. So we waited in the court-yard under the tall tower of the old Greek monastery and the planet Jupiter shining as brightly as ever the star of the Magi could have done, straight up above. Eventually the High Commissioner arrived with a large party and the American consul with another. I followed in and sat down behind Araminta. None of the others managed to get in. It was a bare chapel with three or four rows of chairs for the guests and round the microphone at one end a nondescript collection of waif-like persons waiting to sing. They sang quite well and we sang too. It was very enjoyable.

I slept at the King David Hotel, which is extremely grand and incredibly expensive. I only got a room by saying I could perfectly well sleep in Dan Ranfurly's room for nothing – he being away – though Jerusalem and the King David seemed unusually empty. It was nice to wake up on Christmas Day with the sun shining outside on a dome, instead of in this camp, which in fact was the point of the expedition.

At ten o'clock after a sunny breakfast looking out on the walls, Micky and I went to the Protestant cathedral of St George, a Victorian church, ordinary parish size and ugly. It was a very good service, and the Anglican bishop in Jerusalem preached. I'm told he has only been in the Church ten years and is a very great scholar. He is like a mediaeval monk. He reads his sermons from notes – quite excellent. At the same time he employs gesticulation to a degree which the utmost impetuosity could not save from melodrama. Thus throwing himself back with his hands upraised from his frilly sleeves, he will come to the end of a page of his notes. Keeping one arm absolutely steady he pauses in the middle of a great declaration, quickly turns over his notes, and continues with undiminished vigour. He would be great in a big church where one cannot see all this, but even as it was I was very impressed. His text was 'and there was no room at the inn'.

29 December 1940, Palestine: Letter to Toby

I do hope you more or less like your flying, and the life. I can't say I'm actually frantic to be killed because of the preliminaries and I'm such a funk, but really the possibility of it is a hundred times more distressing to one's family than to oneself, and the great thing is that life in between dangers should be pleasant. Here as you know there hasn't been the suggestion of a danger and life is so easy it is disquieting. At present I am on quite a tough cadre class inside the Regiment, and the very day that finishes I go on a weapon training course and I loathe weapons, but none of that really matters if one has books, friends, warmth, light and sunshine. Warmth is not too terrific at the moment, nor sunshine, and the moment it goes black, depression is apt to descend, fortunately even in bad weather there are intervals of sun and I walk in it and cheer up like a simple savage, and as I say there's a good deal of work.

Three new officers came yesterday. One was a ranker in this regiment, before that a clerk in Flash Kellett's bank, the other two were rankers in the Warwickshire Yeomanry. They are all very busy talking about horses, stags and woodcock, they are much better than the last lot we got straight out from England, and more presentable. Although everybody knows the future of the Division and these three have been earmarked some time for us, their training has been entirely in cavalry.

I don't foresee a very gay birthday [31st December] as I am working on my cadre class from eight in the morning till seven at night, but I have a cake, present from Micky Riviere, and I'm giving him one on January 5th which is his birthday! Our Indian cook makes very beautiful cakes, but they are incredibly expensive (mine is £1 but our big ones for Christmas were £3 each) and the icing is all soft cream so we just scrape it off, and that's the best bit really.

Dallas Pratt wrote, New Year's Day 1941, from New York City

Many thanks for your long and interesting letter. It was strange to hear of villas and sunbathing and sightseeing out of the 'mouth of hell'. I wonder whether things have taken a more grim turn for you? For the first time in months the papers are tolerable reading, and of course everyone is thrilled over the British successes in Libya and the Greek Miracle in Albania.

I don't know whether the situation in America interests you or not. Everybody seems to be getting more and more confused and frightened. When I was at Yale in 1936 everything was perfectly clear – we should definitely stay out of any European war and avoid being dragged in as we were in 1917. We had all read Walter Millis' brilliant book The Road to War, *which proved so conclusively that the Allies were as much to blame as the Germans in starting the Great War, and we felt that by not sending our ships and money to Europe we could keep out of any future conflict. So the Neutrality Laws were passed to save us from ourselves and we didn't need to pass any more rules about not lending money because the Johnson Act was already in force, which said we would not lend to any who had not paid their war debts – and that included everybody in the world except Finland.*

Things then slid along very pleasantly and the sins of the New Deal occupied our attention, until Adolf started to act up. If he had been more subtle we might have been able to say that even he was more sinned against than sinning, but he seemed determined to prove this time the Germans were really the aggressors. So everybody became terribly confused in America and had to cast about for new reasons for staying out of the war (which by this time had started up again). For a time we were very hard boiled and said our 'selfish interests' dictated prudence – we must preserve in the New World what shreds of civilization we could and let the Old go hang.

Our ivory tower philosophy made a terrific effort to bolster itself, and suddenly overnight there was the most extraordinary outburst of fake patriotism. Irving Berlin wrote an obnoxious song called

'God Bless America' which was blared forth from every street corner; ladies wore flag bracelets and carried purses covered with miniature American flags, people hung little signs in the back windows of their cars reading 'God Bless America – we are PROUD to be Americans' (which in most cases they obviously were not), and all sorts of Fifth Columnists and saboteurs were dragged out from behind grocery counters and grilled by the Federal Bureau of Investigation – all, of course, to no avail.

When this effort succumbed to the general nausea, the ivory tower collapsed also, and we began to wonder just how safe we really were, and in a very short time we discovered that our armaments were hopelessly inadequate, that our navy was not really large enough, that our army was non-existent. So the Draft was rushed through Congress, and as a result all men between 21 and 34 are to be called up for a year's service before 1945 – I am number 3,355 and likely to be called up in 18 months. This has very much changed the attitude of the population at large, and now most people think that sooner or later we are going to be involved. When Roosevelt said that France was our first line of defence last winter he was roundly trounced and had to make a public denial; now he says the same thing openly every day about England and everybody eggs him on.

At the moment we seem to be hurtling towards involvement, and yet I cannot make up my own mind. On the one hand is one's intense desire to help the British and have at 'that man', on the other is sheer cowardice and the genuine horror one has at sending human beings into war unless absolutely necessary. Also, as a potential doctor rather than a potential soldier, it is hard for me to say that other men should do and die on my behalf. (Although this does seem to be as much a civilian's as a soldier's war.) You see what a muddle we are in!

4 January 1941, Palestine: Letter to John

My friend Michael Parish's brother Charles, who was my age at Eton, has had quite an exciting time. First he was on the first big

70

raid over Berlin and it was his plane flew low over the Unter den Linden, then later he was sent to bomb Boulogne. There were two Wellington Bombers with a crew of six each. They ran into awful weather and thunder which wrecked the wireless and they had to turn back. The Squadron Leader decided they must bale out, which they did. Charles with great presence of mind blew out his lifesaving jacket as he came down and he was the only one of twelve to survive. He swam for five hours and came ashore near Frinton. He was lucky in being, like all his family, a very good swimmer.

29 January 1941, Palestine

Soon after my last letter, a bombshell was dropped on the Regiment and we were informed we were to revert to our role of last summer [as coastal gunners]. This after the most definite promises of 'most favoured regiment' from every general, as a reward for our box and cox treatment in the past. Consequently my move [to Crete] was put off and the Regiment being rearranged I found myself put down for a new Battery – 'X'.

Michael P was not to be recalled, but to proceed to the place I'd hoped to go to, and B battery was to join them there. I hurried off to Flash and urged that under my command B had won the battery competition in the summer and they were partly my old troop and couldn't I go back. Flash said 'it's not impossible' and then called me back to say 'by the way, B aren't going now too'. However, that night I was sent for and shown an amended arrangement; B was under Sidney Morse, with Micky Riviere and myself, *and* going to the same place as Michael. Ever since then I've been longing to be off before it gets changed again. I am now a lieutenant, but this means absolutely nothing. I become one in any case automatically on 1st March and shall only get paid for it then. Henry Trotter parted with me today with such a glowing reference and apparent regret that my stock underwent a lightning rise. I forgot whether I told you that we subalterns issue stock on our favour in the eyes of the mighty. With any luck I should now make a getaway on a rising market.

I have been reading *Three Deserts* by C. S. Jarvis (John Murray), his first and best book, which I'm sure you would enjoy very much. It has clarified my ideas about the Arabs. As he was 15 years a successful governor of Sinai I think he should know them. His idea is that they should be called not 'Sons of the Desert' but 'Fathers of the Desert' – that they came to Sinai and particularly Libya when these places were flourishing and wiped everything out. The Romans had run channels from the wadis to their orchards and cut great cisterns in the rocks to store water. The Moslems – Bedouin Arabs – were nomads, breeders of camels and herders of goats, who disdain manual labour. They let the water courses fall into ruin and the cisterns silt up, their goats ate all the orchards and they just sat around in great poverty and say 'the will of Allah'. Rather than clear out an old cistern they would send their wives 15 miles for water to a well. He points to the evidence of Lawrence, who was a great pro-Arab, that they had no unity and were purely tribal.

Jarvis also points out that the Syrians and Palestinians are not Arabs, but descendants of the old peoples in those countries and of the Turks, and that they did absolutely nothing to aid the Allies and that it is they who cry out about the Arab cause here today. The real Arabs only think of Palestine as a rich place to loot. He also says that Arab dignity is all my eye, the truth being that on most questions they are completely uninterested, but show them a coin and everyone for miles will be in the fight.

All this seems to me to make sense, and explain one of the big gaps in my grasp of history – how the great colonisation of Africa under the Romans fell into such utter ruin. I am now reading Manson's *History of England*. We are all dumping a lot of luggage and I most of my heavy books.

21 February 1941, Crete

Our journey was much as expected. We left in the morning, reached the canal in the dark, changed again at midnight with a long wait where I slept in the station with a cat on my lap, reached the port named after Philip's son [Alexandria] at dawn, changed again and went to a camp on the fringe of the Western Desert.

We stayed one night, turned back and went on board. Our ship wasn't looking its best and though officers were all right with a stateroom each, the men were four at least to a cabin on the bottom deck where there were no portholes. We were two nights and a day at sea, very calm though a storm the last night, and sunny. We almost ran down one mine and passed another later, firing at them without apparent effect. They were loose of course. We got up early the last morning and slowly the island showed up as it got light – we had by then already rounded its western end – great rumply mountains running down into the sea. Micky and I ran from one side of the ship to the other as we began to enter a sort of fiord and the sun to rise, shining on a long range of snowy mountains behind green hills on one side and an island with an old fort on it on the other, and we steamed on down the fiord to a small town with a jetty. This was the bay we are now defending, if you have a map with names on it, take the first two letters of the names of Sybil D'Elston's second daughter [Susan, used to signify Suda]. I shall go on to a new sheet so that if the censor wishes to destroy any of this he can leave the rest. Nobody can tell me what we are or are not allowed to say about our journey. The island is quite lovely.

It has two main towns, one near the famous labyrinth over 100 miles away, the other [Canea] on the sea not far beyond the end of the bay. Michael Parish is there and has been over twice on his motor bicycle. Transport is a great difficulty, the road is over mountains all along the bay and full of pot holes. Canea is an attractive town, and has a big market where you buy vegetables very cheap, and a fishing harbour. A mile beyond us on the sea is our particular village, to which I ride on my famous bicycle. I early contacted the mayor who speaks a little English and runs everything and is most helpful. He was a sergeant in the last war and then in New York for three years. We fetch our water from here in a donkey cart. Yates yesterday brought back a live chicken and today claims to be producing some mutton. We are told there are no sheep

73

or goats on the island; only shoats, a mixture, this is quite untrue but Micky and I call anything doubtful 'geep'.

Our washing is done by four women whose husbands are fighting in Albania. There aren't many young men left and the place is full of old men and crones. All the men wear high leather boots to their knees, some look like Italian burghers of the time of Dante with black hoods and long white beards, others wear a Balkan get up which Micky and I intend to obtain forthwith – a blue cloak, red inside, embroidered with red and gold, a blue waistcoat with ribbons running from the shoulders to a point, breeches and boots and a little turban hat with a loose end. The women wear black. The mayor entertains every soldier he can lay hands on, and as he was a big exporter of red wine and has a large store, one is liable to be slightly drunk immediately after breakfast.

Micky and I are learning the language and have a futile little book of the 'Postilion where is my post chaise?' type. It is made more difficult by the fact that the mayor definitely pronounces different to the book (which has phonetic spelling). However I can say 'bring six eggs every day at four drachmas each' and get them, which is something. Michael says they all spoke Greek in Cyprus but he learnt Turkish as he thought it more likely to be useful. His lot don't think so much of this place as they say Cyprus was as beautiful and far gayer with riding and dancing and tennis, but this is good enough for me. The only trouble is that we are going to have to leave our olive grove and move into an old prison on the mountain which is full of AA [anti-aircraft] and marine and gunner officers with whom we shall have to mess. We are very cast down about this but no doubt we shan't let it worry us long. It is very sad to be losing our view and solitude. But is all so beautiful and so nice having Michael P again that I feel very happy.

2 March 1941, Crete

Well, very sadly we deserted our olive grove for the prison. It stands halfway up a spur which ends in a point enclosing the bay. The

74

prison looks long and low from a distance, like a big fort. It has a wall round it and several blocks of forbidding buildings, all filthy. It was fully occupied so far as officers were concerned when we arrived. That is to say the Colonel had a house just outside. With him, in the bedroom, sleep his 2 i/c, adjutant and a subaltern. Cosy like. Outside the walls behind the prison is a small village, a church, inn, governor's house (now the Colonel's) and other prison dwellings, on the flat and running steeply down either side of the spur. In front of the prison looking out to sea the land rises for a bit so that the prison walls on this side are actually cut into the rock and above them on a narrow ledge are a row of dugouts. They have no windows, only a door. Some are roofless.

At tea a message came that I was wanted on the telephone about a quarter of a mile away. As I went with the orderly he said he could hear aeroplanes and we saw them just before the first alarm went. They came from the sea towards us very high, without shells bursting round them, and as they were directly over us loosed their bombs. They came down very slowly, the first I'd seen actually falling. I thought it time to go to ground, but the marines whose telephone it was ran up on to a little hill to watch them burst and I with them. They were quite right, they fell a good mile away, and were in the bay and none did any damage. That is the first raid since we've been here, thought they were daily just before. Michael was actually sitting in the cockpit of a plane talking to the pilot when the aerodrome was raided and he hopped out just in time for the pilot to get away while he jumped on his motor bike and made off full speed. We hear the remainder of the Regiment are getting it much more serious, but no casualties.

16 March 1941, Crete

No letters or cables from you since January. I am just back from three nights away with Michael P, to Knossos, travelling both ways in a truck and so saving the six pounds it cost our battery commanders the week before in a taxi. The road is in parts very bad, particularly in a car, and it took them six hours and us only three. Almost the whole way is over mountains, through villages where everyone cheers us and valleys of old scattered oaks and bare stony passes.

There were two other officers there on sick leave from a very ill-esteemed regiment, and we asked them about a bath. They had been there three days. 'We only have baths on Saturdays,' they said. Gesticulations at the servants only brought loud giggles – the servants being an extremely aged crone wrapped in black and some other peasants. So we sent Michael's servant to prospect. I've never seen such a geyser as we found. The servants almost passed out when we set light to it and rushed off for the curator. When he came he admitted that he didn't know how it worked. It produced a small teapotful of hot water at a go, after baleful steamings. It was such a laborious business that the next night we had the servant cook a bucketful over the stove, and that wasn't much cosier spread out in a large bath. The curator and his very old and rheumaticky mother had meals in the villa, though their lodge was infinitely more comfortable.

Next day at Knossos the Governor General came to lunch with his wife, a British-born Cypriot, plus retinue. He couldn't speak English, only one of those with him beside his wife could – a Turkish-born Greek. I am very anxious to find out who Admiral Noel was who helped free the island and is held almost in higher esteem here than any other Englishman. Till the end of last century the island seems to have suffered continual oppression and revolt, and there are still 'Chieftains of the Hills' who in those days led the brigands. As a result, like Palestine, the hills have been pretty well denuded of forest, though there are plenty of olives. The British government has bought all the oil and sultana crop, which is a good thing. I find El Greco was born here, hence the name.

Tonight I played my first game of chess. I was also beaten in the first round of the cribbage tournament while Micky is in the semi-finals after beating the champion, our sergeant major. Micky sits opposite reading the Bible.

76

21 March 1941, Crete

Micky Riviere and I now play chess; we have only played two nights and he has played two with Sidney as well. Last night, without Sidney at my elbow suddenly to move things for me, I beat Micky first in twenty minutes and next in ten, and I almost kicked the floor through with pleasure. So I think it's a good game.

I have enough books to keep me going for some months, so really I have nothing to worry about and I'm being forced to read a lot of books I've put off. One is *Coningsby* by Disraeli, which really is poor stuff after Tolstoy but a good picture of society, then I shall read *Liza* by Turgenev. I will tell you what is cooking for dinner below – soup, fish cakes, French artichokes, steaks. With cheese and red wine this isn't too bad as an ordinary day's meal. The men call the red wine 'crassy' which somehow I think I've read in old books, and I find Malmsey is a corruption of an island wine called Malvesin or something like that.

15 and 17 April 1941, Crete

Since I last wrote things have not been going so easily in Libya and Greece, in fact my poor fish of a General Neame has let himself be captured. I am a little worried about my photograph album, which may by now be at Berchtesgaden. All this of course must affect our future, which otherwise seemed to be panning out quite satisfactorily before.

I have always been puzzled by your stress on faith, which I think self-deception. You cannot deny the fact of empty churches, ridiculous parsons, indifference to religion in literature, and you can only say 'Christianity has never been put into practice'. Is it likely to be then? If it fails to appeal either to the thinking man or to the masses? This man Samuel stresses the fact that philosophy can never be religion, as it lacks emotion and poetry. But religion must have the backing of sense and the inspiration of hope. To me your 'Faith' is uninspiring. And it seems to me that as our religion must wake up or fade out, it would be far better if its renewal came from within and the only people who can revive it are the comparatively few who still support it. At present they are just the people who encourage it to keep going on one leg for old times' sake. Whether our religion can be revived and remain itself I don't feel sure, but it's death or glory. This seems a vulgar, unintellectual age, and a few good ideas brought in to patch the old bottles wouldn't I'm afraid raise the market price much. Fascism's success shows the success of any vivid practical ideal, and I'm sure we too shall find something, sooner or later.

26 April 1941, Crete: Letter to Laurence Biddle in Tobruk

I have two regular openings on Crete. One is the antique, 'here just across the bay, Icarus flying too near the sun melted unbecomingly; here on Mount Ida Great Jove was born; here Theseus vanquished the Minotaur and sailing gaily back to Africa forgot to change his sails, with tragic consequences; here flourished beyond dispute the great pre-Doric Aegean civilization of the Minoan kings'. Or you can have the romanticised version, 'a land of little valleys and great green mountains, terraces of vines and olives overhung by wild crags and a great beaker of snow, and everywhere a million wild flowers and always a blue sea'.

We camped for the first week in an olive grove, my tent looking on to snowy peaks on one side and the sea on the other was almost perfect. But the nanny goat and kid tied to a tree in front to complete the idyll turned out rather a trial as their amiable owner was always dashing into my tent, seizing my toothglass and pumping goat's milk straight into it, his little daughter would sidle in and madly kiss my hand, hotly encouraged in these nymphomaniac tendencies by her mother, who in her turn, the moment I turned my back, placed a small yellow cushion embroidered with a horrid little cupid on my bed and enquired when she might expect to be paid for it.

To our great and enduring regret we had to move from this rustic paradise into the prison which stands at the entrance to the fiord-like bay and had till recently housed 300 murderers. It also once housed M Venizelos. Michael Riviere and I have continued so delighted with the countryside that even the disadvantage of this move hardly disturbed us. Sidney [Morse] however remained for a month plunged in utter gloom and has never been the really comfortable chap you might expect on seeing him in his canvas bath. This comes of 1) Dorothy; 2) homesickness for RHQ; 3) general forebodings. None of these of course are shared by Micky and myself. We are delighted to be away from RHQ and cannot see it as a universal panacea for all minor disturbances, but only as a minor Vesuvius in itself. As for forebodings it is admittedly un-fortunate that they have all come to pass. We live I think extra-ordinarily happily together, we never quarrel at all. We seem to feel almost exactly alike about most things, the only pity is that as the duties have tightened up we now go on duty all day every other day, and so are never free to go out together. On my day off I most often go off and meet Michael P and we climb or bathe.

We have had air raids pretty regularly on ships in the harbour; at the moment there is a strange inexplicable lull as ships are pouring in from the north. You can imagine how much we should like to know how you are and whether you stick to your job or help repel land attacks. The biggest excitement till lately was when we had a one-man motorboat attack – most ingenious with a huge charge of dynamite in the front of the boat. The man sits in the back and at the last moment jumps out backwards on to a raft. The boat goes on, hits the object, sinks with the engine still pressing against the side of the ship and explodes.

I have made great friends with one of the Italian officers off these and now we have a very nice young German who really thinks he is fighting for the Polish Corridor! Micky and I have been making a great outcry about the cells in which prisoners are kept while awaiting trial – old Turkish dungeons, pitch dark all day and airless. We got a doctor colonel to look at them, who said anyone in them would be mentally affected in 48 hours and nothing has been done, to our indignation. Two prisoners have been there five weeks, one a colour sergeant. My theory is that we shall always have wars while the majority of mankind is so stupid.

The Battle of Crete

In the early hours of 19 May 1941, German parachutists and aeroplanes attacked Allied positions on Crete. After a week of fighting the Allied commander General Freyberg decided that his outnumbered forces could no longer defend the island and the order to withdraw was given. As the forces on the island scrambled to evacuate, Myles and his men were given orders to destroy all evidence of their occupation at the prison, and make for the beach at Sphakia on the south coast across the mountains. Gathering other stragglers as they went, they slowly filed down to the beach, only to see the last ships sail.

Toby sent a telegram from Gibraltar to Flintham, 22 May 1941

Don't worry. Myles probably playing chess obliviously in the sun, well away from it all.

Father wrote from Flintham, 26 May 1941

We can't bear to think of what you must be enduring now and it is difficult to write ordinarily. All so suddenly too after your happy days of wandering on the hills in the sunshine with nothing worse than a mad prisoner to cope with. May God bring you safely through it all. If you ever get this He will have done so. We can think of nothing else, but ordinary things must go on and it is lovely here with the bluebells and forget-me-nots out together and both unusually good, a reward for all our labours in transplanting bluebells through this year.

Toby wrote from Gibraltar to Flintham, 1 June 1941

So it has come, but I'm somehow certain Myles got away. These last four or five days have been quite unreal and nightmare like, with work non-stop and the uncertainty all the time. It must have been better than for you, though, at least I was too tired to think of anything much except the job in hand, after three nights running without any sleep worth mentioning, two flying. We did 24 hours up out of 36, which was pretty heavy though some did more, one lot doing 34. I've never been so thankful though for work in all my life. It very seldom comes like this, but it was a godsend. It must have been awful for you though without all that. I think the whole thing was shameful and they did magnificently, but I suppose we will forget it fairly soon once we know Myles is alright. My hunch is so strong I can't worry any more. I felt it very much when we were out on those jobs, probably when things were worst for him, and then we all came back alright and so, I'm certain, did he.

This is only a quick letter as I'm still very tired, but there won't be much on now. Let me know at once anything you hear, it may take some little time I'm afraid. I'll try from this end.

God bless you. Don't worry: listen for me to all of my really good hunches.

Mother wrote from Flintham, 4 June 1941

Such an agonising time. We daren't think of what you've been through, but you have been surrounded by the prayers of so many people. So many have written and all have said that they were praying for you. Please God we shall hear from you soon. I have tried to carry on here as you told me to and Dad of course has been marvellous, but everything speaks of you three and it seems so pointless without you. Still, perhaps the clouds will suddenly clear and you will all come home again.

The War Office, Casualty Branch, Liverpool, wrote to Mrs Hildyard, 13 June 1941

Madam,

In confirmation of War Office telegram of the 11th June 1941, I am directed to inform you, with regret, that a notification has been received from the Military Authorities in the Middle East that your son, Lieutenant M. T. Hildyard, The Nottinghamshire Yeomanry, was reported missing on 1st June 1941, and slightly wounded.

No further information is available at present, but all possible enquiries are being made, both by the Department and by the Missing and Prisoners of War Department of the British Red Cross Society, to whom your son's name has been reported.

Any further information received by this Department will be sent to you immediately, and should any news reach you from any other source it will be appreciated if you will communicate with this Department.

Geoffrey Brooks wrote from Notts Yeomanry MEF to Mrs Hildyard, 30 June 1941

I am writing to tell you how very sorry I am for you and Judge Hildyard in your great anxiety for Myles. I do hope that your suspense will soon be relieved by the news that he is safe. It is a terrible blow to all of us here. You have probably heard that of the party who were in Crete, all six officers are missing and over 100 men. It seems too late now for any hope of their return here and we can only hope and pray for their safety. No doubt Myles will have told you what a cheery party we were in the mess and of the good times we had last year. It was a great disappointment to us when we were split up in February. We had been looking forward to a reunion very soon and I cannot tell you how distressed we here all feel at our great loss. We had received several letters during April and early May, including one from Myles to the Adjutant [Lawrence Biddle] and we had often felt envious of their pleasant station as we were having a rather bad time of it just then [in Tobruk]. Very few of us though would like to have changed places with them during the awful ordeal of the German attack on the island. Under present conditions I suppose it must be some time before any correspondence can get through from those left behind there, but I sincerely hope by the time this letter reaches you, you will know of Myles' safety and whereabouts. Till then, please accept my heartfelt sympathy in your great anxiety.

C. W. Parish wrote from Batemans, Burwash, Sussex, to Judge Hildyard, 17 July 1941

Your letter of 13th July arrived here today. I hasten to tell you that I have had no word regarding Michael officially since the War Office telegram reporting him wounded and missing.

I have already told you of Lady Ranfurly's letter which unofficially reported Michael and one other young officer slightly wounded, and which we so earnestly hope was true. So much turns on this word 'slightly'. I presume that your boy was this other young officer.

You tell me that the four unwounded officers are now officially reported as prisoners, and of course it is very distressing that our two are not included with them. We can, however, only hope, as you say, that this is because they were wounded and are presumably in hospital. It is certainly encouraging that neither of us has heard; if one had heard and not the other it would have been even more disquieting.

I do not, however, think we should be unduly apprehensive, though of course Lady Ranfurly's letter was entirely based on reports brought back by the men, and anything may have happened after they left the island; but it is no good meeting trouble half way. We must quietly and calmly await events and hope that sooner or later telegrams will reach us via the Red Cross, and that both boys are alive as prisoners. If and when this glad news reaches me regarding Michael I will at once send you a telegram, as letters

83

take three to four days, and I shall be very grateful if you will do the same.

Robin Hildyard wrote from 149 Anti-Tank Regt RA MEF to Mrs Hildyard, 11 September 1941

Aunt Sybil, I have met an officer of Myles' Regiment, name unknown to me, and have been in communication with the Adjutant, Captain Biddle, by post. While there is no official news of his present whereabouts, the Regiment have not the slightest doubt that he was captured together with Captain Morse, now known to be a prisoner in Germany, and Michael Riviere whose whereabouts are also not known.

They have told me this story, which you may not have heard, so I will repeat it anyway. Myles' battery had to retire near the mountains from Suda Bay to Sphakia, they had a difficult time getting across but arrived with practically no casualties. Here they performed valuable work in carrying rations to the rearguard who were defending Sphakia. On the night of 31st May, the last night of the evacuation, his battery were supposed to embark from the beach. When last seen they were on the beach and it was anticipated that they would have no difficulty that night, but evidently something went wrong with the embarkation arrangements and they got left behind. So far news has only been received of Captain Morse.

I have spoken to Red Cross HQ out here and they say no news has been received of most of the Crete prisoners, so the fact we have no news of Myles is in no way a bad sign, but is the general rule.

I have been to Thomas Cook & Son in Cairo and seen Myles' list. A large metal trunk, a wooden box with rounded top and two suits. I could not open the first two as they were locked, so I cannot tell you what is in them and whether they are worth sending home. Apparently it would cost about £6–7 to send them home to you and they would not be certain to arrive, as they might be sunk; so that it seems to me best to wait till someone can take them home with him, which will probably not be till the end of the war; what do you think? I think it would be cheapest for someone to take them with him and safer at the end of the war. I could do anything you would like about this. The Regiment have got a letter for Myles with photos, I think of Flintham, which they are holding to send as soon as they know of his whereabouts.

Excerpts from Myles' Journal, Beginning from Mid-May 1941

I had slept the night in Micky Riviere's house instead of in my tent, where from dawn onwards there had lately been a struggle between my love of bed and a certain restlessness as enemy planes started the day's work overhead. Now, calm and well dressed as usual, Sidney came in and woke me up to say we were off in an hour. Crete was to be evacuated. He disappeared and I yelled for Yates to discuss the situation. In my haversack, ready for all eventualities, were already some tins of sardines, my compass and so on. I added a few things and told Yates to destroy everything else. Down at the guns we destroyed everything we could with hammers and with bars, and threw the breech blocks into the sea.

During breakfast I went through my papers and gave Yates a mass of intelligence stuff to burn in the oven in the garden. That attracted our friends who zoomed over the house machine-gunning. Meanwhile, the men had collected in the gateway of the prison. Some had had close shaves when the BOP and gun positions were machine-gunned after I left, though nothing like so severely as a day or two earlier when bullets went through the telephones, wireless and both officers' beds, and blast from rear bombs blew the whole of the front in. At the same time the Port War Signal Station got a direct hit and Commander Salisbury and his staff vanished completely.

I was told to lead the way out of the prison. We ran from house corner to house corner, and once out of the village from ditch to ditch and patch of corn or weeds or olive tree, while the enemy planes passed low overhead, machine-gunning when they saw anybody.

85

After a mile or two we reached the river and followed the tree-fringed bank. Michael brought up the rear, and very soon he was in difficulties. Men who in a period of tension we had not been able to take off the guns and exercise, some who long before Crete had never walked further than the mess room, now began to collapse. It was with difficulty that at midday we reached a village, Neo Xorio, on the main road to Herakleon, intact. Here our truck with food and ammunition was to meet us; Sidney went off to find it.

All the 15 Coast Regiment was there, and instead of letting us go on, the Adjutant said we were to stay till dark as no movement was allowed. Micky and I sat with the men under olive trees and were machine-gunned continuously. Then a message came from Sidney. We were to meet him and the Colonel two miles up the road. As the road was obviously suicide, we led the men up a dry river bed and so to a point we judged to be two miles above the village. We hid in a pine wood against the road and Micky and I looked and shouted for Sidney. No sign of anybody. So we led the men down again into the river bed and there we lay till dark, protected by a cliff behind us and hidden by leafy plane trees while aeroplanes passed continuously just above our heads, spitting and crackling.

A little further up was a good spring. We refilled all our water bottles there just before dark and moved off in good order with strict instructions as to discipline on the march. The road was a streaming riot of flying troops, hurrying along in the dark. It was difficult to keep our column together and yet push our way through the stragglers past jammed lorries. We came to a village in flames some time before midnight, and at the rumour of water our men fell out in the darkness. We had to halt and try to collect them. The water was in fact an illusion. I jettisoned my heavy overcoat, and we went on. Soon after Matheson, Micky's servant, fainted – a tough man who had trained the battery's boxers.

Men began to drop out hopelessly, and Micky and I gave up all idea of keeping them together. We went on with a few of them, becoming very thirsty and weary ourselves as the road began to climb. In the ditches all the way along, men were resting or asleep. We pressed on, for our reading of the map had made us expect to reach a mountain plain, where we might get food, water and room to disperse off the road. But the road circled up and up in long sweeps and we felt thirstier and thirstier and were practically alone.

Just before dawn we came to a place where the road crossed a small open flat, and there was a well. We tied together all the water bottles we had and let them down and had just got water when General Freyberg, the C-in-C, arrived with Force HQ in trucks (which they drove into the undergrowth and covered over) and he ordered me to disperse the men collecting round the well before planes began arriving. We took our men as far back from the road as we could get and settled down for the day. I slept on a ledge of rock, camouflaged with branches and tufts of grass.

In the afternoon I was sitting talking to Micky when a plane dropped bombs just below us. Buckingham, Sidney's servant, got a piece of shrapnel in the arm. We put him on an ambulance with Force HQ. When it got dark we moved out again and when we reached the top of the mountain pass we began to look down and listen for the sea.

We came about one o'clock to Imbros, a village on the road used as a collecting post, and there we found Sidney. The stony fields were crowded with sleeping men, but Sidney got us permission to move on and we marched out down the road, pretty well up to strength, for the stragglers who had not joined us during the day had mostly walked on and joined Sidney.

We didn't get far before we were stopped and told we must take cover as there were already too many men on the road to the sea. So we went into a gorge off the road and slept very coldly on a rock till it was light and then told the men to hide where they could for the day. We officers found ledges on the cliff side, but it became too hot and Micky and I moved into a cave full of New Zealanders, charming people we thought. There we finished my sardines. We found we were eating very little. All day planes were over and we covered our faces in the mouth of the cave as they passed.

At dusk we collected the men and formed up ready to march down to the sea. This was now more or less organised – everybody had to be in a band of 50 under an officer, with a gap between each

87

band. But we moved at about 1 mph, stopping every 50 yards, and when we reached a counting post we were chopped in half and I was given a band, half our men and half of the band next behind.

Next we stopped for a talk from an Australian officer, who told us that the evacuation had gone well the night before, that if we made a sound or lit cigarettes we should be fired on by our posts on the mountain overlooking the road, that terrific air-raids by the RAF over Germany all week would keep the German air force off Crete for the next few days, and that we had had great success in Libya and reached Tripoli! *All* untrue.

We marched on, halting every instant because of the crowds ahead and to let rearguard parties go through. They were begging water as they passed, but we had failed to get any all day. Only some rum which a parson was doling out. The road began to swing down hill, and became much worse. Every moment in the darkness we expected to see the sea.

At one of our halts I was sitting on a stone wall by the side of the road when to my great surprise I got a bullet in the leg. Randall with me was hit in the hand. Two men had been shot and were lying also hit quite close, one very bad. But it is puzzling, and I accuse a Colonial, who is indignant! We put on first field dressings, and as at that moment some trucks came along with wounded on board, we got on them. They gave us to drink petrolly water and liver salts. I thought it was the best thing I ever tasted. We bumped and jolted downhill past bombed and burnt-out trucks and ambulances.

1 June 1941

At last we can get no further, the road is blocked by discarded trucks. I am on one of a lot of trucks with walking wounded. We get out. Nobody knows where we go next. We walk off down the road which twists down a steep hillside, embanked at the corners and finally just stops. All round a dark rocky hill, and far away a flatness which is probably the sea. But in what direction the evacuation is going on no one has any idea. Randall and I walk downhill, tripping over rocks and bushes, till he has a fall which all but knocks him out. We feel hopeless about it and decide to lie down and sleep where we are and wait for daylight.

Hearing a voice I shout out, and it is Bob Laycock, the commander of 'Lay force' – our commandos. Another voice in the darkness ceaselessly calls for help. When it gets light we find we had stopped on the edge of a gorge, and climbing down into it we find that its cliffs are lined with caves, already full of soldiers. In the village on the further side of it we get water, and we go into a cave full of Australians. None of us have any food at all. There are caves all along the gorge side and in the bottom olive trees, and all chock full of troops, 'Bomb happy' troops at that, shouting if anyone moves out into the open, for fear of attracting enemy planes.

In the morning there is a conference of officers in the village at the end of the gorge. There I find Tony Holden. They tell us at the conference that very few troops would be taken off that night. Tony tells me that Sidney and B Battery are right down on the beach, so I decide to go off and join them again, which means leaving the Australians who want me as an officer to lead their party. However, first of all we manage to get a bit of food from the dumps on the beach – biscuits and marmalade – which we draw for the whole party, and tinned stuff too, which I make them hoard. Then Randall and I go off to find Sidney. On the way we meet Colonel Downes of the 15 Coast, who tells us to find Sidney quickly as he should be getting off tonight. We find Sidney in the village, very exhausted as they have had no sleep but spent the night taking up rations to the rearguard. Micky Riviere is there and Michael Parish, and they have a pot of golden syrup and some tea and biscuits. Michael Parish has spent the last three days as Liaison Officer for General Weston, riding a motor bike between him and the other generals, who have now all got themselves off. Michael however is sticking to B rather than Y battery, which isn't together much.

We form up about 11 p.m., and with some difficulty and jostling, get into our position. But unfortunately about then the rearguard begins to arrive and pass through us. (Lay force – Bob just cut in.) We move slowly down towards the beach, down a steep and stony path, in bursts as a load is taken on board in front, and long halts. It is very slow and the fatal hour when all ships leave for the night comes closer and closer. We are getting quite near the water when there is a complete stoppage. At last officers are summoned to the front; we are told that the boats have gone and will not return, and that we will be surrendered in the morning.

We felt pretty tired when we heard that. We collected the men, told them, and said that from now on it must be every man for himself. We officers went down to the sea in the dark. We could see a couple of half-swamped rowing boats in the water. I threw in my revolvers and everything else heavy and unnecessary. Then we went back into the village for a bit of sleep. We slept in a house – deserted like all of them – high up on the outskirts of the village. It was quite empty. In the morning we went down and bathed – the best bathe I ever had. From the rocks on the shore that water fell clear and very blue and very deep below us. We felt a hundred per cent better. There was a young commando officer bathing too and we began to plan our escape.

There were fairly large boats on the beach, but either rotten or machine-gunned. Our idea was to go to the next village along to the west and look for something there. As we walked up to our house again, German bombers came over and dropped bombs on us and on the village we had planned to go to. As we knew we had been surrendered we hadn't reckoned on this. We sat under a great ledge of rock till they had gone, and then went up to the house.

Almost immediately we were being machine-gunned there by planes which patrolled the village backwards and forwards, firing all the time. It was impossible to leave the house. We had looked at the house next door in the darkness and turned it down in favour of ours which had a nice vine-clad verandah to sleep on. But we regretted it now as the other house had vegetables and every kind of thing in it. It had since been occupied by Australians, and we were a bit frightened of them. However, when I saw a chicken walk into their front door I hurried in after it and said it was mine and cornered it. It was quite a young chicken and I found it quite difficult to pluck. Then I had to cut its head off with Micky's souvenir Cretan knife, and its insides out, which I thought the worst thing I'd seen in war yet. I filled an earthenware pot with olive oil from a great jar, put in the chicken and some potatoes and onions and made a fire under it. Meanwhile Sidney went out for a bathe and to look for some wine. We felt irresponsible and gay. After twenty minutes I took the pot off and it was done to a turn. We had just begun to attack it when Sidney walked in. 'Quick, give me some,' he said, 'I'm a prisoner and can only stay five minutes.' We looked out of the window and there was a German on a roof top below, pointing a tommy gun at us. I shouted something to him and we settled down to the chicken, which was excellent, though we could have dealt with a couple each. Sidney rushed off and we followed. The Germans were a small party of Alpine troops in green uniforms. They searched everybody's haversacks and took weapons, binoculars, compasses, etc. I talked to them in German, handed over my cigarettes and was not searched, thus saving two compasses as I had Michael's in my bag too. They let us go and get some water, at a well we had been to in the dark, and which we found now to be graced by the most revolting corpse I ever saw.

Really I was tickled to death at the idea of being a prisoner. We sat in the sun while the Germans rounded everybody up. There were very few Germans; we watched one party coming in from the mountains to the west at a terrific speed, leaping from rock to rock as though they were at home in their native bergs. They were very neat, or seemed so besides us, in green hats, short coats and shorts, and all blond and well shaved and simply loaded with paraphernalia.

We were moved higher up into the upper part of Spakia village and all the officers put together. I got permission from the German lieutenant in charge to go and look for our men. When I found them it was to face disaster. Deserted (as they obviously and openly felt) by us the night before, they had climbed back to the little valley at the entrance to the village where they had been encamped for several days. There when it had got light they proceeded to cook the little food they had, and they were sitting around doing this, thinking themselves prisoners and perfectly safe, when the German planes came over and machine-gunned them. One of our men was killed outright. The wounded were in a little church, and among them was our Sergeant Major Fountain with twelve bullets in him. We heard later that he died. Three Germans who ran out shouting and waving to the planes to clear off were also killed.

In the heat of the afternoon we set off on the march back, a mile-long column of men and planes overhead photographing us. We passed a few Germans going south, laying telephone lines etc., they mostly carried cameras. I talked to our guards and all came from around Berchtesgaden and Munich. They were the nice peasants of the Lederhosen and looked very much the same except they had no feather in their hats. Their doctor was bitter against us because his best friend was killed while tending a wounded man, knifed, but he thawed. And the rest were perfectly friendly and unconcerned. They told me of their walks into Poland and France and Greece, and how they'd like to be home. The only thing against them was the way they all had of shouting, in the most brutalised voices. Pappy [Graf Zu Pappenheim] always used to say that the Bavarian peasant really let loose was the most brutal fellow on earth.

We walked along parallel with the sea and into my valley of caves and from there back again north-west up the hill to the road where it ended meaninglessly, and up and up, taking every time the short cut where the road made a sweep. Everywhere on the road Germans were getting our discarded trucks moving again. It was said that every parachutist had in his equipment the small part in the dynamo of our trucks which our men are taught to take out.

We became very tired. We came to a chapel and I lay down in it, it was cool, and was turned out by a German soldier. Micky Riviere was all in and dropped behind. 'A little further on', the Germans kept saying, 'there's a rest camp and food.' We passed under some trees. Germans with commandeered horses (a thing we never thought of doing) and a few German graves on the road below Imbus along the gorge, and blown conduits and bombed trucks and hideous smells. The German graves with a cross and inscription and the dead man's helmet and cartridge belt on it.

We reached Imbros in the dark and there were big marquees but not for us. We were tired and thirsty and the road seemed endless before we reached Lassithi plain. There in the first village crowds were fighting for water round the wells against the road. I knew one off it, and got water there with great difficulty, for the peasants saw themselves waterless and the summer before them. I walked on to the next village, for it was too cold to sleep, and there there was a staging camp, and officers all sleeping together in a field and Sidney and Michael there. But no food. I asked for a drink in a house and they had me in and gave me tea and a tiny bit of meat. They were refugees from the town and all sick from exposure.

2 June 1941

We marched on in the morning. Our feet were becoming very sore and our shoes giving out. The bottom of my feet hung in places in shreds. We walked all morning; up the mountains and down again. And at midday we came to the village which was burning as we streamed south. And here at last we were given food, a tin of bully beef and some biscuits between four; and there was a shallow river in which we could bathe. A fair-haired boy, a soldier, gave a bit off a loaf – he had exchanged it for his gold watch.

Suddenly we found that the place was full of released Italian prisoners, taken in Albania and brought to Crete. They had refused to make use of the arms which the Germans dropped them by air, for which they were bombed. Now instead of standing and jeering at us they were all friendliness, and drowned us in red wine, which no doubt they were stealing in the village. We all had as much of it as we could drink and filled our water bottles with it, and when we moved again it was in high fettle.

But the long, hot road wore that off, and as it got dark we were almost past going on. In fact I tried to persuade the others to fall out, sleep by the river and get back to Kalame and our officers' mess, food and clothes. But we did get to the next night's lodging place, by the village of Stilos. It was foully damp, and bitterly cold though I shared the heavy fleabag Michael had carried all through. He tried to escape from here and couldn't.

3–6 June 1941

In the morning again we moved on. Michael and I dragged further and further behind till we seemed to lose sight at the tail with a few Germans. We passed through a grim little battlefield with bombed trucks and corpses under trees, sprawling about, and so to the road along Souda Bay. Souda was a complete ruin. The cruiser *York* and plenty of other ships still lay in the harbour; but all out of action. Between Souda and Chania the road was completely jammed. Off the road were thousands of Italians, apparently shut up by the Germans for looting.

Chania was an amazing sight. Every house apparently had some damage, a large proportion were completely destroyed. And this was not the old and crumbly part of the town. The streets were blocked with fallen stone. For two days Chania had been bombed all day. It had contained hardly anything military, but when after almost a week the blitz had failed to make headway, the Germans revenged themselves on the towns, which they destroyed systematically, in waves, attacking one quarter at a time. Herakleon suffered the same.

We were marched on, on the road to Maleme, and at last we reached our prison camp Galatas. The Germans had bombed the field hospital and set light to part, then parachutists had captured it, destroyed the medical stores and made the walking wounded there work for them – and, I believe, walk in front of them as they attacked. Now the tents were full of men, and as the later arrivals came in they camped in the open ground. The officers were more or less together. There was practically no organisation. We slept in the open that night, and it was cold and damp by the sea. Sharing Michael's fleabag was such a tight fit that any movement disturbed the other. We were right on the sea, and the first thing we did was to get into it. Throughout our long hot thirsty walk a bathe seemed the ultimate bliss, and yet when I got into the water I shivered with cold, swimming slowly with raw stinging feet, and hurried out again, disappointed. I was feeling too tired to be braced by it.

Next day we found a tent – Sidney and Michael P and me, Alexis Casdagli and Derek Gilbey and Venables the RC parson, and a few others. We had one or two beds and mattresses in our tent, but I had only the sandy floor, and it was dirty to say the least. There was no water inside the camp, it had to be fetched from outside, and we were all in such a futile state that this seemed an unparalleled and impossible effort. Most of us possessed nothing; brushes, combs, plates and spoons were the most needed. I found a case of glasses which had been twisted but unbroken by the fire, and some hospital bowls, enamelled. We cut spoons out of wood and began cutting wooden sandals. I still had my knife, though they were supposed to be given up.

Apparently the Germans, finding we had people who enjoyed organising things, simply left everything to them; which means to say that having chosen a site for the prison camp, on which a few tents already stood and buildings for themselves, they started to wire it in. They made no effort to provide further accommodation. They provided no food or blankets or beds or latrines. Our guards were parachutists and resting from their labours. When they were dressed they wore our uniforms out of our stores and our topees. But most of the time they were lying browning on the beach.

Meanwhile Milne was organising the thousands of men into camps of about 500 each for feeding etc. Casdagli in a truck under guard was fetching ordnance stores which Teddy Parker and his REs [Royal Engineers] were installing so we got food and stoves to cook it. But it was very little. There was none for about a day and then we got some tea for one meal and some rice for another, and some stew for the big meal of the day. We were madly hungry. We would queue up and wait ages for our bit of porridge dumped in an enamel spittoon, and return and queue up hoping for a scraping more. And we would slip into the German cookhouse and see if there were anything to be pinched. The Germans were eating enormously on the verandah, their officers on white tablecloths and all; while we looked like nothing on earth – half unshaven for lack of water and blades, unbrushed, dirty with sand and no change of clothes, ill with dysentery which began almost immediately.

From the first, Michael P had talked of escape. Nobody else did. Everyone was sick or exhausted, shoeless, fed up. Teddy Parker, a most brave and tireless man, who himself blew all the bridges as the Germans came to them on the road to Spakia, and walked back barefoot, too proud to take a lift, a man moreover who knew all about sailing, said that it would be madness to try to sail away on our own. Crete seemed to most people as much of a prison as any prison camp. The Germans were presumably everywhere, their planes seemed to spot anyone who moved. It was difficult to realise that blitz conditions were already over. There was a feeling of resignation, at best of putting off any effort till a better opportunity. When we mentioned the word escape to Derek Gilbey, he said, 'Would that be quite playing the game, old man?' Meanwhile, Milne put a stop to organised scavenging parties which had been getting out of camp and searching nearby fields and villages. Anyone trying to escape, he announced, would be put under close arrest. He was obviously not the man to ask for help. We needed money, but rather than broadcast our intentions, merely got what we could from Sidney, about £10. The Germans announced that anyone trying to escape would be shot.

Among the prisoners was Tony McCraith, Pat's brother. He asked me to join him in escaping. His idea was to get out of the camp and go to Maleme aerodrome which was quite close. He had an RAF Sergeant Pilot, and they planned to watch their opportunity on the aerodrome, jump into a plane and make off. It was a tempting idea because if it came off you'd be in Egypt that same day. But Michael and I decided to stick to our old idea, which was to walk to the eastern end of the island [the port of Sitia] where there had been no fighting, which we had not garrisoned and which most likely would be free of Germans and unblitzed, and there get a boat.

96

Michael and I slept four nights in the camp. We had our own doctors and MI room, and I had my leg and feet dressed and my wrist which I had cut jumping away from a bomb on the way to Spakia. The sanitary conditions in the camp were awe inspiring. Everyone was beginning to get what we thought was dysentery but really was a glorified diarrhoea. Sidney was down with it, unable really to appreciate Casdagli's treasure or think of escaping with us. Micky was too weak. We thought in any case that two was enough together, and we didn't even tell Jos and Tony (who would have been furious at the idea). Casdagli gave us tea and sugar. We hung on one day to fatten ourselves on his food. Michael pinched some tins from the German stores.

All this time we saw little of the men. One of us would go and lead them up to get their meals, otherwise there was nothing to be done for them. We were as badly off ourselves; we only wanted to lie quiet all day. The Australians and New Zealanders stayed in the camp only one night and then marched on to what had been the Italian POW camp up in the hills. Which left three or four thousand in our camp – marines, RAs [Royal Artilleries], commandos and oddments like ourselves. We learned that the officers were to be flown off almost immediately and that the Yeomanry would be in the first batch. So Michael and I had to get moving.

7 June 1941

With practically no plans in our heads we set out after breakfast. We both had bright blue hospital coats. I had also pale blue pyjama trousers. We jettisoned tunics, belts, fleabag etc. I carried my haversack containing compasses, tinned food, handkerchiefs, pull-over, pair of shorts, extra shirt (from Venables), socks (from Casdagli), three books, chequebooks, photographs, all inside a sack over my shoulder. I also carried a spade. Michael had a blue coat, shorts, his big Infantry haversack, a spade and a bucket, and on his head the leg of a bright blue pyjama. We climbed through the wire, wandered across a vineyard in the direction of a well where prisoners were washing and drawing water and German guards sitting round talking. The atmosphere charged with unconcern and innocence we meandered on, looking under olive trees and crying, 'Is this the place – is this where we left it? It looked I do believe like that clearing over there.'

We crossed the main Maleme road. Among the olive trees were the trenches of the battle, and parachutes and ammunition cases. We cut bits of green-grey silk off a parachute. After a bit we came to a village on a ridge. In the well below, children filled our water bottles for us. We walked up into the village to ask for food and, rashly strolling into the main street, we met two German soldiers.

'What are you doing here?' they said in German.

'Do have a grape,' we said in English, handing each a bunch of unripe grapes about the size of green peas and devouring them ourselves.

How hungry we are. Notice our bucket, we fill it with these uneatable grapes. Notice our spades, we are a work party; our clothes too, so striking. And we are so pleased to see you, anyone can see that.

'Where do you come from?' they said. 'Where are you going?'

They point, we point, all in the same direction, back to the camp, of course, where else?

They walk on up the village, stop, look back at us. We sit, eating the uneatable grapes. They walk on and we leg it.

We get into olive groves again and look down on the valley through which runs the road to Meskla. Among the trees by the road we hear German voices, no doubt of soldiers collecting parachutes etc. We run across the road just in front of an empty German truck. Almost immediately we come to a river, with trees and rushes and high banks and we lie down in the shade.

We found some little Bakelite boxes there of stuff to put in contaminated water. Dropped by parachutists, I suppose, who filled their water bottles there. It was difficult to read the labels but it seems to work in ten minutes while ours takes half an hour. I threw away my razor as I had no more blades, and the spades and bucket. We went on towards the hills, with a gap in view, but lost it as we came to the foothills and began to climb. We passed German telephone wires laid among the vines, but saw none.

We began to feel very tired, and Michael, who had boasted of never having been in such good form as after the march, suddenly crumpled up with diarrhoea. In the groves of the great old olives at the foot of the hills it was difficult to know which path to choose. Towards evening we lit on a lone farm hidden away among the trees – a most attractive place, built around a courtyard with a chapel in the middle. It all looked very old and peaceful. We walked in. There were people sitting in one corner. They gave us chairs. We asked for water; they gave it us. 'You are Germans?' they said politely. So we said, 'Of course not.' We shook our heads, pointed to our clothes, our bandages. They only half believed us and were none the more friendly for that. It was a big family, swollen by refugees, and there was a town-bred granddaughter who spoke French. They thawed a little but told us the Germans often visited them. We asked for bread and they gave us some with miseethra – whipped cream cheese, which we still had to learn to like. We then took our leave for we were obviously unwelcome. It was the one and only occasion that we were not welcomed by the Cretans.

After that we climbed uphill, up and up, till we came to the top, and we were on a ridge looking across a valley at further ridges. In the valley were a river and a road. It was the valley of the gap we had been aiming for. As the sun set on the hillside opposite, ourselves already in shade, we climbed diagonally down. It was covered in stiff under-growth, over which we tripped and fell painfully and miserably. It took a long time to reach the valley bottom and it was already getting dark. We decided to sleep a bit. We lay down but there was a cold wind, and by midnight it was altogether too cold. We got up and moved on. The path led us into a gorge which narrowed till it formed one of those 'natural phenomena' in which Crete is, I believe, rich – a narrow cleft between towering perpendicular cliffs, running for miles, sometimes in bright moonlight, sometimes in darkness. The path became a stone causeway built at some time at enormous trouble alongside a river bed, which from the size of its boulders must in spring be a rushing torrent.

99

We stumbled along till I could go no further, and despite Michael's determination to keep going, I lay down under a rock and slept an hour or two. It was protected from the wind there. Then as it began to get faintly light we went on again. The gorge ended and a path went left and right. We took the right and it led west, the rising sun told us – we hadn't thought of using our compasses.

So we turned back and on the other path we came to signs of cultivation again, fields and olives, but no houses. We sat down in a grove and there came along the hillside a flock of goats and their shepherd. I rushed to him, while Michael sat, feeling very ill. He was a nice friendly man, filled a bowl for me and another for Michael. It took not quite three goats to fill our bowl, which was quite a good size. It tasted wonderful.

We lay for a bit and then, before the sun should get too hot, walked on. Neither of us felt too good. So following a rocky path we came to a village – Panagia – and we went up to the first house. They were the nicest people in the world. A boy from Canea spoke a little French, otherwise communication was difficult. They made beds for us and we lay down while they prepared a meal. The house was really all one room with a gallery for a bedroom and some store rooms under, but all open with the living room. It was nice and clean. The woman was charming, her husband back from Albania with frostbitten feet, full of spirits. And the food! Fresh eggs! Chips! Hot marrow! Salad!

When it was all over the men took us down into the village to the cafe. It was Sunday and the café crowded, and the barber in one corner plying a great trade. People sent us drinks over. We got shaves and our hair cut. The barber had been in America. We pressed them to find us someone to mend our shoes, and he made quite a good job of them.

And then we returned for supper. People we had seen at the café drifted in and out. Conversation was a little difficult. They made us beds on broad couches built out from the walls, sheets and pillows, quite wonderful. And they mended our clothes, and gave us wine to take with us in the morning when we left, and were all the time so friendly and generous and helpful that they seemed the best people we had ever met. For we didn't know the Cretan people at all.

8 June 1941

We left in the morning and took the valley east. But immediately villagers clutched us, crying 'Germania', and they led us up the hillside. There we met a man of the night before carrying a bucket to the well, and he dropped everything and said he would guide us. So we followed him through a nice pine wood with bracken underfoot, and up and down the steep ridges of the foothills, by paths which we should never have known to choose ourselves. But he was going homewards to where he was born, and even he lost his track, or perhaps there was none. We walked across country, through brush wood which tore chunks out of my bare legs. I was to curse that walk as long as I remained on Crete. The wine came unstoppered and leaked, and we by drinking rid ourselves of it.

We climbed down into a village where a white church stood by a dry stream full of oleanders in flower, and as we toiled up the farther side a Greek policeman passed us. We distrusted the police, but he took no action. We followed a steep wooded valley running into the hills and at midday came to a village buried in olive trees. It was a small place and everyone turned out for us. A schoolmaster and his wife, refugees from Canea, gave us lunch, fried eggs and bread and wine, and after that we were taken to see an English refugee – Parry Shaw, a retired sailor with a Cretan wife, who was living next door, surrounded by his wife's relations. He had been working in the Cipher office. We talked to him about our chances of escaping. Everyone begged us to stay, and a man with two pretty daughters, refugees again, made us wait at least till he brought a chicken freshly cooked, and eggs and bread.

Then we moved on up under the trees, crossing and re-crossing the little dry stream bed, till we came to the village where our guide's wife and children were living. It was some time since he'd seen them, they were with a sister, and he led us to the house, promising us beds there. It was incredibly squalid. Everything looked filthy. It swarmed with children. Michael collapsed inside. I took a chair and sat in the yard. Lots of women walked in, none seemed very pleased to see us. Our guide seemed to lose interest in us altogether. There was one woman who obviously wasn't a village woman, wearing quite a nice dress. She asked us to her house. She was staying there with her husband in the house of her parents. We followed her gladly. She had some children too, and everybody lived and slept in one small room with two big beds in it. The husband looked like El Greco. They came from Canea. We lay down on one of the beds. When it began to feel like mealtime we offered our chicken to swell the feast. It was accepted gratefully, but we were a little disappointed when for our supper we shared with the whole family our chicken and nothing else. Still, she was a very nice woman. The old people, her husband's parents, real old villagers, were put to sleep somewhere outside with the children (under a tree we discovered next morning) and we were given one bed, quite a big comfortable one, with sheets. But hardly had we settled in for the night, and the woman and her husband in theirs, than we began to scratch. It was alive with fleas. I stood it as long as I could, then I got out and lay on the floor. They were there too. I sat in a chair. There was no respite. I got back into bed and at dawn, when they tired, I slept. It was a dreadful night.

9–21 June 1941

The next morning we walked out of the village, following the valley. We soon met up with two friends – a very good-looking boy and a young soldier just back from Albania, who guided us. We were both weak and found it hard climbing. A party of refugees we passed gave us handfuls of the almonds they were picking. We came to a village high up all in one straggling block, like a fortress, and at last, above it, to one lone house, the boy's uncle's. It was a really nice house, a little concrete chalet for the summer with proper rooms and windows, the owner having done

102

well for himself in America. He was a nice man, but he offered us only water.

Here the boy left and the soldier took us on, down now into the next valley. He was obviously nervous, kept us up on the hills off the tracks, and after a bit he too pointed out our way and left us to it. Across the valley before us, straggling up the further side of the hill we could see the roofs of another village. He told us to avoid that (for we were making for Stilos on the road to Heraklion). But Michael and I as we stumbled downhill, over vineyard-retaining walls, and stopping and falling heavy from weakness on the rocks, began to see the next village as something of a haven. Particularly I. We climbed down and up again to it and turned into the first house. They were a bit scared till they recognised we were English. It was nicely whitewashed; we sat down and asked for milk. There were lots of goats tied up outside, and they produced a bowl of it. So we showed them how to make hot bread and milk of it, and they gave us plenty of sugar, so that it was grand. I ate enormously of it.

Then Michael lay on a couch and I on a blanket and sheet on the floor and the house was cleared for us. We felt better after that, so we thanked them very much and went on through the village. It was less like a village than a number of scatter hamlets, all having one name, Cambus. As we left one of these, we were surrounded by people who seized us by the arm, asked us where we were going, assured us that we were walking straight into the Germans, begged us to stay. One extraordinary little fellow, with an Apache cap over one eye, the most appalling squint I ever saw, a face all twisted to one side, and an excellent flow of French, assured us that if we cut open his veins, or the veins of this sister of his here (a fat old woman) or that sister there (a fat younger woman), or his brother-in-law here, we should find some English blood would flow out. Such was his and their love for the English, as anybody could tell us. He begged us to stay a week, a month, a year, we should want for nothing. No, we said, we must press on. An old Cretan like the Ancient Mariner adopted us as his children. Michael began to weaken; I longed to sit down anywhere. So we said, Right, if we might stay a day or two and rest we should be very grateful. For

103

every day now we got weaker with a sort of dysentery. The little Frenchman led us off. He was a chauffeur from Canea, and with his two sisters and his brother-in-law, he was taking refuge with his aunt. 'Thea' was a fine old lady with a bad leg, widow of a captain of the hills in the eighties, who lived in the filthiest house I ever saw. It was a part of a conglomeration of hovels, all of whose occupants were cousins, and the ancient mariner was the 'papous', the grand-father.

In one small room on the roof of Thea's house lived her nephew Georgio with his wife and four children. He was a handsome ruddy creature, young and jolly, with a stick of a wife like a ghost, who never uttered. There was a sweet little girl, Katina and three boys. We lay down on their one bed and at night they gave us blankets and sheets on the roof. One-eyed Kosta, our host, disappeared that night, so no one remained to whom we could talk. But Thalia, his fat unmarried sister, dealt most efficiently with my wrist, which was in a pretty good mess, having gone septic and spread.

They were all terrifically friendly and kind. People poured into the house to sit and stare at us and describe with much gesticulation the fate of their homes in the bombing of Canea, and what they would like to do to the Germans. 'Germania!' they shouted, with hideous grimaces, and drew their fingers across their throats. We nodded brightly back. There was one bearded giant of a man who like most of the men had fought the parachutists when first they landed. We were taken to dinner in the house he was living in, a very nice clean house and piles of food, and we said that if we could find a nice clean room like that we should like to stay a bit and help them in the fields for our keep. They wouldn't hear of that. So we slept very comfortably on the roof and next day rested mostly on Georgio's bed.

Our insides became worse, and we felt pretty feeble. I decided to do Geoffrey Brooks' cure and starve for two days. Meanwhile they took us down to Thea's well and vineyard, where the effort of collecting a few dry sticks for a fire almost killed me. There was some kind of feud between Kosta's family and the Papous. He had, like most of the old men, been in America and retained a few unintelligible words which he fired off at us, and at one moment we gathered he was trying to warn us against our hosts, but why we couldn't make out. Later, it really seemed that he longed to look after us himself. He was a strange, fierce, bone-headed old man. His main attraction was that he had 'crassi' – red wine – and our hosts had none. He would disappear with a dirty old bucket and return with it full and pour it partly into a decanter and largely on to the floor, assuring us that it was his last.

The day after I began my starvation cure, Michael started on it too, and that morning, as we lay on our bed, in came Papous and ordered us to come to his house and eat. We tried to explain that we weren't eating; he tried to drag us off. Finding us quite determined he retired, and reappeared with fried eggs and red wine. We were horrified and began all over again, begging him to take them back and eat them himself before they got cold. The fierce old man burst into tears. Horror struck, we got out of bed and to appease him drank some wine, followed hurriedly by water to save the cure.

That same afternoon Thalia came back from visiting in a distant part of the village with the news that she had met some Australians there, and brought back one with her. He was a good-looking self-confident fellow, and told us that with two friends he had escaped from the Australian prison camp. They walked across the mountains and they met a man who handed them a note. This note was addressed to any free English, and adjured them to keep their hearts up, for the writer was working to get them off. It was signed illegibly, Lieut. Commander R.A.R. They were expecting to meet him that same evening in Cambus.

This was wonderful news, and Michael threw up his cure and went off together with the Australian. I had our bed on the roof to myself that night and revelled in it, for we always quarrelled over our just shares in it. Michael was gone all next day. He met the naval officer that night and returned very early next morning to collect me and our things. The naval officer was a Greek, which explained the slightly odd tone of his note. As owner of a salvage boat he had been working in Suda Bay salvaging and on the Booms. Because he had his wife and children on the island and they couldn't

105

go too, he didn't leave with the fleet, but had taken to the hills. Now he was planning to get a boat to take them to Egypt, and with them a party of ten British soldiers if he should find any hiding in the mountains. He told Michael what he must do – move immediately right up into the mountains and stay there till they found a boat. Michael was impressed with his energy and confidence and we moved at once.

My cure had done me good and I made the climb quite easily. Georgio gave us one blanket and some food and helped us into Cambus with it where we met the three Australians and a guide with a donkey, who was already loaded with a great sack of potatoes and more blankets. Walking carrying nothing was a hundred times easier. After the first hour it became really mountainous and steep, climbing up the side of a ravine. After two hours we reached our new home – a cluster of amazing dome-shaped beehive dwellings built of rough stone. Here lived the shepherds from Cambus in the summer months. A little further on was a second cluster, of two beehives and a pen, and this was handed over to us. Michael and I took the smaller house. Inside half was built up a couple of feet above ground level to make a seat. There was just room on the ground for the two of us to lie, and it was already covered in fairly clean-looking branches. The rest was filthy and had recently contained goats.

The Greek officer, Emmanuele Vernicos, whom we never called or spoke of as anything but 'the Captain', had assured us we should do well on his potatoes and the milk and cheese we should get from the shepherds. Fortunately, however, we had brought up with us presents of eggs, bread, chicken, etc. We had a good deal of tinned stuff, but we wanted to keep it for our eventual voyage. We added considerably to our stock of this, as we were given some by various villagers. In the first days of confusion after we withdrew from Chania the villagers went down and carried off all they could find in our NAAFI or anywhere else, and they all had British boots and oddments of equipment.

We were high up now in the mountains and at night it was cold. Michael and I had one blanket under us and one on top, and all our clothes on, and we were very cold. There was only the doorway to give light or air to our beehive; it had no door and opened straight on to our feet. The bigger beehive with the three Australians in it had such a small doorway you had almost to crawl in. We kept all the food in our house and issued it out. Our three Australians – two corporals and a private – were very nice fellows. They had all been through the great attack in Libya, followed immediately and without any leave by Greece. In Greece their Battalion, the 2nd/2nd, did the withdrawal on foot with terrific hardships, besides which our walk to Spakia and back paled. They failed to get taken off, escaped from Greece in a caique which took them to Chios, got another sailing boat there and were brought to Crete. They were one of the completely disorganised units which came to Crete from Greece, but should never have been allowed to stop there.

22 June– 4 July 1941

Life up in the mountains is extremely dull. My legs continue to fester and I feel very dull and feeble. Water has to be fetched from a spring about a mile further up the mountain, a very good walk on the bare rock. The valley where we are has a little scrub, but it is the last, and above us there is nothing but naked stone. It is awful ground for walking, all rough stone ledges. All the plant life seems tough and prickly and unfriendly to my bare and tender legs.

After we've been up in the mountains for a bit, Michael and I go to Cambus to forage for food and news. We go to the house of the aunt of an English-speaking girl named Phyllis. At Phyllis's aunt's we meet the Captain, which is the first I've seen of him. He is a smallish perky little grey-bearded fellow like a youngish Shylock, with a loud voice and an authoritative manner. He hasn't left yet for the south, which saddens us, as mountain life has palled. Our forage for news is equally exciting, for the Germans have just attacked Russia, and no one can help speculating on 'the beginning of the end'! In any case we imagine it means the withdrawal of many troops from Crete. They tell us also that all the prisoners have now

107

been taken off the island. [This was not true.] We get hold of a German newspaper printed in Crete in German and Greek, with fantastic claims of success against Russia. We learn from that for the first time definitely that we have never retaken Libya. The German soldiers told us of great British successes there, God knows why. They told us, too, that General Freyberg had been killed, crash landing in Egypt (a universally popular piece of news) and that Mr Churchill had been succeeded by Mr Attlee!

There is no doubt that the Germans are simply loathed by the Cretans, who tell one all the time of people being shot. We reckon it is always the same people. But though I continue to give the Germans the benefit of the doubt (particularly after their treatment of us prisoners, which was at very worst neglectful) they appear to be doing their best to put the population against them by shooting civilians – for firing on parachutists during the blitz – burning houses and robbing everything.

5–11 July 1941

A fortnight after we went up into the mountains, Michael and I go down to Cambus again. We sleep the first night at Phyllis's aunt's, on real beds brought from Chania; mine breaks through. Next day we visit the Captain's English wife, blonde, beautiful and cold. She isn't at all pleased to see us, as too many escaped prisoners visit 'the Englishman' on their way through Cambus, and she is terrified of being betrayed.

Next night we sleep at Thalia's, of whose displeasure at our daring to sleep one night away from her we were very afraid. The following day there is a scare. Just as we are starting out for a meal with Phyllis's cousins, one of them, the nicest, Eleutheria, comes running the whole way, almost two miles, to say Germans are entering that end of the village. So we spend all day in the rocks. Papous's son, Lambros, brings us the stewed remains of baby rabbits with which Michael played the day before, and eggs, and a dear old man gives us our first grapes and big pears from the plain, and kisses the pictures in my *New Testament*. We're amused to watch the Cretans running out of their houses with all their arms and English or German equipment and hiding them in the rocks just when one might suppose they could be useful. Michael is suffering agonies from a festering foot and not at all amused by scares and scamperings. This is purely some silly child's imagination.

We are made to spend the next day down by the well, where Thalia brings us some very mediocre food, but we sleep on the roof as usual. We decide to stay till the Captain returns and we know definitely how things are. In the mountains we feel so very out of touch. By the well, Michael holds court and a procession of passing escapees are led up to him and discuss identical rumours and projects and possibilities. It is most difficult for us to advise them what to do, as we are at a low ebb ourselves. The noise of tree locusts is everywhere terrific and nerve-wracking. We long to hear a radio as the most fantastically contradictory reports of the German-Russian campaign continue to come in. The Cretans exaggerate everything past belief and will invent the most impressive tales without foundation. I ceased believing anything, but we heard that the Russians were in Rumania, Poland and Bulgaria; that Berlin was in ruins, that the Germans were using gas, that they were tearing the gold out of the teeth of our prisoners. Such rumours were repeated and believed enthusiastically.

At moments I appreciate the simplicities of Cretan country life: Georgio with his half-dozen goats and his cow winnowing the chaff in a small rocky field, around him his wife and children and female cousins. One sits under a tree spinning wool on a distaff. There is not overmuch work to do and it is done leisurely. The sun makes everything pleasant, and in the mountains it is never overly hot. But here in the winter with many feet of snow it must be appallingly squalid – the houses dark and dirty and uncomfortable to a quite unnecessary degree.

Thea leads her goats through the house into the yard behind and a donkey has its room in a further corner. The isolation brought about by the broken rocky nature of the country, the green of olives and vineyards, the friendly intercourses between the inhabitants, their generosity, simplicity and kindness, the quiet certainties – it is Eden or Arcadia. But I only long for a suburban spring clean. It is no doubt my lack of health and companionship; for this is the life I thought I loved. I think our house is quite unusually dirty (and the food unusually poor). We received such kindness at our first coming that we fear to appear ungrateful by moving elsewhere. But in fact Thalia has great difficulty in getting any food at all, and lives as much on us as we on her. We are becoming critical of her one and only dirty dress and her pigtails and general squalor – and say 'Do something. Don't talk about bombs and what you *used* to have. Make a *new* dress. Sleep with the door open; of course you get headaches. *Buy* food – here's the money.' And she is annoyed. But that one room of Thea's, where three women sleep with everything shut, and the floors rock and dirt, and the fleas jumping up your legs like puppies, and there's no furniture at all but a tin or two and half a chair. What does Georgio *do* all the winter? And they like us to sit, sit, sit, long after midnight and listen to them talk like Niagara. By the light of an oil lamp such as the Romans used.

Oh! the tedium. Oh! the stifled irritation – and they are so incredibly kind. Unfortunately they go into fits if we take walks away from their sight – they are all dead scared of the Germans, for all their pantomimic throat slittings. We are picking up quite a lot of Greek at last; baby talk. I find that the animals which annoy me so much by their chorus in the trees are a sort of moth with transparent wings, quite easy to catch. The boys hold them in their fists and they go on chirruping, but I squash them. In the trees they start up screeching all together with intervals of silences – like a nest of starlings trying out a fret saw. The Greeks say they are crying 'The grapes are ripe.' Which they aren't up here.

12–16 July 1941

After a week the Captain arrived back from the southern coast, with the great news that he had got a boat. But he had gone west first and then south, and in the villages to the west of us and south of Canea he found hundreds and hundreds of Australians and New Zealanders, which has altered all his ideas. Now his suggestion is that four Australian sergeants should go in the boat and we remain in charge of this new army. The sergeants would carry a note asking for an evacuation to be arranged. We decided in a week's time to walk over with him to the south and see the boat off.

We tried and failed to get the BBC on a hidden wireless, but next day we got it. It was very exciting. They said the German claims were very exaggerated and their losses very heavy, and then they began talking about Lord Byron. Next morning early I went off up into the mountains by myself and down again in the evening with the rest of the party and all our blankets and stuff. During the day there had been a Germania scare in the village. At midnight we were woken up by my worst enemy, a revolting Greek from Kaleni who stank, raising a hell of a scare. At dead of night very unwillingly, we were hustled off to the mountains. I led a party of nine. On the way up a young Englishman who had appeared at Thalia's the night before with Greek pseudo-parents who had saved him from the Germans, packed in and turned back. We were pretty bored to see our mountain again and this time we had a record small amount of food. And the milk was going dry. During the morning there were sounds of machine-gunning in the far distance. All the week there had been explosions somewhere beyond the hills in the plain. From up the mountain I could see some going off in a village north-east of Chania. But now a terrific explosion well our side of Chania made the whole mountain shake and clouds of smoke rose slowly from below the foothills far up into the sky. The constant sound of aeroplanes of the previous week had completely stopped. They were probably carrying away German troops. A convoy went out, said to be carrying English prisoners, most of whom we think have now left the island.

17–29 July 1941

Lambros came up with food for the Australians he was looking after and we all went down. He told us of great Russian advances.

111

Three RE (42 Field Coy.) NCOs have arrived in Cambus, having escaped from Galatas just before the prisoners were shipped off. They say that the Bavarian and Hitler Jugend troops who took over the prison guard from the parachutists maltreated the prisoners disgracefully. They shot indiscriminately, knocked out people with their rifle butts and beat them with iron rods.

Two days later we were to dine with Eleutheria but there was a scare and we were hustled off into a hole, where we slept. We left with the Captain next day, very full after lunch with Eleutheria, with whom we left everything we didn't need to carry. With us we took one of the REs Corporal Bert Murfet, in theory because he was dark and could spy out the land before us dressed as a Greek, but in fact as a pack horse. We walked west across the mountain valleys. The Captain is a great walker in spurts – that is to say he dawdles and then runs. We sat for a long time on a charming loggia shaded by vines overlooking the olive-clad valley of Thernia and then ran to Dracona. The country was the most beautiful I ever saw in Crete, with many pine trees, but the sweat blinded me. We picnicked by a well and a dry stream beneath a plane tree, and hung our shirts out to dry. Excellent cold veal and bread and cucumber and cold water and hot tea. Then on, and as it got dark we reached Therisso. On the way we picked almonds off the trees. Therisso was always a great stronghold, which the Turks never once reached. It has over fifty soldiers living somewhere outside and a few whom we met inside. All the women carry them food, and they do some work in return. There was a big party for supper in the house of a friend of the Captain's who had been an officer in the Greek army, and afterwards we were given blankets and sheets on the roof.

We made an early start next morning and crossed some very steep hills to reach Zourva for an early lunch or late breakfast. Very exhausted we reached Omalos, where we found the Captain's four Australian sergeants, living with a charming Americanised gentleman named Steve. One of the sergeants was in bed with jaundice, but they performed on him their famous and apparently invariably successful operation of cutting the thread under the upper lip, and

112

in two days he was well enough to leave with the Captain for the south coast and the boat.

With them went Fred Embrey a captain in the 1st Bn. AIF, whom the Captain had met on his first journey to the south (and suspected of being a German, exactly as the inhabitants of Lakh Omalos suspected the Captain himself of being a fifth columnist and very nearly shot him). Embrey was a bore but tough. Michael and I tried to persuade the Captain to let us go instead. He said it was a forlorn hope and he needed us where we were to deal with the troops on the island, and it was after all his boat.

Michael and I remained in Omalos alone. Steve gave us the most excellent food and my first cigarettes for a month, smoked most economically through a cigarette holder cut from a grove of walnut trees just by his house. Under them I lay most of the day. It was hot there in the sun and chilly in the shade, and at night really cold. We slept on a threshing floor which made a fine bed, though we got up looking like lunatics with our hair full of chaff. Neither Michael nor I had shaved by this time for over six weeks, and I had a handsome chestnut beard and Michael a fair Renaissance affair which made him look like Christ.

Omalos was the most pastoral scene I ever saw. Shut away from the world into a little world of its own, there seemed an extra-ordinary patriarchal dignity in the great herds of sheep led by colossal billy goats, in the groups round the wells down the centre of the plain, in the yoked oxen moving round and round on the little threshing floors and the men throwing the chaff and grain into the air with wooden forks, most of all in Steve's nieces as they took the crackling chipped potatoes off the fire in the dark smoky room and beckoned us to sit down to them. Steve in the morning would sit on a wall quietly watching his chickens on the hillside behind his house, to see where their nests were hidden. Now we were to reap the benefit of his patience. We sat with alacrity.

A few days later the Captain returned with the whole party. The plan had failed. The Germans in the south, perturbed probably by the news of stray parties of English, had properly scared all the fishermen and put sentries on their boats. The Captain had made arrangements with a fisherman who had to report to the Germans twice a week, that he should take off our party immediately after reporting, when he would not be missed for several days. Now he was afraid for his family and would not play.

We had decided before that if this plan should fail, we should try the north, and if possible leave together with the Captain's wife and children. We left Omalos now for Lakkos to put this plan into action. It was a long rough downhill walk, and I rode the last part proudly on a sleek cream donkey on a red saddle and wondered why I'd ever used my feet. We entered the village in the dark and were led by Lefteris to the house of his father Nicolas, just a few yards below the main road to Canea which ends in front of the café. The road was used by German patrols but no one seemed to mind.

The Captain is the first person I can ask about many things that have puzzled me or interested me here. He says that the Greeks fight for two things – their family and their religion. Their family life is very close, their religion very real. I guess Greece is very backward. No one seems to have any money. They get up early and work off and on all day to produce enough to live on, squalidly. They could in fact easily produce more and make themselves comfortable, or if comfort is nothing, pleasant, more interesting. Just as they could wash more if they chose and rid their houses of fleas. But long years of brigand life have made and kept them rough. What of it? The cattle trample the grain – muzzled for all the law of Moses, the men cast it to the winds, the women sift it in sieves, everything is serene, slow and laborious. They go to bed tired, not needing Miss Dell or gramophones or cinemas. They sleep in their clothes. Their food is very poor, though they can and do manage a fine meal for strangers. But mulberries, almonds, pears, apricots and plums drop almost unpicked from the trees. They make no jam or preserves, no cakes or pastry or biscuits.

In the summer the sheep are in the mountains, in winter they are driven down to the plains by the sea. I loathe sheep but they are wonderful, really, entirely self-supporting and producing milk, meat and wool. Goats are more trouble, though they produce more milk. The Cretans make exciting kinds of cheese miseethra and yoghourt and the big expensive cephalitiri and graisara. I used to hate cheese. The Captain says that on his island, Syphros, the poorest houses are better than the best here, and all the tracks are earthen, not rocky, and in the villages they white-wash the pathways every day. No hotels are allowed there, for such is the tradition of hospitality.

In the other islands the women are housewives and leave the hard work to their men. In Crete the women do practically all the work. They wait on the men and eat after them. They give up their chairs to them. (Michael and I made a point of rising for a woman, to their consternation.) All this is a remnant of the days when the men were all fighters and the women did the work in the village. The Captain says that in Greece they have good women and bad men, and in England it is the other way round.

We love Lakkos. The side of the valley is covered in the most magnificent olive trees with fantastic Dulac boles and of a great height, quite hiding the houses. There are mulberries too and walnuts and plane trees and the houses are scattered among them. German patrols visit the village along the motor road, but we have never been so free. We can sit and play backgammon in the café on the square, and eat grapes and drink coffee and cognac. Here we meet all our friends. The barber works ceaselessly in one, our good friend Paul the Mayor plays backgammon and there is a continual cocktail-party atmosphere. About six the bus arrives from Canea, with fruit and news, an appalling old bus but a great event in the day. At present there is no work till the grapes and the olives ripen, so everyone is café society. We are feeding magnificently. For breakfast the Captain cooks us tripe soup, filthy looking and not particularly good. Fortunately, tripe is a great treat. They are great on soups – broths really, into which they always put lemons and eggs. The latter seems almost a sacrilege; they look so much more satisfying on a plate.

Lakkos has many quite important inhabitants, who only confirm one's impression of the democratic character of the country. For indeed here all are really peasants, and there is nothing to choose

115

between the general's family and the shepherd's. Because they treat all men as equals they can afford to be really courteous. Continually they are on the lookout to do someone a service; to such an extent that one has to preserve a numb passivity, for one's least move is interpreted as an unspoken cry.

We pay rather a state visit to the house in the village where Madame Skoulas, the Cretan C-in-C's wife, and other women run a mess for English soldiers. It is a very fine effort; they are feeding about thirty just as they'd be fed in barracks, all together, regularly, under a roof. On the way back by the church we are given our handkerchiefs full of an odd food by a woman out of a basket. Damp swollen grain and chopped almonds, sugar and eucalyptus – very good. It is some kind of mourning rite whose origin no one could explain. Grapes are now very plentiful though they come still only from the plain. And we have a few odd figs. The grapes are the small yellow seedless variety which make the currants, and we pop them in like a machine gun. They are not yet fully ripe and so not too sweet.

30 July–1 August 1941

We lunched with Theodore Tzo Tzolakis, whose son was Greek liaison officer, and afterwards he brought me a pair of breeches to try on as he had noticed how bad my shorts were, and shoe soles of really good leather for Fred Embrey, which Theodore had got with great difficulty for himself – and we know well it is absolutely beyond price. They regard such generosity as a duty. It is most shaming to us. When one thinks of all they do for us (and how little we deserve it), one cannot but wonder whether strangers would fare as well in our homeland. Would our mothers give them the bread for lack of which their little children will starve this winter?

The next day I dined with the village priest, a handsome young man with a beard, who spoke only Greek. I intended accompanying him to early service the next day, but it was very early; there was a difference of three-quarters of an hour in our watches. Orthodox services are very long, and somehow I was still in bed on 1st August when I was told that there were Germans in the village. So I got up and dressed and drank a glass of milk and retired into the trees, regretting my breakfast. I had been two hours in a ditch when Athene rescued me, and took me to a house where I got some milk and on to another house, Carolambris's, where I had more milk and for no comprehensible reason was just left there.

Then men begin coming in, obviously excited, and tell stories to the accompaniment of female groans. The Greeks are habitual groaners and sighers; they will sit all day doing nothing else, so when they really mean it they say 'Pew Pew Pew'. They all come in armed. Carolambris, who is a fine oldish man, wounded in the blitz attacking parachutists, has loads of arms. Apparently the Germans are up to something bad. We begin lunch and then Marika comes to fetch me in rather a state. We return to Nicolas's house and I find the others all set to move off and am worried about how many of my things are going to be left behind. We set out with Lefteris and several of his friends and a long string of villagers making for Omalos.

Apparently at four o'clock that morning the Germans had surrounded the neighbouring villages of Fournes, Skenes, Alikarnus and Prasses, pulled the men out of bed and, after making them dig their own graves, lined them up and shot them. Those who ran away they machine-gunned. The village of Skenes, where the Germans had met resistance, was burnt to the ground. Some English, dressed as Greeks, shared the fate of their hosts. In one place they held a sort of trial and let out three who were not from that village. They have somehow obtained lists of names. What the trial was about the three had no idea, but everyone had to sign something, presumably an admission that they attacked parachutists. One hundred and twenty men were shot in Fournes alone, including the Mayor and the priest. There seems no reason for this sudden new outburst. But when a deputation visited the German commander not long after the blitz and asked him when the persecution of civilians was going to end, he replied that there were still very many parachutists unaccounted for and that everyone would be revenged.

117

The Germans at the start demanded eleven Cretan lives for every dead German, and at another time they threatened to kill 20 per cent of the male population.

We don't go very far on the road to Omalos. We rest in shady places, while Lefteris goes back to Lakkos for news. In the evening we all climb the nearest hill, high above Lakkos, where there is some water. There were a lot of people up there. We have blankets (and a donkey) and bed down in a small sheep pen. Suddenly we are woken by the most terrific explosion imaginable. We leap up and through a gap in the hills we can see the sea and Maleme aerodrome, on which there is a red glow. More explosions follow and we can see distinctly the tracer bullets of our aeroplanes firing on the aerodrome. The explosions are so heavy, although fully ten miles away, that the Cretans all throw themselves on the ground. We were thrilled.

Next day we move on to a place on the road to Omalos where there are several wells and corn under trees. There are a few shepherds' houses. The news from Lakkos is that the Germans have come into the village and are apparently settling down there. They pretend to be very friendly and ask where all the men are. They are told they are out with the sheep. All the men have left the village and are now high up in the mountains above us. They are all armed. Their women bring them food at night. There is much talk of starting a revolution.

In the evening the Captain arrives to join us. He leaves us in Lakkos and goes over to Cambus with Bert to collect his wife and children. He has a mass of clothes, food etc. in Cambus, papers as well, and with his wife pregnant, they have had a pretty tiring journey. Just short of Lakkos they stopped the night and there they heard that Lakkos was full of Germans and we'd all left.

2 August 1941

The Captain calls an officers' conference and suggests we start a revolution without waiting for the Greeks to make up their own minds. Michael and Fred have been discussing revolution all morning, right down to medical supplies. They are full of it. Very largely in desperation, I say that in my opinion we should still try to get off. The conference decides to carry on with our present plans for leaving the island, unless the Greeks rise in the meantime. The position seems to be that the local Greeks will rise if the Germans attempt to advance further into the mountains. As they point out, they would rather die fighting than be shot in their beds. Personally, I don't think the Greeks would make a good job of a rising. They might carry on guerrilla warfare in the hills. But their villages would be burnt, and where would their food come from?

I believe that under the Turks, when the Cretans contemplated revolution, they sent their womenfolk to the mainland, and the Germans are as unscrupulous and far more efficient than the Turks. The Cretans have arms, but very little ammunition indeed. Practically no one has a decent pair of boots, and leather is unprocurable – and without boots, how can you carry on guerrilla warfare? The same with our men if we joined in with them. As we are now, without any connection or hope of aid from Egypt, we should in no time be out of food, ammunition and boots. We should be exhausted by the rough country. Admittedly we could cause damage to the Germans. But it would be a suicide squad. It would be much better to combine a rising with a proper British landing, or at least time it to coincide with British advance in Greece. Of course all the Cretans are certain that we will send troops to retake the island. At present that would not be very difficult if our information of the German troops is correct. But it's a most expensive island to hold.

It now appears that the Germans killed 500 in this district yesterday. Nicolas's wife walked up in the dark from Lakkos (which it is a death sentence for women to leave), carrying on her back our heavy radio and news that the Germans have given the men five days to return or they will burn the village. Any women caught leaving with food will be shot.

3–10 August 1941

We pressed the Captain to get a move on and so it was arranged that we officers should set off before him, making for the peninsula beyond Maleme. Michael and I each gave the Captain a cheque for £50 and a letter for Cairo (mine to Longmore, Michael's to Wilson) in case we got separated; we kept all the time in separate parties. We were to take the boy Lefteris with us, right through to Egypt; but at the last moment he wouldn't go. We started at dusk and our guide went off to leave his rifle in his house. Nicolas led us the first bit till we should meet up with him. Nicolas didn't know the way, there was no sign of the guide. It was quite dark. Within one mile of the HQ we lay down on a cold windy ridge to sleep. What it was all about we couldn't understand but we were very cross.

On the morning of the 6th, it transpired that our guide was deterred from going with us by his womenfolk. The Captain arranged for another but he had to go off and get his shoes mended first. I may say that we actually bought shoes for yesterday's guide, who failed us. Michael, certain as usual that he would do something splendid, cooked flour in water and produced a glutinous dough. We had some rice, cheese and a little yoghourt, and continued to feel cross.

About tea time, just as we were about to cook a leg of goat the Captain sent up, Steve arrived looking almost warlike, and after eating a little miseethra of his we followed him up to Omalos. We were amazed that we should take this route to reach the north coast. The Captain joined us in Omalos with our two guides, one of whom is Carolambris and the other the famous 'Fire Dog'. We had a good dinner of rissoles and chips and heard news of a Russian advance. We slept up the hill, which all the people there are doing for fear of the Germans.

At dawn, a very cold misty morning, we set off across the plain, leaving it by the pass at its western end where there is a little lone white church, and so downhill mostly on a paved road to Agia Irene which lies in a wide valley. It is the highest village in Crete, very rich and quite delightful. Houses scattered along the village, a stream

120

fast running between flowering oleanders and large trees, walnuts and chestnuts and sycamores and mulberries, loaded with the biggest and juiciest mulberries I ever hope to see. Lady Macbeth's hands were nothing to mine, and little fields of marrows, potatoes, maize, all watered by little runnels and channels.

For a long way we followed the crests of hills with little gullies and springs of icy water. We stopped in one at a shepherd's hut and were bitterly disappointed not to be offered milk. His dog, an Alsatian, which from the start was a summons and six months from the RSPCA but which had now been banting continuously for a week and looked like something stuffed in alongside his royal master in an Egyptian tomb, chased and caught a lamb. He didn't eat it but neither did he improve it. Towards evening we looked down on Rumata and rested, eating cold goat's meat produced by Carolambris. The Captain went on ahead again. We officers followed with Carolambris down into the valley. Arrived at a stream in the bottom, Carolambris made 'what do we do next?' gestures at us. Which infuriated us, and we made 'you're the guide blast you' gestures back. Immediately after, villagers appeared and told us there were Germans in Rumata which we could see a little further down the valley. In fact all the male villagers were sitting under the trees, toying with rifles. The Germans had only come in that day, and were apparently settling down there. We had thought we would find the Captain somewhere in Rumata; now we didn't know what to do.

We discovered a Greek who spoke English and was wanted by the Germans; he was very discouraging about our chances of getting a boat. Just as it was getting dark a little boy came from the Captain and we climbed the mountain again, simply furious with the Captain for keeping his plans to himself and letting us get into such a jam. It was apparently impossible to go through Rumata, and we had to climb right up to the top of the mountain in the dark, looking for some other village. It was a murderous climb, very steep, rocky, prickly and abominable. Arrived at the top we followed the crest till we found ourselves at the end, looking into space. All the way our two guides quarrelled. The famous 'Fire Dog'

121

sat down like Satan on the Mount of Temptation, and we left him there. Down we climbed again. It was very dark and very steep indeed and the undergrowth had been burnt. As a result it was all black stumps about knee high, completely invisible but agonising and irritating beyond words. Arrived at a more level bit we sent Fred to shout for the Captain, German or no Germans, and he was found and led us into a small village.

On the way we passed a deserted shepherd's hut, with the day's milk hanging up in a great cauldron and a poor little puppy tied up. What was really in that cauldron I don't know. It was half way to being something else, but we attacked it with spoons. In the village we went to the house of a poor woman whose husband had fled to the hills. She was going to have a baby and had several already. We found a basket of figs and they were gone before you could look round, and we devoured some wheaten cake and felt very gay and light headed. From there we went to another cluster of houses, one of which we woke up and it contained among others a crazy woman who kept beating her breast and tearing her hair. I think her husband had been shot. From there a woman led us down into the valley, though she was also going to have a baby, and sick and risking her life. We crossed the valley and climbed up the further side.

Halfway up this new mountain there ran a main road. The Captain was certain it would be heavily posted with German machine guns and, as Cretan roads end just nowhere on the mountain, he wanted to find the end of it and creep round. However, a road was good enough for us, and we walked along it, finding imaginary machine guns in the shadows to please the Captain. We left it after a bit and climbed again up to the very top of the ridge and begging I was to know when this marathon was going to end. Just over the top there was the main road which we crossed in a desolate burnt-out village where no doubt the Germans had met resistance on their way to the south.

As it began to get light we made down into another valley, and to a village, and knocked up a big house. I longed to lie down; we had been walking 25 hours. They led us down to a secret place, where

122

we slept a little. We were in a river bed, opposite us high perpendicular cliffs with oaks leaning out and over us from the cliff's edge and the stream forming a pool beneath our feet. A bit higher up the pool was dammed to make a long shallow pond, where I bathed with a boy from the village. We were very tired and stiff. It was shady all day in our little gorge and wonderfully pretty. The villagers brought us a marvellous lunch – chicken soup and potatoes, chicken, pears and grapes and watermelon and most excellent wine. And bread and boiled eggs and a chicken for us to take with us and they sent to warn the villages ahead that we were coming. There was one English soldier in the village, with the priest, who was a grand man with the head of a world-loving Mazarin and helped us enormously.

In the evening our spy returned. We went first to the house in the village, where our clothes were ready washed for us and they gave me a new Khaki shirt, mine being in rags. The village hadn't a window pane in it after being bombed for holding up the Germans. It was only just off the main coast road. Our spy's news was that, as we feared, the near port was patrolled by the Germans, but that the further one was quite hopeful – the far point of the peninsula. We started off about eight o'clock in the evening and crossed the main road. Just across it they showed me where the Germans had taken the village priest and some men and released them and made them run and shot them, so that they could say they were trying to escape. Though why they bothered I don't know. We climbed in the dark down into a rocky valley and crossed a stream. Our guides were going all out and we were strung out and falling over rocks and cursing and sweating. The hill above the stream was much worse, all shrubs and prickles clutching at my bare legs. I sat down and nearly cried with vexation. But at the top we all sat and ate a boiled egg and a little further on we came to a shepherd's hut where we were made very welcome. We sat in a row and they passed along sliced cucumbers and wine, buckets of it.

The moon had risen as we rose to go and I went rolling. Some of the shepherds came with us, and helped carry our things. We passed through the only two villages on the peninsula. In the bright moonlight the first was charming, sloping away from us to the sea out of sight, across shadowy fields and orchards. Just beyond it we met our next guide and with him the lawyer cousin I met at Carolambris. I was amazed to see him and still more so to be told quite calmly that he was coming with us. He was nicely turned out in a grey suit, panama hat, overcoat over one arm and a suitcase. He had no food. It had all been arranged by Lambris and sprung on us without a word. The Captain was livid. In the next village, the only other one on the peninsula, big and straggling, our new adjunct sent a message back to his family. This enraged us as our movements were supposed at least to be secret. In point of fact Lambris talked in every village like a burst gas main, and while we were only passing through, we said, because it was such nice weather for a walk, we could hear Lambris explaining to anyone who would listen that he was going to Alexandria to see General Skulas.

After this village we got on to a broad paved track. Midnight was just striking in the village. They said this was the old Minoan road leading to the Minoan port at the end of the peninsula. It is in a remarkable state of repair if that is so. At least 12 feet broad, paved with large stones, but foul to walk on as the stones now lay at all angles; with our practically soleless shoes it was most trying. We had the most amazing guide. He insisted on carrying practically everything we had. He told us quite accurately how long the walk would take. Not that we believed anything so hair-raising as that we still had four Cretan walking hours before us. For definitely on the map the peninsula was a snub little affair about five miles long. It was mountainous but a series of level plains lay down the centre, which we thought could have been put to better use than sheep grazing. In fact it occurred to us to move all the escaped prisoners there and raise vegetables. We stumbled along, with the Captain ahead giving Lambris hell over his cousin. The unfortunate Nicolas was very soon completely out and I'm certain as sorry as a live man could be about it all.

Passing over a ridge and entering a small plain we saw a body of men ahead of us. We approached them carefully. On the moonlit path we eyed one another with hostility. They were Cretans from

Greece, landed that very evening. Such concrete evidence that we were not on a fool's errand was wonderfully heartening and sent us hurrying on. But their news was not altogether good. They had been without food for a week in Greece before sailing, though they had plenty of cigarettes and pressed whole boxes on us. When they landed they were attacked by a German patrol boat. They ran off, but they believed their boat was captured. They were full of stories of Germans on the end of the peninsula. We hurried on.

The next people we met were a band of Cretan Muleteers with loads of olive oil, returning disconsolately from the sea after failing to get their olive oil on board because of the Germans. We longed to hear that we were nearing the point; they said it was still two hours. Our fantastic guide told us that we must keep going, because having brought us to this point he was going to hurry back and intercept the Muleteers before they could reach their village and spread the news of our movements. I kept on kicking one ankle with my other foot, till I had it so raw that the least touch was an agony and sent me swerving across the path. I stuffed my sock with handkerchiefs. My shoes were in tatters, the Captain's had no soles at all. Only Frederick had good soles, given him by Theodore in Lakkos. Michael had a good pair of army boots, but one was at the shoemakers when we fled from Lakkos and now he wore one black and one of his practically useless buckskin tennis shoes. They were already held together by string when we lived in the White Mountains. It was really typical of British officers that for our evacuation walk Michael chose ten-year-old buckskin tennis shoes dyed brown and I a pair of Fortnum country shoes to which I was devoted but which had long reached the annuity-and-a-cottage stage. I gave a pair of new boots to an Australian scrounger, the only Australian I ever knew salute. The Captain was more exhausted than I ever knew him before.

It began to get light, and there was no point in going much further. Our guide went off and found two cousins who lived alone with their goats at the end of the peninsula, and leaving us to them, he hurried back. We were in an open valley and the shepherds led us down into a little gorge in it to hide. They were afraid of a villager

125

who had not yet returned from the beach with his olive oil. His small son was going to a German hospital and they got a lot of information out of him there. Twenty thousand men are said to have passed along that Minoan road in the last two months. Cretans returning to Crete and Greeks to Greece. All I suppose like us hurrying and struggling along in the dark, doubtful of the future, wanting only to get home. There is something weird about these walks by night, the whispering, the hidden cigarettes, like bands of smugglers.

All night the moon had been cloudy. It was an unattractive little gorge – all rocks and prickles and not a level yard. We had hardly found a place to lie down when there was a downpour of rain. I had crept under an overhanging rock with about 18 feet of headroom and only I kept dry. We slept, not for long, for the sun rose and there was no shade, so we sat up and ate our chickens, and slept again. Lambris said his shoes were too bad for him to go back to the last village for more food.

Just before dark we moved down towards the sea, turning east. We were furious with the Captain for waiting till it was dark, so that we should lacerate ourselves with the going so bad and our shoes terrible. But he had been right the way down once already to reconnoitre. We slept under a lotus tree not far from the sea, while the Captain and Lambris watched by the shore. We aren't allowed down on the beach because there are a lot of Greeks there waiting to get off and the Captain is terrified of our being betrayed. No Greek trusts another Greek. About midnight we could plainly hear a boat's engine, but no message came. It was a German patrol boat; they said in the morning that two had been around. However, later we discovered that one was a caique which saw the Germans and landed round the point instead.

11–12 August 1941

Our lotus tree is infested with flies which make life almost unbearable. The Captain brought small limpets back from the sea and

126

cooked them in rice with tomatoes. I can't say they tasted much. Due east of us about a mile is a little hole in the rock cliff, where caiques also sometimes put in. In the afternoon we went down there and bathed, one of us keeping a lookout for German patrols. It was a difficult climb down to the water and must be desperate at night. On the way down to the sea there is a German glider. Two landed here in the blitz. It has very clear thick celluloid windows, the men sat one behind the other down the centre. It is pretty big, and very light, but well built. Near it is an unexploded shell, probably fired by a 25-pounder from Maleme. We tore off bits of canvas to tie round our feet and cotton binding which was proper ersatz and useless. I keep on wounding my head on the lotus tree and that goes septic too.

That night there was no German patrol and no caique. To our fury we hear that one came in somewhere else on the point.

Next day just as we were cooking a rather dreary lunch of dried beans, there arrived Lefteris [Rosmaris], brother of Michaelis, one of the two shepherds. Lefteris was even handsomer than Michaelis, and he brought a donkey from the village, with a huge basket of grapes, tomatoes, pears, eggs, figs, wine and bread. The biggest grapes I ever saw and the finest bunch was sent specially to Emilio (me) by our guide along the peninsula, but Michael seized and ate them, saying he was Emilio, and other white grapes, very sweet, like the iced sugared ones I used to love in London. Michael took greatly to Lefteris and when he left Lefteris kissed him warmly. He was quite beautiful. Our grapes attracted hordes of bees like hornets, but they cheered us up greatly. I only discovered the bees really were hornets very much later. They were cannibals. Nothing would keep them out of the fruit, no matter how carefully you plugged up the baskets or haversacks, when you opened them you found a seething horde of brown and yellow savages.

13 August 1941

The Captain came back with the news that a caique had come in at 4 a.m. and that it was waiting for him till nightfall. It has a German

127

permit and is flying the swastika. At breakfast the shepherds came shouting and the Captain and Lambris ran off after them down to the bay. A caique with an engine had come in and they were just in time to prevent it taking Greek soldiers on board and making off again. Instead it moved round to the end of the point to await us by night. We sit and pray for no German patrols.

We hear now that the Germans have taken 800 women and children from the villages they shot up on 1st August to Chania, presumably as hostages against a revolt, though possibly to bring the men down from the mountains. Near Lakkos apparently the Germans met some armed Greeks. There was no fighting, the Germans merely told them to return to their villages, which naturally they have not done.

We had a fright during the day when we saw a boat in the bay of Chania, but it turned out to be going away. Lambris and Michael went off to locate our caique and came back to say they couldn't find it. At 6 p.m. the Captain went down to Menes bay and soon after we saw the sails of a boat being rowed slowly northwards below the cliffs past us. At dark we all packed up and followed down to Menes.

There was no boat.

There had been a muddle.

The sailing boat understood we had sailed on the motor caique and so has taken on 33 Greeks and it was her we had seen passing. The motor caique never appeared either for us or for the 500 okes of oil waiting on the shore (to be exchanged for cigarettes). We realised that this was the boat we saw out in Chania bay, it had evidently taken fright. A friend of the Captain's, the Master of the caique captured by the Germans, has been put on board the motor caique by the Captain to hold the fort for us, so we felt very betrayed. We climbed up again out of Menes valley and slept on the top of the cliff. During the night we heard a German patrol boat. In the early morning we returned to our lotus tree, discouraged.

Two hours later Stratis [Rosmaris], our guide along the peninsula, appeared with a basket of grapes, tomatoes, beans, olives, five loaves of bread, wine and cigarettes. Stratis had been told to find out about boats, and he brought news of one for sale for 30,000 drachmae. The Captain told him to go back and arrange for it to come to us. His other news was that the Germans had been into the peninsular village and threatened with death anyone feeding Greek soldiers, and it looked as if they meant to wire off the whole peninsula. He also told us that all the women and children of Lakkos had gone up into the mountains, which was good news for the Captain, who feared his wife might be among those carried off by the Germans.

During the night, two caiques came in on the other side of the peninsula and went straight out again.

14–17 August 1941

We got a whole side of meat. The Captain loves cooking which is so lucky. Given half a chance he would produce really excellent food, and as it is he makes the very best of everything we have. I particularly approve of him because he says it is quite wrong to cook meat in olive oil, which Michael loves to do and I loathe. The Captain tells us he paints. He has decorated an hotel. I don't actually know of anything he can't do.

The Captain went down to Menes for the night and learnt that quite unknown to us a caique had come in at 8.30 in the morning and taken off all the Greeks. The English had been away getting water. Thirty fresh Greeks had arrived. Early in the morning we all moved down to Menes. It was obviously hopeless being so far away. We only did it to content Stratis and his cousins, who were afraid of English being so near the port, but it cost us two good chances of getting off.

In the night two more caiques come in on the other side and the Captain says they would always be coming in there now because of the German patrol our side. The Greeks all left Menes and we are in two minds. For there is a high wind and Menes is a much more likely place for boats to make for in rough weather. Also the sailing boat Stratis told us about has been bought and paid for and should

129

have come here to Menes yesterday, loaded with provisions. All that has been arranged for us by a priest, we don't know what has gone wrong. The other English are staying here. The New Zealand officer says he has heard the news lately and reports big successes in Libya and Mr Eden saying the war should be over in three months, which is cheering. [Though absolutely false.]

Nicolas, the Crown Counsel, has packed his bag and left. He wasn't a bad old thing really, but it isn't his line of country.

The other English tell of an RE in the 42 Field Coy. who found a suitcase at Spakia, and opening it, found it was full of money. He was just going off with it when he thought his CO was eyeing him, so he contented himself with a handful of notes – which he counted in the prison camp – and there was 46,000 drachmae. He escaped, spent it all, walked back to Spakia, found the suitcase again, and three times as much still in it. Generally speaking I think the prisoners in Galatea camp had very little money, though unit funds were in many cases left with those who could not get off. The Paymaster was bombed in his truck in Kalyves on his way from Herakleon to Chania and 24,000,000 drachmae went up in the air.

The next evening we walked over to the western side of the point. It seemed the more hopeful. From the shepherd's house on our road was down a gorge, in a dry river bed. We had been told it was the worst road in Crete and we knew that must mean something. All the same we were surprised. The river bed was all huge boulders, and there were enormous falls to climb over. I had our earthenware cooking pot in my sack. Lambris has the water pot, full. His survived.

Just before we got to the sea we met Lefteris coming back from chasing a whore (with the Greeks) who had stolen the water tins from his well. We stopped and as it was cold I changed my wringing shirt and put on two dry ones. But in fact we were still some way from the sea and when we got there after some awful climbing I had three wet shirts to keep me warm for the night. The sea as the Captain had feared was rough and breaking against the rocks.

No boats came in during the night.

We decide to stay, hoping the sea will go down, and we try to arrange for the boat we have bought to come round here. At midday we hear that a caique has come in to Menes. Lambris and Fred go off to investigate, and soon after we hear that there is definitely a caique there and follow. Up the confounded river bed. At the shepherd's well we meet Fred urging us to hurry. We rush on, Bert runs all the way. Standing on the last hillside we can look down into Menes cove and see a sailing boat on the beach and many Greeks. It is a great sight.

In no time the Captain is on board, sitting on the bows like an *Arabian Nights* sailor. We bathe, slightly modest before the whore, who is back too. The New Zealand officer is there with his two men. Six other Britishers have been displaced on the boat on our account because they weren't going to pay. We climb over the hill and down the cliff to the water's edge and wait. Then there is an altercation between the Captain on the boat and the Greeks on the shore. We can see that there are too many of them for everybody to go. First we hear that the boat is going to take only the English. An olive-oil seller turns nasty and the Captain goes mad. He draws his pistol, screams at us to leave as we aren't going in the boat and begins to get off himself. The Greeks round us tell us to stay where we are. The Captain climbs along the bowsprit, falls off still clutching it, drops his revolver in the sea, and gets ashore green with rage and still shouting. The Greeks all seem very friendly, and the quarrel dies down without our knowing what it was about. Half the English are to go. We had expected trouble from the Australians who had to remain, but they take it very well. Lefteris is with us and we owe it to him that we are taken on the boat. He insists on Michael getting in first. Altogether six of us, the New Zealand officer and two men and 34 Greeks get on board. The boat is 200-foot long. At dusk we leave, the sail is hoisted. Lefteris kisses us all and fires off his revolver. We sit round the edge of the boat with the Greeks huddled into the hold in the centre. The crew row the boat out of the cove. We eat some bread and cold pork, given us by Lefteris. It is all unbelievable.

We get out of the cove and there is a heavy groundswell as we move very slowly up the coast, one oar aft and one astern and no breeze at all on the great dhow-like sail. We pass over a sunken German plane which they say was pulling the glider we saw. It lies shivering pale green on the rocky bottom. The Greeks waste no time in being sick, and press forward to the side one after the other, shoving their heads between us. Apart from the hold, into whose bottom the Greeks begin to subside like corpses in a common grave, there are two tiny holds. The whore is in one with her beau. We are all sick, me last of all, but I don't feel bad. Our bags are in the hold and buried under Greeks and I can't get at the extra clothes for the night. We huddle together on the edge of the boat and doze.

18–20 August 1941

As it gets light, we see a mountain rising out of the sea a mile or so behind us. We ask what that is. It is the end of the promontory, and all we have done during the night is tack across the bay to Chania and back again.

We try to row the boat, taking turns on the oars and feeling wretched. Just as we begin to think we are going to look extraordinarily stupid lying there by day, a breeze gets up and we run for the island of Anticythera. Opposite Anticythera the wind dies. It is a rocky and deserted island. Further on we can see a tiny island called Prassa and the Captain gets us to row towards that. The boat does not seem to move. The Greeks lie in a ghastly heap and won't help on the oars. The sun glares down on our bare heads. There is no shade. Practically no food, but we don't want that. It is terribly uncomfortable. It is all frightful. Apparently the boat doesn't move because her bottom is so weedy. She is owned by a shoemaker who bought her for the profit to be made out of the job. He charges 1,000 drachmae each passage, and the profit on olive oil and cigarettes is very big. It is definitely the worst thing I've ever been on. During the night a breeze springs up and takes us past Prassa and halfway to Cythera.

Next morning, I am more or less in a stupor. We run in a high wind for Cythera, the sea very rough and splashing against the side all the time and soaking us. This was rather good for the sack containing all my possessions, which I had recovered from the hold definitely worse for its sojourn among the Greeks. The boat's side where I sit is only two feet above the sea, but she rides very well and ships no water. It is a huge sea. Suddenly the sail boom gives a crack and looks like breaking any moment. We turn into the wind and lie rolling horribly. The Greeks stir and those that are conscious cross themselves desperately. The Master of the ship remarks that he is a shoemaker, not a sailor. There is grave danger of the sail being carried away, and he can only think of turning and running before the wind. The little foresail does carry away. Our Captain takes command. We are almost out of water. If we turn and run before the wind we shall not hit Crete. If we hit anything it will be Bizerta. More likely we shall die of thirst somewhere in the Mediterranean. So the Captain turns the ship once more towards Cythera and battles on. The mast stands it, and suddenly to our salvation the wind veers round to the west and we run smoothly forward. It has been a near thing.

The Master of the boat swore he would never sail again. But in the crisis he remained very cool. He climbed the mast and roped up the boom while we lay flapping and rolling. And they certainly were rollers. The Captain's plan was to try and get within rowing distance of Cythera before the sail went. The wind changing saved our mast and sail, and when it died completely away we were not very far from the island. She might be a monster to row, but very few boats would have stood up to that sea. Now we had to row her.

During the evening we moved slowly up to and along Cythera. We'd hoped to land there, but with a slight breeze the Captain decided to go straight on for Greece. He said we'd be there in three hours and he'd be cooking us dinner. I laughed for the first time, sourly, and shared a tin of M. & V. with Bert.

In the night a wind got up and we used it to run into harbour in Cythera – to get news of patrol boats, apparently. We ran in in the dark, like smugglers again. We had passed close to an Italian destroyer during the afternoon and now passing a hulking rock in the dark I could have sworn it was another. We crept in, past the dim shapes of boats, and the Captain whispered to us to be ready to swim for it if we ran into Italians. There was a light we aimed for, which seemed to be on a jetty. In fact it came from a house of friendly Greeks, in a small fishing village. We anchored and the Captain went ashore and got fresh water. Michael managed to get into the boat with him but it was the wrong side for me and I sat longing to be on dry land, if only for five minutes; when Michael got back he said there had been a peach waiting for me. But we crept out again, quietly still, for they said there were a great many Germans and Italians on the island and machine guns on the cliffs. They said we must get round the north cape before dawn. The wind had dropped entirely and though we rowed till dawn, we had only just reached the cape and we had to turn east and coast along the north side of the island. And we never saw a man or gun.

We went on rowing slowly along, in a broiling sun, and the sight of vineyards on the island made us sick. We decided to put into a bay for shade. Just as we'd dropped anchor among some rocks a breeze got up, so out we rowed again and the breeze sent us speeding towards Greece. We could see the mainland now, and it looked extremely like Crete, all bare mountains. But after a short crossing – when we saw some big caiques – we entered a beautiful sound, the water as clear as anything. We tacked up it and passed a fisher boat from which the Captain bought some fish. After what seemed a desperately long time tacking about in the sound, the Captain found a spot to land the Greeks – and the other English (whose plan was to get across Greece by train and into Turkey). The last we saw of our Greek friends was a lot of naked men wading ashore and the whore on one of their backs, and very glad we were to have the boat to ourselves and be able to move in it.

We sailed across to the island of Elaphonisi ('Deer Island') where a fishing village stood on a sandy beach and a white church above by some trees on a sandy spit running out to sea. The houses were all creamy with pale tiled roofs and as the sun went down the sea was pale blue and then pink. The Captain went ashore, after battening us down in the hold lately occupied by the whore. To

134

which we objected, and it was unbearable, and so far as secrecy went Lambris was holding royal court on the bows with a crowd on the beach. Lambris did not enjoy the crossing. He lay near the tiller like a corpse throughout. When Nicolas went we couldn't help feeling it would be better if he went too. He hadn't proved himself a very good guide and he rather objected to being used as a hewer of wood and bearer of water. He had left his wife without a word and there didn't seem much advantage to either side in his coming with us. But I think he saw himself as an ambassador to his cousin General Skulas and he said fiercely that he'd made a promise to accompany all the way and he meant to keep it. He'd never done anything of the sort, but we left it at that.

Very soon after we landed there was a heavy firing the other side of the island. We heard later that a submarine had sunk a large caique full of currants. (For, days afterwards the villagers were bringing in salt damp currants in boats from the wreck.) We went ashore in the dark and ate our fish in a house in the village, with lots of watermelon. On dry land I felt quite dizzy and light in the head. We were given blankets and pillows and slept on the sand dunes by the sea. The Captain got his beard shaved off and re-appeared looking completely different and twenty years younger.

While we were in the house in the village a young man came in and asked us what our business was. He said he was from Athens. He was in fact a 4th Hussar, the only Englishman on the island. The villagers gave the Captain a letter which had been written to this soldier by the man who brought him to the island, but which no one had been able to translate to him. It was a most damning letter. The writer, an Archdeacon, said how out of love of England he had aided this soldier to the utmost, but that he had to risk his life and position and leave his diocese which he was forbidden to do because the soldier was so nervous and afraid. So he had brought him to safety on the island – on which the soldier was living comfortably like a Greek, in nice clothes, and obviously intended to remain there.

21–23 August 1941

We stayed under some trees on the dunes, and fed on watermelons, very unripe sugar melons and grapes. There were vineyards quite near, but the grapes were very poor. A shepherd gave us a bit of bread and tomatoes and for tea we cooked some bully beef, rice and onions. Some Cretans waiting for a boat to take them to Crete came and sat by us during the day and insisted on giving me not only cigarettes but money. Caique owners are frightened at the moment, because of the submarine (which would never bother with small boats I'm sure) and no one will make the crossing. Nor can the Captain get hold of a motor boat for us; all we hear of either have something wrong with them or their owners are afraid. We ate in the dark under the trees, a whim of the Captain's. He is not well. He cut his leg to the bone during the storm on the way across, falling on the anchor, and now he is sick inside as well.

Next day the Captain announced that for 50,000 drachmae he has bought the very pretty newly painted blue sailing boat which is tied up alongside our old horror on the beach. The wind has been favourable since we have been here and we are to leave in the evening. Lambris got a lot of figs and I started to wash my clothes at the well furthest out from the village but was stopped because a policeman had come over from the mainland. Actually he was Harbour-Master and came about the torpedoed caique. In true Greek fashion he had given the villagers time to pinch what they could. The Captain of this boat was killed, because although the submarine gave the crew time to row off, the Captain went back for his wallet.

During the day the Captain changed the boat he was buying and for an extra 10,000 drachmae got a pink boat (scarlet when it was wet) with brick-coloured sails. We loaded her with two big baskets, one of grapes and one of vegetables, and at dusk we rowed out black against the sky and along the island for five miles. Then we waited a bit hearing the engine of a patrol boat and there being no wind. We rowed across from the island to the mainland with the sail up but not helping much. Michael started off rowing in fine Eton style; it was very tiring after the first hour and we decided the others must learn to row. My oar was a brute of a thing, all warped.

As there was no wind we fell asleep where we sat, but about 4 a.m. the Captain heard another patrol boat and woke us up, and we rowed round the end of the cape and eastwards along, hearing patrol boats all the time. We came at last to a little cove and rowed quietly in just before dawn. There was a building on the cliff which the Captain thought might be an Italian post and boats in the cove he thought were patrol boats. So we made out again, but outside we ran into a fishing boat and they told us it was quite all right. We stayed there all day and it was lucky we stopped there for they told us that further along the Italians were stopping every boat passing by day, even fisher boats. It was the most delightful place. A charming little cove, with cliffs full of caves and a little white church built right out on a ledge of rock which gives shade to the fishermen mending their nets by the water below. There is one house up on the cliff where they gave us grapes and pears and figs. Finding nets and a sail in the church, I slept there on them. We lunched off the most delicious small fish – two fisher boats went out at dawn and fished with explosives. Last night we saw my first comet with a blaze behind it so bright I thought it must be a searchlight. Shooting stars are very common.

My hands, which I scraped getting off the old boat in deep water, have gone septic and are very stiff. We ate fried aubergines for dinner and tomatoes, laying on a rock looking up at the church and at the white, pink and yellow boats in the clear deep water of the cove, an absurdly peaceful picturesque scene. I bathed in the cove in the afternoon, diving in off a rock. The rock is all just like concrete, splitting in flat surfaces and made up of conglomerate.

23/24–26 August 1941

We slept on the water's edge. The Captain was very taken with the story of Italian watchers, and decided we must cross the cape on foot while he brought the boat round by sea. We were also to try and get bread on the way, which he assured us would be easy. So early next morning, Michael, Fred and I left with two boys. We made first back north-west to the village of Agios Nicolas at the foot of the mountain range. There we had some milk with honey in it in one house, and bread and milk in another and in a third Michael was just settling down to a huge meal when our boy guide dragged us off.

We climbed and crossed the mountains, which were greener and less rocky than those we were used to, and reached a valley on the further side, where we sat down by a well in a vineyard. We were given the best grapes I ever ate, huge bunches of black ones, and figs. In the village we talked to the Mayor, who was long in South Africa and we thought probably a very rich man. But a tiresome one. He took us to two Englishmen who had just arrived; they were in fact two of the Australians we left behind in Menes. After we left, the Germans had machine-gunned Menes from the sea and practically everybody had left. Then a motor caique came in which brought them across in ten hours. The Mayor tried to make us take them with us, but we told him we hadn't room. Round here all the villagers have been either in Australia or South Africa and have relatives there now. They save a lot of money out there. But they are very short of food.

A bit further on we came to Kastrinia. We were pretty full of grapes, but we were determined to get some proper food here. Nobody took much notice as we entered the village, so we sat down on the road in the shade of a house and started in on some cheese Michael had. A crowd soon began to collect and from one person and then another there appeared bread, then tomatoes, hot potatoes and marrow, cheese, finally scrambled eggs and superb grapes and figs and wine. We almost burst, watched all the time by a friendly crowd three deep. We were led from the roadside to a house, the crowd following, and there Fred and I had ourselves shaved and I had my first haircut for two and a half months. Curiously enough it had hardly grown at all in that time, and Michael was the same. We were given beds in the house to rest and then went on down seawards, to the little village of Agia Phocas near Monamassu where we were supposed to meet the boat. We thought we had seen it setting out from the mountain above Agios Nicolas and again rounding Cape Malea, but when we arrived very exhausted at 6 p.m. there was no boat there. We went to a house in the village and were given a very good meal and blankets, and slept down below the house in a field. During the night the two Australians arrived from Kastrinia, having been told by the wretched Mayor that there was a boat waiting to take them off. He longed to get rid of them.

We breakfasted off figs which were very fresh and good but some acid in them stings one's lips. Then we were taken down to a small bay where there was shade all day and fresh water within a yard of the sea. The villagers are as usual afraid of the Italians, who declare they will kill anyone helping the English. Michael and Fred were already discouraged and making plans for getting on without the Captain, possibly in a large lifeboat there, which brought eight English soldiers ashore. At the same time three bodies were washed up and the villagers have a strange assortment of eastern banknotes and cheques and photographs off them.

A party of about six Australians arrived, on the same goose-chase as the first two. They had just got off Crete from the peninsula of Cape Spartha just before we got on to it, and had landed at Cape Malea right under the Italians' noses. They waved gaily to them in fact and it was some time before they realised they were being fired on. They were chased when they landed but got away, as the Italians were resting and had no shoes on. They are collecting money to buy a motor boat and want to get 250,000 drachmae. They have been given a lot already. Which goes to show that the many English hiding in Greece are not making the most of the possibilities of escape.

Pressed by Michael the Captain left soon after lunch instead of waiting till midnight to see how the wind would be and mending the big sail as he had first intended. We ran fast out to sea and everything seemed splendid. But after an hour the wind veered to the north-east. Just the one we didn't want. It died down, and we rowed towards the bare rock which lay between us and the Aegean

Islands. The wind rose again in the evening and we sailed, but it became impossible to sail anything but north and after a bit it was only north-west. In fact at one moment when I was steering I found it was going west.

At dawn it turned very rough with an easterly or north-easterly wind and a big sea. It continued all day and the Captain feared we should have to turn back. He was afraid particularly of our southerly drift, which might make us miss the islands. Then if the mast carried away we should be lost. Like the Greek sailors of old he wasn't really happy out of sight of land. At dusk the wind died down and we rowed for five and a half hours and then a little wind got up and it was north-north-easterly. With our rowing this took us a bit north and saved us.

27–28 August 1941

In the morning there was a very strong wind from the north-east and the sea was terrifically rough again. We were thankful to God just to make the south coast of Milos at midday. In weather like that we all have to lie in the hold to balance the boat, and it is like an aquarium with the sea continuously pouring in. We none of us think much of sailing. We sailed along the south coast of Milos and then the wind dropped and the Captain made us row for a cove at the south-eastern cape.

We had no food and no sleep. I persuaded him to put in at a little creek and cook some food and rest. It was a charming well-hidden little place and we dashed off to look for firewood to cook our aubergines. I hadn't gone far when I heard cries from the Captain and turned leisurely back thinking he had bumped his leg as he was always doing and making the usual absurd fuss. Instead Michael was lying at his feet, while he wrung his hands. Michael had climbed the cliff, which gave way just as he reached the top and he had fallen backwards on to the rocky beach striking his forehead, which knocked him more or less unconscious. His wrist was obviously out of place. Bert was most efficient, and my curly-handled Cretan walking stick, which I had clung to as a souvenir, went for a splint and his head was bandaged up. We moved him to a more comfortable place, covered him up with our coats and rugs and returned to our aubergines. We slept the night there.

Next day at dawn we got Michael on board, walking on to a rock supported on each side. He had no idea when he was upright. There was no wind and we rowed for three hours till we reached the Captain's bay. He went off to a village and with difficulty got some grapes, for money. The people of Milos are well known for their general unfriendliness and inhospitality, being spoilt by their valuable mines. I went ashore and showed myself and was given some fine grapes. The Captain was livid at my going ashore though he never said anything to me. There are about 50 Germans on Milos, on the aerodrome they have built. From there we sailed quite well to the end of the island and rounding a cape saw all the islands like a litter of sea cows cluttering up the sea and Syphnos, the Captain's own island, and our objective, not so very far off in the distance.

We headed for Polyvos. But there was no wind and after rowing all afternoon with the sail up the drift had taken us far to the south. There was a current running against us and the Captain despaired of making the island and we thought of turning back to Milos again. However, we rowed on and just as the moon rose we entered a little cove. The beach of smooth white stones was merely an end of a dry watercourse. The island is not inhabited, but when we leapt ashore we met lying spread-eagled on the moonlit beach a month-old corpse, clad in British shorts and shirt. I fled from his welcoming smile. [Almost certainly Oliver Barstow, killed when the yacht *Kalanthe* was dive-bombed on its way to Crete with Harold Caccia and his wife Nancy (later Lord and Lady Caccia). Oliver was Nancy's brother.]

29–30 August 1941

We woke to stormy wind of which the Captain was afraid, but it died down somewhat and after burying the lonely corpse we rowed out and into the channel between the islands. We tacked slowly up it, with a high but unfavourable wind. It was too fresh to allow us to reach Syphnos, and so we made for harbour and food on Kemalos. There we could see quite a town on the hill and a little port. We put into a cove just beyond the port. There were no Germans or Italians on the island, nor food either – they had had no bread for three weeks. A doctor came and looked at Michael on the boat and he was got up into a cottage on the cliff and into bed. They all spoke well of the doctor, who seemed to know his business and put Michael's arm in plaster and dressed all our various wounds.

Fred and I went for a walk up the hill, avoiding the town, and the first person we met sitting on a wall was the Greek Sergeant of Police. He looked rather like Count Ciano, but seemed friendly, so we invited him to walk with us and let him talk a lot. I reckoned he was saying that we put him in a very unenviable position and the Germans would shoot him if they found out and the town had two well-known spies and there was a telephone to Milos, and really we'd better not stop. So I patted him and said we wouldn't and we parted friends.

The Captain slept the night in the town. By some wizardry he got masses of food although the people were almost starving – seven loaves, cheese (a special local brand), 30 eggs, fish, beans, grapes, pears and tomatoes. He also arranged for the motor caique anchored below us to tow us as far as the furthest island. It was great news. No more rowing.

Kemalos is a very poor island. They produce very little but grapes and figs and of course they catch fish. On Syphnos apparently you get olives, tangerines, oranges and lemons. But I'm afraid we look like missing this idyll of an island, particularly as we hear now that there are Italians on it. The story is that an Italian troopship was sunk on its way to Rhodes and the men on it were first landed on Paros and then scattered throughout the islands. If we couldn't land openly on the island and go inland to the Captain's village and dance on his whitewashed streets and revel in his spring-mattressed beds, there wasn't really much point in going there.

31 August–2 September 1941

The Captain decided not to wait for the motor caique, but to use the south wind, and the boat was loaded up. We only wait for the priest to come and bless it. We christened the boat by the holy name of Agia Irene, but we put down our ill fortune on her to the fact that she has never been blessed.

Last night the BBC announced that in Crete British soldiers were fighting side by side with the Cretans. We rather doubt this.

The priest came, a big old man with a grey beard, in a long blue gown, followed by his little daughter carrying his grey umbrella. He sat outside the cottage and watched while the fish were cleaned for us to take cooked. Then he climbed down over the rocks on to the boat and us after him. Standing in the hold, with in front of him on the water barrel two candles and incense on charcoal, he read Mass and afterwards special prayers for the ship. When he took off his high black hat, a pig-tail fell to his waist. Round his neck he had a red and gold stole. At the end he blessed us all and the boat and scattered sacred water over everything, us, the boat, the pink sails, the great basket of blue, red and golden grapes and we kissed his cross. With many good wishes he departed, his little daughter behind him, leaving with us holy water and bread to take tomorrow, as today we have already eaten. The fish of every kind, soles and red mullet, some fishes redder still and of every shape, were cooked and pickled in a special sauce which should keep them good for a month,

Michael got down to the boat without too much difficulty, and at 1.30 we left, our host and his family in their boat circling round us and blowing a trumpet encouragingly as we dealt very inefficiently with the sail. The wind was high and soon we were away and past Syphnos going fine. The sea became so rough that it was difficult to keep the huge following rollers from splashing into the boat. It was fortunate we wanted to run before them, for we could have done nothing else. As it got dark the wind was reaching gale force. We averaged seven miles per hour for 45 miles that afternoon. It got dark very early and we sailed along the island of Paros. There in the dark we made into a small bay for shelter. Taking the sail down it caught and tore and the Captain mended it by the light of holy candle ends and the clouded moon.

Next day, the wind if anything increased. It is annoying not to be able to use a south wind now we have it. We moved the boat into a good little cove, where we found a trickle of fresh water right on the sea. Next day at midday we set sail. We passed the famous Delos, a very low uninhabited little island, and crossed over to Mykanos. In the evening the wind veered to north. We could see Chios in the distance and at nightfall we were opposite Samos. We ate our preserved fish, which all tasted exactly the same, i.e. of preserved sauce. After a wretched night of veering and disappearing winds, ending up with our lowering the sail and merely drifting, we found ourselves 15 miles further to the south off the coat of Nicaria. It was beastly cold at night. Michael had the blanket. We had discovered a colony of young bed bugs on the woodwork of the hold and Frederick made the most of some lice.

3 September 1941

There was a little wind in the morning. It rose in the afternoon and we had to go under hatches. They were most ineffectual and water poured in over us. We steered north-west and by tacking got up near to the cape opposite Chios. All day it was cloudy, like England almost, and at night it was very cold and damp and we were one and all miserable.

The Captain couldn't find a suitable landing place on the cape and so at dawn we steered south along the coast for Ephesus opposite Samos, which was marked on a map we had found on the beach in Crete. We reckoned we were in Turkish territorial waters. A big convoy passed us steaming north, under a Turkish destroyer. It was a lovely day, smooth with a good breeze, and the boat swam along nicely. Samos and the mountains of Turkey were far greener than anything we had seen for many months. A little town climbed up a hill from the sea, white with red roofs, a little island before it with a Venetian fort, and a mosque and a minaret near the shore. We hid under hatches and anchored opposite the harbour-master's house. As the hatches covered only two-thirds of the hold, we were perfectly visible to anyone above us on the quay. The Captain went ashore. We came ostensibly asking for provisions before carrying on to Cyprus, but he soon returned with the glorious news that all was well.

Within an hour we were on land and free. It had just begun to get rough, and we had some difficulty getting the boat up to a jetty. Food on board, which a few hours before had seemed priceless, was discarded. We were led before the harbour authorities and spent hours with them and the police. Everything was normal and apparently efficient. In the ridiculous what-is-your-father's-christian-name-taken-down-phonetically-in-Turkish manner. We were helped enormously by the Greek Consul, who had dealt with many hundreds of escaped Greeks. Free at last we made for the hotel, stopping to be photographed in the main street and myself darting into shops as I saw meringues and chocolates in the windows. The Turks seemed friendly but uninterested. We ate in a restaurant, pilaff; the hotel was quite clean, with bedrooms all round a central hall which was crowded with a party of Greeks also passing through on their way to Egypt. I managed to get a hot bath about two o'clock in the morning.

3–4 September 1941

We breakfasted and got ourselves shaved and the naval defence officer arrived from Smyrna, a typical jolly old RNR Commander. We are in trouble over a steel box of papers which the Turks want to hold for examination and from which we refuse to be parted. The Turks have also seized Fred's diary and my photographs for further examination. My photographs could hardly be more innocuous and include a tiny leather folder I won as a prize for a three-legged race at St Neots with photographs of Toby and John aged seven and two respectively and nothing else. The tin box offered more possibilities. Its history was as follows. The staff of the British Embassy left Athens in the yacht *Kalanthe*. It was thought unsafe to sail by day and arriving at Polyvos most of the party landed and spent the day ashore. At midday German aircraft came over and bombed the yacht. The crew were on board and a few others, including a friend of mine, Arthur Forbes [Wing Commander Viscount Forbes]. His plane was held up waiting for a woman passenger and destroyed on the ground, so that he had to go on the yacht. When the ship was hit he was nearest to the bomb and sent to the bottom of the ship. The boiler burst and shot him up to the surface again. Several of the crew were killed which explained our friend on the beach at Polyvos. Most of the secret ciphers on the ship were saved, but all the embassy plate and jewels to a great value were lost. The party were chased by Germans but had time to tell a fisherman on Kemalos (whence they left by caique) that there were important papers on the yacht. If they should be found they were to be handed over to the first trustworthy person to be carried personally to General Sir Maitland Wilson, our C-in-C in Greece. Hearing of the Captain's arrival on Kemalos the fisherman came by night bringing with him an iron box, full of papers. His story was that he had salvaged the box from the only partly submerged yacht. He reported his find to the Greek policeman on the island, who told him it was of no importance and advised him to throw it away. The Greek police did however report the matter to the Germans who in the meantime were using divers to try and collect papers from the yacht. The Germans therefore sent for the fisherman who told them that he had thrown the box into the sea, as he had been told to do. Now he brought it to us. When the Captain opened the box he found it contained the secret orders which passed between our ambassador in Greece, General Wilson and the King of Greece regarding the evacuation of Greece by the troops.

The Turkish officials at Kusadasi refused to return us this box, and eventually we left for Smyrna with the box attached to a Turkish officer, whose turned up mustachios cut across his eyes in the most intriguing manner. We drove to the police station in Smyrna in two cars, and were kept there till midnight. The main trouble being the famous iron box. The wires to Ankara are humming.

There is a detachment of REs in Smyrna busy building aerodromes for Hitler to use and they took charge of us. They wore civilian clothes of course and were charming, but while we wanted to go to the most gaudy hotel they insisted it was full of Germans and we must keep hid with them. At least till we had proper clothes. So they took us to their colonel's house and a pension next door, where we ate and I shared an attic with Lambris instead of the bridal suite at the Smyrna Palace Hotel on which my heart was set. I was driven mad by mosquitoes and an itch. We all itch. It started before we landed and we scratch night and day and rub our backs on everything we meet.

Most of next morning we spent again with the police. We sent cables home and after lunch we were cross-examined by the RE Colonel and the Vice-Consul [Noel Rees]. We made a short expedition to buy clothes and I got a white coat and a pair of grey trousers I can't get on.

We went ten kilometres outside Smyrna to tea. Civilised life had begun again.

7 September 1941, Post Office Telegram to Judge Hildyard

Safe and well after Odyssey. Cable all news care Longmore.

Miss Grace Cooper wrote from the British Embassy, Ankara, to Judge Hildyard, 15 September 1941

I met Myles the other day whilst on holiday in Smyrna and he asked me to write by the next diplomatic bag to give you news of him as this is quicker than the other way.

He arrived with Michael Parish, rather exhausted and swearing never to go yachting again. I think they had a wonderful time in Smyrna, which would be a delightful place were it not for the

Levantines (though I think they were not there long enough to appreciate all their vices!) and I gather that Myles was altogether surprised to find Turkey so nice. He asked me particularly to send his love to Toby and also to tell you that he only spent two days as guest of Captain Milward's son [Gerry – i.e. German prisoner of war], but Sidney Morse and Micky Riviere stayed on. Myles it seems climbed the mountains he was always telling you about [White Mountains, Crete] and he says he made quite a study of them, but mountaineering is another thing he can do without.

They will both write fully on their arrival in Cairo and in the meantime are eagerly awaiting letters from home. Should you need my address it is The British Embassy, Ankara. c/o Foreign Office, Whitehall London SW1 ($2\frac{1}{2}$ d stamp).

PS Of course Myles sent all his love and is longing for news.

The War Office Casualty Branch, Liverpool, wrote to Judge Hildyard, 16 September 1941

In confirmation of War Office telegram dated the 15th September, 1941 I am directed to inform you that a report has been received that your son, Lieutenant M. T. Hildyard, The Nottinghamshire Yeomanry, Royal Armoured Corps, is safe in British hands. Unfortunately no further details are at present available and it is not possible, therefore, to advise you as to his whereabouts or of means of communicating with him.

General Sir Maitland [Jumbo] Wilson wrote from Headquarters British Forces, Jerusalem to Clement Parish, 21 September 1941

Your boy Michael has turned up here and came to dinner with us two nights ago. He was looking very battered from a fall off a cliff that he had on an island near Mylos. Since then he has been taken into hospital here with sand fly fever which they say is rather *aggravated by the strain he has undergone. They will look after him well there, as they have a very good team of surgeons and physicians. One eye is bunged up and he has a broken arm.*

His experiences are really worth listening to and I expect he has let you know them. From what he told us the escape was only too easy, as they did it with buckets over their shoulders saying they were going to have a wash, and never came back, but he had an exciting two months or so up in the mountains where sometimes the village he was in was raided by the Germans, until they could get away. The Greek Captain, M. Vernicos, who seems to have taken charge of the party, seems to have done extraordinarily good work, and it was a very good idea of theirs to go back to the Peloponnese instead of going directly to Egypt. Vernicos told me he thought Michael was killed when he fell down the cliff, but the young seem to have wonderful powers of recuperation.

The tragic part of Michael's story is the appalling conditions for food existing in Crete and the probability that no children will be able to live through the winter owing to lack of vitamins, whereas the older people will be able to survive. They must be a great hearted people for doing what they have done, and they have certainly made the Germans pay for attacking their island.

We are settling down in Syria now that the Vichy French have gone at last, but I would very much like to be rid of the Free French as well. Of all the despicable nations, I put them as low as any, and it is not to be wondered at that they collapsed as they did in the spring of 1940. They trust nobody, not even themselves, and are as corrupt and deceitful as they can be. It is not surprising that de Gaulle chose the double cross as his emblem. The best of luck to you.

4 October 1941, Cairo

Of course you will say that it is monstrous to wait one month before writing. I should almost pretend I have written and it's gone down – to save your feelings. I stepped ashore from my yacht on 4th September and cabled you soon after and arranged for you to be sent some photographs and a note which I hope reached you (via the diplomatic bag) and I reached Aleppo and the Middle East on 14th September and Cairo a week later. We had great fun in Smyrna and you might think our return here would be a riot. But really the end of our saga should have been the old homestead in Ithaca and an old muse or two instead of the dreary old Middle East. It hardly seemed worth it. So at first I felt dazed and above all I cannot abide writing sometimes – *vide* when I was very low in Haifa last year – and particularly when I have so much to say that I don't know how to start about it! These letter cards are a great relief, as obviously there's no room to say anything in them. All of which is most unfair to you who of course will long to know all.

Here I have seen the head of the intelligence three times and all his satellites and have been nominally on duty reporting to him till today. From tomorrow I begin a week's leave and then return to the Notts Yeomanry. There seems no alternative to this as I asked Flash Kellett what the position would be if I was offered a job here and he said he would do everything he could to prevent my getting it. Very complimentary but due only to a momentary glamour and I'm sure tanks will give me indigestion.

Of course Flash is quite mad. He has in consequence of our return turned out Pat McCraith who alone of the Regiment has any experience of war, and practically all the original officers have gone. Anyway, the report is that the Regiment is very keen, hard-working and dull. For the present Cairo is fun. Michael Parish is here now (he got waylaid in hospital in Jerusalem) nominally in hospital but largely free. Mrs Marriott has invited me a lot. At one luncheon I met Prince Peter of Greece, so English-looking that, not listening to the introduction, I began by shaking him warmly by the hand (he is said to have an eye on the throne) – Randolph Churchill who is the most unpopular man in the ME and very unattractive, but he censors the parcels I send you which is something – Princess Ali Khan who I knew already – and Ralph Ingersoll, a very important American newspaper man who used to run *Time* and had just made a complete trip round the world. Most entertaining and encouraging about Russia.

150

Here all of us are still posted missing (myself wounded and missing) but I gather that news of officer prisoners reached England months ago now. I'm afraid it must have been a worry to you (and hear so from Pat McCraith). I regret very much that Michael Riviere is a prisoner. He was much the nicest person I've met out here. He was too exhausted unfortunately.

PS As for the wound it was a shot in the leg and very slight and I'm sure it came from my own side.

12 October 1941, Cairo

After I had been here a fortnight I was told I wasn't needed any more for interrogation and I could have a week's leave before being posted back to my regiment. That is up today, but as the doctors here have failed to discover that I had scabies till halfway through it, and I have had a wisdom tooth out, I am staying on a bit longer.

I met last night the young Cameron, son of Lochiel. I was sitting, God knows why, on the sort of stage of a nightclub and he was against the light which made him almost invisible so I wouldn't know him again, but it seemed as though he wrinkled his nose in the most charming way when he smiled. He told me he had what he wanted – a job with the minimum of work and the maximum of society. Don't though tell that to the Camerons as I don't believe they like him. I can only suppose he hasn't wrinkled his nose at them, because it is devastating.

I am now getting a boil right bang in the armpit which is going to drive me mad. Otherwise I'm very well. I've been able to replace everything I want and have made a nice fleabag out of a camel-hair blanket. Michael P is in hospital still, but I think better.

4 November 1941, Karkur: Letter to Toby

Of course any suggestion of getting back to England makes me sick. I hadn't quite the face to demand it when I got back, and probably wouldn't have got it, though Michael was offered it on account of his injuries. How long would it take? Could I for instance do anything in a fortnight or three weeks with certainty of not over-staying the time applied for on account of lack of transport? It would be incredible.

When I first got back I was really very healthy but mentally quite numb and Cairo did me a lot of good. Michael and the Australian officer both had to go to hospital. I had intended going either to Syria or to Akaba via Petra with Billy Brooksbank, but realised that what I wanted was the whirl of the city. Actually if I had come back to the Regiment just a few days sooner I should have been taken to Syria by the Colonel [Flash Kellett], who made a trip up to the Euphrates and waited some days for me. I get on very well with him and with Donny Player.

We are supposed to be training, but with practically nothing to do it on. Two things make me mad:

1) that I know the Germans would have built an artificial Caucasus in the plain here and covered it in artificial snow and charged it day and night with a thousand tanks
2) that one day we shall be given some equipment, told we've been training for months and are obviously ready to meet the enemy next week. Which we shall do and be massacred.

11 November 1941, Karkur

Two men up for a court martial have both asked for me to defend them, very misguided as the Regiment is now full of legal talent. I bought Ernest Hemingway's *For Whom the Bell Tolls* in Haifa for Michael P (but am reading it first) which they say is the only good book written since the war, all about guerrilla warfare in Spain, for which I can sympathise as it is among wild folk in the mountains and I might easily be doing the same myself now. The last few days it has turned cold and cloudy which I prefer except I know the sun is the only thing which keeps me going and I miss my evening bathes.

This court martial is *un peu difficile* as they pinched a car and are charged under a section of the *Army Act*, which is in no manual of Military Law, with an offence under the *Road Traffic Act 1940* which absolutely no one possesses. We have so many officers now it is unbelievable, new ones come every day, none are gents.

16 November 1941, Karkur

A wonderful thing happened this week: I saw Baalbec. We drove up the coast to Beirut, stopping for lunch and a bathe by a little sandy bay where the water almost immediately fell away deep, the only bit of sand on that coast and I'd noticed it 18 months ago driving back as fast as we could go to reach the French frontier by dark. It's a nice drive along the sea with hills on your right, but near Beirut it becomes divine, gardens and orchards and a sea of olives overlooked by pine-covered mountains with red-roofed houses among palms and flowers on the terraces of the lower slopes. Beirut itself juts out into the sea.

Instead of taking the main Damascus road we climbed further north, through the pines and the little villages, up to skiing resorts where the fresh air brought memories of the Tyrol and how one felt there. Then the pines stopped and we drove past edifices and palaces of rock and gorges and a little green corn sprouting and thousands of white croci, and that changed to rolling ironstone and so over the top and down into the plain with Anti-Lebanon rising beyond.

We lunched in the plain down a lane of tall mimosa by a stream. The stream fed a tannery, but it was peaceful. Our ears buzzed with the heights we had crossed. In that wide bare plain the ruins of Heliopolis dwarf plain and mountains and sky. But it is not the hugeness (and there are single blocks of stone 60 feet long and 12 thick) nor the baroque splendour of capitals and mouldings, the titanic columns, the extravagant extent, which made me stand alone before the stupefying mass when everyone else had left. It is its colour, which is sublime. I stood in the shadow of the 66-foot columns which are all that remains of the largest temple and which hid from me the sun, thinking that thus I should rob them of their power, of their sunlit honey colour – and they glowed, flushed through with radiance, golden like alabaster on a verdant pedestal, flooding with colour a subservient sky. I bowed in spirit before Baal the eternal. A cold dark drive and I slept in Damascus. Next morning we left the green gardens for plains and white-robed Arabs on white betasselled stallions and then a horrid basalt wilderness falling to Lakes Hule and Tiberias far below sea level. In the latter I bathed and ate and read under eucalyptus trees. So through Nazareth, home.

19 November 1941, Karkur

I dined last night with our brigadier and today went up to Jerusalem which I have been longing to do to see about my accounts. My claim for lost kit was returned because I failed to put in the month in which I bought each article originally! Fortunately my arrears of pay covered my expenses in Cairo and my purchases with quite a lot over (to my great surprise) so I have a packet coming in. I can also get a pound a day for three weeks while I was at the disposal of the intelligence and the higher rate of ration allowance from the time I escaped till I got back to ME, and I suppose Captain's pay now, so I ought to be rich and may send you something towards the park fence. I carried my two chequebooks throughout and used several cheques on Barclays en route! [One had reached Westminster Bank, Newark, and when they telephoned to ask whether it should be honoured, my mother fainted. It was the first news of me since I had been reported missing.]

I lunched today with Princess Eirene of Greece, Prince Peter's wife, a red-haired Russian, very intelligent and a great expert, I am told, on religions. She took Kurt Gottlieb and me to lunch with Dr Eisenger the psychologist, a pupil of Freud's. He gave us a very good lunch, in a house full of good modern pictures and a fine library, and we loved him and long to go again. We think it must be expensive to be psychoanalysed as he's obviously rich, and he says altogether in his life (he's 65) he has done 500 or 600 people (only). I do love meeting these sort of people – not the sort one finds in Newark market.

My poor batman, Hill, got a telegram from Myrtle Kellett to say his wife has run away. They have three sweet small children. This is always happening these days. I think it's monstrous.

25 November 1941, Karkur

We had a frightfully amusing lecture the other day from a young man who was captured in Syria. His yeomanry failed to take a fort so they left him with his troop to watch it and went on. After a few days a British supply convoy drove up to the fort in Chevrolet lorries, having been told it was in our hands and got into a lot of trouble. The same day a line of Chevrolet lorries came out from the fort towards him flying a white flag. When they reached his forward section they shot the lot up and the lorries turned out to be full of Arabs under French officers and led by a very famous Arab who led the Palestine and Iraqi revolts. This boy ran for it and made a trench and was surrounded by armoured cars which ploughed up the ground all round him but couldn't depress their guns enough to hit him in the bottom. Eventually a French officer lent over and took a shot at him with his revolver. He wasn't wearing his revolver, being a typical yeoman, but he grabbed a rifle and fired back and the Frenchman made off. However, eventually he surrendered and was taken by air to Greece and so by train to France through Germany. There were quite a lot of them and they were badly treated [by the French]. He said he got a good view of Belgrade and apart from the station there was no sign of bombing! We were told it was flat. And in Munich he said the railway marshalling yards were floodlit all night and there was no blackout. They passed in the train and talked to a party of British soldiers captured at Dunkirk walking in the fields and quite cheerful.

I had an excitement in a truck the other day, when on a newly built and rather narrow road we passed a Jew donkey cart and ran two wheels on to the verge and they wouldn't go back again. As there was a concrete bridge ahead our driver ran down the seven-foot embankment at full speed and a terrific angle and after crossing a small wadi landed us all safely but rather surprised in a field. We have 33 officers actually with the Regiment now I believe, of whom eight were with us when the war broke out! It wouldn't matter if they were what Spencer [Forbes] calls O.C.D. (our class dear), but they aren't.

You will think I am become a story teller, but I still dislike talking at meals. I have had an appalling cold but it is better. I am slightly fed up with the war, are you? However, having read that book *If Hitler Comes*, I should dislike peace now even more.

7 December 1941, Karkur

Happy Christmas! This is supposed to get you in time. I got your cable 'John passed Board' which is excellent news and I suppose now he'll go and be trained. Give him my love if he's at home. I hope he is. I got a letter from Toby today, dated 23rd November, saying he hoped to be in England next day, so that must have been nice for you. I am sorry he was worried I might be in the present Libyan show, I hope you were able to dispel the idea. [This was the Allied push across the Egyptian frontier into Libya. Tobruk was relieved and Benghazi recaptured.] I don't think I've ever told you that Michael P and I were recommended for MCs and though I don't think we shall, Auchinleck told our divisional general that we should get something.

I wandered the other day into a Kibbutz – a Jewish communal agricultural settlement. I think about a quarter of all the Jews in Palestine live on the land, as the population has increased eight times since the last war and most of the newcomers probably went into towns. I imagine that it was originally intended the proportion should be higher. In a communal settlement the land belongs to the community who go in for very intensive methods (and research). They get no money at all. The profits go back into the land and into buildings to replace the original shacks, and the new buildings are very good. In them a couple would have one room. Children live together communally, all adults eat together. After the day's work they have their children with them till bedtime. I went into a children's house, they were all six years old, and obviously very happy. It was very clean and modern, with trained nurses, little tables and chairs, flowers, very nice supper of hot milk, scrambled eggs, tomatoes, bananas, bread and butter, all grown on the place. I came away very impressed. They were Poles but children are taught Hebrew and Arabic. At a further stage they go to a school in the settlement and then to a school in the district. Geoffrey Brooks who was with me foresees this sort of thing in England but I don't think anything but the most pressing necessity would start it or that it would be bearable if it wasn't self enforced.

I went to the races in Cairo purely for the pleasure of seeing the famous British phlegm in action. The Libyan battle was raging and the first news of heavy casualties had just come in. The Egyptians who took their children to see how the 'upper ten' behave were treated to the spectacle of Peter Herbert of Muckross and the Ali Khan quarrelling like mad for 15th and 16th places and complaining to the judges of one another's behaviour.

20 December 1941, Karkur

I have been made second in command of B in place of Pat as he's away now, and the Colonel too. I don't know what's going on. I look like having a busy next few days. I have got to learn the work of 2 i/c, I am down to defend someone on Tuesday, and I am to lecture on Crete to the Lifeguards in Jerusalem. I plan to investigate the Caesarea aqueduct tomorrow which is full of mysteries. I am in charge of Christmas decorations for the men's Christmas lunch in the very large cinema and the officers' mess, which means finding Christmas trees among other things, all before Christmas. So I want to finish my letter to you tonight and I haven't begun yet on why I should be wearing a coat of many colours.

157

Flash is a great friend of an extraordinary woman called Mary Newall, who is commandant of the MTC [Motorised Transport Corps]. I'd seen her in Cairo and heard a very great deal about her. She was definitely Cairo's female sensation. She collected £30,000 and bought ambulances and brought them out with 77 girl drivers, trained to do all their maintenance themselves. I don't know much about her but she was a great beauty, divorced by one husband in the Irish Guards and married another in the navy, of whom she was very fond but he blew his head off in his dressing room not long before the war. She is about 50 and has a bad duodenal. Anyway, she went up to Turkey and left her car here and Flash was sending it up to fetch her from Aleppo so I asked if I could go in it. Just as in Whitsun 1940 I won a battle for Flash and was sent on holiday to Syria on the strength of it, so this time a tank experiment I organised with A and C Squadrons went well and Flash decided I was an amateur strategist of the first order and I left for Syria again.

After Tripoli, leaving the gardens of bananas, the high hedges of fig trees and pampas grass, and the Lebanon itself, we came out on to an open windy plain of grass and sparse villages and little men wrapped in black, bent before the wind like gnomes, and then we came to country like Palestine, arable and stony. We passed the island of Rouad about a mile off the coast, entirely covered with houses and surrounded by sailing ships, and came to Tartouss (the ancient Aradus and Antaradus of the Phoenicians) where there was a fine basilica, now deserted but once a great place of pilgrimage. I lunched under grey, bare fig trees with the sea 50 yards on my left and so warm I almost bathed and, crowning a ridge two miles on my right, the great Crusader castle of Markab. The hills were all green and I ate my buzzard cold and hot coffee and croissants.

I had a letter of introduction to the chief of the Alunites at Lattakia, but instead I headed into the mountains which had been reported to me as a marvellous snowy road like Switzerland. There wasn't a trace of snow. We crossed country like green wold, and hills of firs and russet shrubs and streams, within a mile or so of the Turkish border, following a canyon down to the valley of the river El Kebir and up again. There were oleanders but not in flower and

158

the men we passed wore high jack boots and square goat-hair coats, often belted, and cone-shaped hats. We crossed uplands of stony hills and then fell down into a plain where we crossed the famous Orontes by a long, old stone bridge. Here the men wore black embroidered coats lined with sheepskin and their hair was long either side of their cheeks and they carried lambs in the panniers of their donkeys. On the hilltops were Bedouin tents, shared by camels. We reached Aleppo as it got dark, a great city of Arab houses round a castle on a colossal mound of earth and not a tree or a garden. However, a good hotel.

Next morning I met Mrs Newall. On her way into Constantinople at night there was a train crash, eight people were killed and she had to walk miles in the snow carrying her bags, barefoot to save her shoes! I had been warned she wouldn't sit still a moment and sure enough she wanted to go straight on. Half her fame is of the rows she has had, but she was so extraordinarily beautiful that one had to forget all the things one had heard. She has white hair, and wears a very smart uniform. Everywhere we went Arabs stood and gasped and soldiers saluted her (a thing quite unheard of). We went first to the souks. There are 13 miles of souks, all arcaded in stone and not a gimcrack European thing in them. We did great bargaining for the shoes for Toby, though when it came actually to buying Arab clothes for myself I rather wilted. I wanted to have a soft camel-hair gown, embroidered with gold, and we got one down to £5 but no lower, and I wanted an embroidered black silk gown with scarlet on it and lined with fur, but all I got was my striped affair. We were frightened of getting lost but we came out again all right.

27 December 1941, Karkur

I failed to finish my letter just before Christmas. But everything else went all right – my lecture to the Household Cavalry on Crete went well except that I agreed to make it three quarters of an hour and, reaching the time when Michael and I moved up into the mountains,

159

I looked at my watch and found I had been speaking an hour. So the remaining three months had to be skimmed. Anyway I made them laugh a lot.

I rushed back from Jerusalem on Christmas Eve to do the decorations. The mess dinner was in the cinema, a very large wooden building. I did the wall supports alternately with cypress trees and orange branches with the oranges on, and paper streamers and lanterns. The tree was very fine with electric lights, icicles, tinsel, stars and balls of silver paper on the end of string. I had a smaller tree for the officers' mess (but all the same its head lay along the ceiling) and very good streamers and lots of narcissi and even some sweet peas! The men's dinner was a very great success. Turkey and roast beef together with tons of stuffing, cauliflower and potatoes, Christmas pudding and brandy butter, a bottle of beer each. The officers and sergeants served, and as it's a big job dishing out for 600 most of it was done with our fingers. The men were staggering about the place for the rest of the day. Squadrons were supposed to parade full strength for church on Christmas morning; most had had parties the night before, and C marched in six strong. I never saw anybody look so sheepish as poor Stephen Mitchell. Rather a good service, alternate carols and readings from the Bible.

I told you I had my arm in a sling at one time; after returning from Syria I had them both in slings alternately – with sores on one and boils on the other. In Syria I got four new boils or carbuncles, one an extremely bad one on my hip, and when Geoffrey [Brooks, the Regiment doctor] saw that he said really I'd much better go to hospital. So now I'm lying in bed in the Scottish Hospital at Sarafand. I didn't mean actually to be in bed, but I seem to be there. The young gentleman in the bed next me gets up and goes out after breakfast and doesn't reappear till 11 p.m. Nobody knows where he goes or what he does.

I hope that my diaries will be rescued for me from the safe in GHQ where Michael deposited them and delivered to Mrs Newall, and if this is done successfully she is going to send them to you via Lord Moyne. I feel very bad about the long delay, which is entirely due to Michael's nervousness. I have been made Welfare Officer to

160

work between the Regiment and Mrs Kellett's Society. I have already left B Squadron and shall go back to C. I have brought my Fortnum's biscuits and cake to hospital with me and thousands of books.

Kurt Gottlieb up in the 9th Army scheme got quite a lot about Hess from an intelligence man who was in on it at the time. According to him, Hess and Goering tossed up which should come and Hess won. Such a pity as Goering would have been much funnier. Both were very against the Russian campaign and brought peace plans of their own. Goering has had all power taken away from him in consequence.

You ask if I am still thinking of agriculture. I definitely am. I don't know what the world will be like after the war but I don't think country life will change all that much; it doesn't matter to me what happens to fox-hunting. I want to live at Flintham and preferably in the house or on its site. When I come back I want to go to an agricultural school. Flash who is really my greatest friend in the Regiment these days and is an MP says I should go into politics. I had an argument with him (and was worsted) about the place of ambition in politics. Anyway I know I myself have no ambition. My friend Tommy Dugdale looks like being Chairman of the Conservative Party one day and I know hopes to control the choice of candidates in place of the local associations. But I don't think politics should be a full-time job – in which case it has all the disadvantages of business, and no cash. I am assured that there must be Party Politics if there is to be a Democracy. Not that I'm keen on democracy. And the demos regards 'the government' as a sort of upper-class machine and doesn't like it either. Nor do I like the way we choose our candidates from the leisured class and the stupid members of it generally. But what is the answer with such frightful examples of non-democracies? But democracy cannot plan ahead and it is petty. I only like the idea of state control when I think people of our class will run it, and probably they won't get a look in at all.

What other ways can one 'play one's part in national life'? Will county administration (farming etc.) be at all important after the war? Anyway, I want to dig myself in first. I live among very unintelligent people, except when I'm in Cairo, and hear no ideas for post-war life, or even government. I think I shall see chaos all my life probably, and can live in it or out of it as I choose, and I'm not conceited enough or ambitious enough to want to throw away the chance of a quiet, definite life.

28 December 1941, Karkur

The doctors, after a very superficial glance, seem to think that my affliction is scorbutic and therefore I ought to go to another hospital not far away, but much less pleasant. I am annoyed about this.

To continue my Syrian visit. After the souks we went and saw the citadel. Aleppo lies on a dead flat plain but in the middle of the town there rises a colossal mound, with walls and towers, and a very fine entrance indeed – a steep high arched bridge over the moat and two towering gatehouses, a lovely warm sunny colour with enough Arab decoration to prove that this was a Saracenic and not a Crusader stronghold. We left Aleppo after lunch, with the snowy Caucasus on our right, and drove the 98 miles to Hama in one and three-quarter hours.

Hama is on the Orontes, and according to my guidebook is the Faubourg St Germain of Syria. We saw nothing to substantiate this. We crossed the Orontes and watched French colonial troops pretending to practise pontoon bridge building, and a pied king-fisher hovering above the bridge drop like a stone in the river. The natives here wear saffron gallabias, with embroidered waistcoats, fur-lined black cloaks and high red boots. After this we passed Crac des Chevaliers, the most famous of all Crusader castles out here. By now Mrs Newall's duodenal was screaming for food and she devoured a steak in an Arab hotel which she declared to be camel and I left aside. She almost died of it later.

We drove on to Beirut – along what is supposed to be such a lovely road along the sea, but I am spoilt by Crete – past the old Byblos where Ashtoroth was worshipped with orgies of a very

162

degenerate and exciting nature, and stopped at the Nahr el Kelb (river of a dog) between precipitous hills. In front of a café, under trees by the river, we had tea. The Nahr el Kelb is famous for the inscriptions on the cliffs which you may have seen in illustrated papers at the time of the Syrian campaign, left by conquerors on the high road to or from Egypt – Tiglath Pilese, Nebuchadnezzar, Pharaohs, Marcus Aurelius, Caesar, down to Napoleon III and ourselves in the last war. Mrs Newall and I stayed the night at the new and very comfortable Hotel Normandie.

Next day we drove to Damascus, over the Lebanon and Anti-Lebanon, a very fine drive, and got to Damascus for lunch. The Lebanon is like an Austrian mountain range, with pines and red-roofed villages. The Anti-Lebanon is red and rocky sand stone, colourful and deserted till you reach the river which feeds Damascus, with its poplars. Damascus itself lies at the foot of great sand coloured hills, but surrounded by green gardens in a very flat plain. We went to the souk after lunch, it was dirty after Aleppo, not vaulted but only covered in tin, and full of western junk, but the people I found as varied and fascinating as ever.

We visited Saladin's tomb and noticed it had been narrowly missed by a bomb, ours presumably. We next went to the Azim Palace, which I hadn't seen but of which I had heard much. Ali Khan tried to buy it for his girls. It consists of several grey and white plain marble pavilions round a garden full of citrons, cypresses, various roses and jasmine. The rooms weren't really so good as those in Gayer-Anderson's house in Cairo but he has no garden. This was very serene and peaceful. Many of the rooms were painted or lacquered with flower designs, like a peasant chest. Mrs Newall came over very faint here. We walked through the souks to the car and drove off to the best but very second-rate (except in its charges which exceed all others) hotel where I put her into a bath and to bed and hoped very much she wouldn't die on me. Her temperature moved from 95 to 101. It was very cold indeed.

After Mrs Newall's second husband shot himself in his dressing room she took to building and decorating. She did the decorations for Vice Regal Lodge, Lutyens' great palace at New Delhi, working with Lutyens, and among other houses Hugh Seely's cottage at Brooke. Next morning in Damascus she was still mercifully alive and insisted on driving herself, and we drove south through the very unattractive larva belt to the Palestine Frontier, by Lake Huleh. Before going down to Tiberias we turned west on to the Safad road to Acre. I'd never been on it before and it was a marvellous drive, very high up, looking over Lake Tiberias, the Moab hills, and all the mountains of Judah, ridge after ridge to the south. Then through old olive groves to Acre and so to Haifa, where I left her.

On my way back to camp I saw something going on in a village and stopped the car to look. It was an Arab wedding. The bridegroom in his best clothes was sitting on horseback. In one hand he held a bunch of jonquils, in the other a pale pink and blue frilly parasol, on top of which stood up a great bouquet of flowers. In front of him the young men of the village in a row, arm in arm, were doing a mad and noisy dance. There were some draped female figures round the bridegroom, but they made off and I saw the female element processing in another direction. The bridegroom dismounted and sent to ask if I wanted to photograph him seated. He sat absolutely impassive, without a smile, his face very made up and his eyes ringed with black.

No news of Robin [Maugham], but his brigade have remained out throughout after the original brigade had to be brought in. We had to send up very heavy reinforcements of tanks. As you know we had a startling success, catching the Germans completely unprepared and everyone says Shearer was brilliant (for a change) but Rommel returned from Germany and sent out his flying column and Cunningham lost his head completely. The RAF have been absolutely terrific. No definite news of Bob Laycock, who led his commandos and was last seen swimming ashore under fire and none were there to be picked up next day. They went by sea to land and blow up Rommel.

31 December 1941, Karkur

Geoffrey came this afternoon bringing your birthday cable. So that was clever of you and frightfully nice. We ate your Fortnum's Ceylon cake, which was very much all right, and a thing one doesn't see once a year here. As a result I couldn't eat any dinner. I am also very oppressed by your news that Toby has probably gone to Singapore. However I am telling myself that I am always timid, morbid and unpatriotic and that when one is afraid for other people it is really one's own happiness one is afraid for.

I am sending you a cable which I hope somehow you will find a means to forward. Although it is tiresome getting on to people in their hour of greatness, of whom you made small fuss before, I do think it would be a good thing if you somehow made friends with the Baron Sherwood [Hugh Seely]. There is no doubt whatsoever that the easiest way to get things done is by using the right people. I think he would be very helpful in keeping touch with Toby, which being so, do use your best endeavours to make use of him. If you can't, I can from this end. Both Flash Kellett and Mary Newall are close friends of his, and I know would write to him for me.

I've just finished Arthur Bryant's *English Saga*, a very much more interesting book than I expected. It embodies many of my own ideas, particularly re the Empire. I think it vitally important that people should be educated into regarding the Empire as a second home, and a monstrous scandal how little we all know or care about it. By developing it we could replace our foreign trade, give security to a definite number of workers and an opening to others in the dominions. It is incredible that the dominions should be so under-populated and under-financed. Under Germany they would be something very different.

3 January 1942, Karkur

Did you really faint when you got my telegram [of 7 September]? If you did you might have told me. It is no wonder your children are

165

so disastrously emotional when away from home. I may tell you my upbringing has stood me in very poor stead. The reason Flash wouldn't hear of my looking for a safe job outside the Regiment was that I am considered so sound, unemotional and dependable! When I say above 'it is no wonder', I do not mean because you are capable of fainting, but because you are capable of fainting and saying nothing about it. Long years of unshared childish sensitiveness have not made me less timid, shy or emotional but they have made me act the exact opposite. Certainly most English children are brought up to hide their feelings. But I think that makes them dull and of course that famous word, 'repressed'. Anyway, the fact that I don't burst into tears at the sight of a tank, I blame entirely on you.

My last and most sorrowful letter was from Toby, dated Gib 21st December, saying he would be passing though Alexandria but couldn't warn me in time. I am extremely sad. If only I had guessed he'd travel this way, I would certainly have been allowed to wait a week anywhere on the chance of his coming through. God knows what we shall be up to this summer. I suppose we might conceivably be sent out his way though. Certainly I'd much rather fight the Japs than the Germans. I continue to prefer the Germans both to the French and the Americans, and though I don't know the Russians, I'm sure they're awful.

8 January 1942, Karkur

This morning I was sitting on a fence in the sun outside the camp and I heard some shouting and saw some Arabs fighting two or three hundred yards away. Then a woman began making an awful row and went on and on and I went down to see what it was all about. I found an Arab girl, her face hideously tattooed and the back of her head covered in large silver coins, simply rending the heavens, one or two Arabs looking on quietly, and on the ground another woman whose head had been split open. I didn't examine her but an Arab told me he thought she would die. Some Arabs

166

went to the camp for a doctor and I went off to see if he was coming. On the way, I asked two Jews who spoke German, whether they'd seen anything and they said a man had come running past with a chopper and was now sitting by the camp gate. There he was, sure enough, sitting with a blood-stained chopper. I couldn't get anything out of the Arab sentry who politely presented arms to me, though I was carrying my coat and wearing the old peppery pullover I always wear at home, and let me in, though it was strictly forbidden in that particular area without a pass. I discovered that the man had come to enlist! He was smiles all over, but said there would be relatives of the girl after him. She wasn't his wife, it seemed to be something about land. I had him arrested. He said he reckoned she would die. They are very extraordinary.

4 February 1942, Jerusalem

I've been in Jerusalem several days, at Lady MacMichael's Convalescent Home for sick officers, and have done a great deal of walking. Yesterday afternoon I walked down from the Mount of Olives to the Garden of Gethsemane and into the town through the St Stephen's Gate where the Via Sacra (Dolorosa) starts. The old city is all on a slope, perpetually sunless, incredibly cramped, entirely undrained, mediaeval, thronged and sinister, like no other place I ever saw. Entirely unchristian. What Christianity there is, is tawdry beyond words. I talked to a monk who was sitting reading Dostoevsky. He was American, very young. We sat and argued in the Garden of Gethsemane. My American astounded me. His motto was 'My Country Right or Wrong', and in support of this he quoted 'render unto Caesar the things that are Caesar's'. When I said that this didn't hold out much hope for peace, he said 'there will always be wars and rumours of wars' and a man could but confess his failings and ask forgiveness and continue the fight. I told him I was deeply shocked and departed.

167

18 February 1942, Jerusalem

Lawrence Biddle came up with me for a sitting with Robitschek who is drawing him. I sat and looked at his portfolio and as practically everybody in 1st Cavalry Division seems to have patronised him I decided to also. The results are quite good, the method most extraordinary, i.e. he photographs you, you choose the one you like, he makes an almost complete drawing from one of those things you look through with two slightly different photographs in it. Then you sit while he puts in light and shade and details. I sit tomorrow.

25 February 1942, Darmanhur, Western Desert

I left Jerusalem very early on Sunday 22nd and so far as I know only left behind my last lot of washing and my new knife which I'd got to replace yours, anyway till it arrives. I got my picture finished by Robitschek. I think it is very good indeed, and he took a lot of trouble over it. You will make up your mind when it comes whether you want to frame the original. I feel sure you will be pleased with it. [It is now at Flintham. No one likes it.]

This place [Darmanhur] is very easily described. It is flat, gravelly sand, quite hard, thank goodness. The horizon is only a mile or two. During a sandstorm it's very considerably less. The sand is dotted with half dug in and very scattered tents, in which everything is covered in sand deposited by the last storm. There is practically no running water. There are three to each tent, big ones. I'm with Kurt Gottlieb and next to the Colonel. There are camp areas (we have noted 76 to date, one for each regiment) all round. If not occupied these consist solely of latrines surrounded by matting on which I have my eye for the floor of my tent.

Did you hear about the recent Battle of Abdin Palace? The King of Egypt was unusually tiresome so Miles Lampson [ambassador to Egypt] staged a coup d'état – guns in front of the palace, palace gates unhinged by a tank, men with tommy guns. In walks ML plus

Myles Hildyard at Flintham Hall with labradors
Greta Garbo and Gary Cooper, 1939

Flintham Hall

(left to right) Micky Riviere, Flash Kellett and Patrick McCraith, Dover,
c. December 1939–January 1940

(left to right) Stephen Mitchell, MH and Donny Player, Palestine, *c.* 1939–40

(left to right) MH with Rhona and Henry Trotter
and Michael Parish, *c.* 1939–40

4th Troop C, Hadera, *c.* 1939–40

Haifa, after bombing, *c.* 1939–40

MH's troop, Palestine, 1940

Archway in crusader
wall, Castle of Athlit,
Bay of Acre, 1940

Billy Brooksbank and Minta MacMichael, Palestine, 1940

MH and Bambino, Tripoli, 1943

MH in Turkey, on his way to Cairo, September 1941

MH with Billy
Brooksbank, Ein
Karem, February
1942

MH in Sabratha,
*c.*1943–4

MH in Tripoli, 1943

(left to right) Toby Horsford and Richard Wingfield-Digby, *c.*1943–44

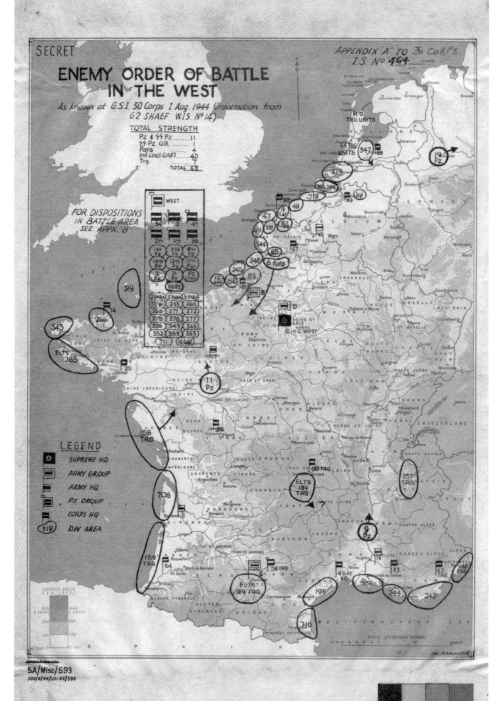

SECRET

ENEMY ORDER OF BATTLE
IN THE WEST

*As known at G.S.I. 30 Corps 1 Aug. 1944 (information from
G2 SHAEF W.I.S. Nº 14.)*

APPENDIX "A" TO 30 CORPS
I.S. Nº 464

TOTAL STRENGTH

Pz & SS Pz 11
SS Pz. GR. 1
Para. 4
Inf. (incl GAF) 40
Trg. 7
     TOTAL 63

FOR DISPOSITIONS
IN BATTLE AREA
SEE APPX. 'B'

LEGEND

SUPREME HQ
ARMY GROUP
ARMY HQ
Pz. GROUP
CORPS HQ
319 DIV AREA

SA/Misc/593
300/8/44/531 RE/593

Landing in Normandy, 1944

B. L. Montgomery
Field-Marshal

General Montgomery with troops in France

Jimmy Burridge, Holland, 1944

Martin Lindsay with intelligence maps, 1945

Russian guard, Berlin 1945

MH, 1945

MAJOR-GENERAL L. O. LYNE CB. DSO.

COMMANDER BRITISH TROOPS BERLIN

REQUESTS THE PLEASURE OF THE COMPANY OF

Capt. Myles Hildyard M.C.

AT THE VILLA LEMM, GATOW.

FRIDAY 17TH AUGUST 1945

R.S.V.P.   COCKTAILS 6–8 PM

The war is over

abdication form and an armoured car waiting outside to take the King to India. Knocks on the door and they say the K is out. So he marches into the harem. Still no king. King returns and comes into line with a new pro-British government. But everyone outraged by the display of armed strength and the insult to the harem, so Egyptian society has resigned from the Gezira Club! Trouble is that the next heir is a childless uncle and no one much after that. It's all very stupid and all it's done is to make Farouk quite popular in the country.

Not much news in these parts. Kurt, an arch intriguer and news worm, was told on enquiry 'never in the history of war have so many people known so little about so much'.

26 February 1942, Western Desert

Returned for tea (food disgusting these days) and found two air-graphs still not saying you'd read the diary. If you could conceive the trouble and fatigue it was writing it out and getting it home, you would have been slightly more tactful. I should only have been court-martialled if it had been opened by the censor. And I even thought the part you have quite interesting. I shall take it for granted that you will use part two to wrap apples in.

I'd got thus far with this letter when Donny came and invited me out for a drive in the desert. He wanted to experiment driving by compass using the compass inside the car, which I wasn't very keen on as of course the car affects a compass. Added to this, we talked busily and I forgot to watch the compass and before we knew we were miles away and lost. Fortunately he'd brought whisky and biscuits so it was fun.

Last news of Michael Parish was 15th February and 700 bills reached GHQ from his last port of call and a telegram to his father intercepted by the censor giving his exact position by reference to the Bible. His boss was tearing his hair.

2 March 1942, Western Desert

I am very pleased about Uncle William and have sent him a cable. [William Temple had just been appointed Archbishop of Canterbury.] If I should ever want to marry I can do it at Lambeth like Colonel Thoroton and Miss Whyte. I have had a very pleasant two days in Cairo staying with Lady Russell. Sir Thomas Russell Pasha is the famous Egyptian chief of police.

Russell is a sweet henpecked big grey-haired man, frightfully keen on birds. He was the only man in Egypt whose name I knew before we came out, principally for the work he's done against dope trafficking. The latest trick is to make camels swallow it in containers which aren't magnetic nor affected by the stomach juices. The camel has to be killed to get them out. They have now got an X-ray to find these. The hashish is grown in Syria illegally and very difficult to stop. He told me the name Assassins comes from hashish. He has a parrot and he is rather liable to make strange bird noises to himself during meals and wander off. The parrot is loose in the drawing room.

I think it is too wonderful your collecting £2,000 in Flintham for Warship Week. I told Lady Russell about it, just to take her down a peg when she was talking about what the English in Egypt had done. But if to be really good and efficient you need to be a Lady Russell, Lord preserve us. She is quite terrifying. She is bursting with plans for hostels, co-ordination councils, grants, buildings. She has almost finished writing a most learned book on mediaeval Cairo. I am told she spent two years trying to prove a barony. Anything you say is immediately sorted out via *Encyclopaedia Britannica*.

I see in the *Field* that a Sir Charles Trevelyan has given his place and 13,000 acres to the National Trust. He is a socialist and believes it better for the community to own great estates. I cannot see this. It seems to me that it is now certain we shall become more socialist, and that wealthy people are fairly ready for it and the important thing is that education should underline socialism as a great effort to provide a fair and secure life. We don't want everybody to get a public school education just because till now only rich people have had it. If we do want it, it should be because it is a very good education suitable for everybody (which I don't think it is).

The man Robitschek, who drew me in Jerusalem and only spoke German, was interesting about the Germans. He particularly stressed their great physical courage (developed in the upper classes in his day by duelling), their love for heroics and sacrifice and their unvarying treachery. He wouldn't agree with me that they were a naive race, easily persuaded and lacking in a sense of proportion and perspective. He was a Czech.

4 March 1942, Western Desert

How tiresome you are. Your airgraphs of 12th February arrived today and now I have covered with writing and wasted two of these valuable letter cards on the text 'unshared shyness and sensitiveness'. But really what does it matter? If you take every-thing so seriously I shall stop writing to you and as I enjoy writing to you we shall both be sorry. There is only one way to decide whether our upbringing was successful – what we are like at the end of it and what we feel about you. The first you must decide for yourselves and if you don't like it no doubt you will lump it, the second I hope you can answer for yourselves, as it seems to me you have unusually affectionate and really quite appreciative children.

I have generally had someone to whom I could write whatever came into my head, and I write like that now to you. In these days, when answers take so long, it is probably a mistake to say anything which can start an abstract discussion, or which could worry or hurt you, and my only excuse is my far too great interest in my own character and its development. One hasn't a great deal to think about here. Quite honestly I shan't begin to consider the question of the problem child till I have one of my own. I should have been unhappy at moments whatever you had done because I was extremely timid and boys' schools are no place for that. Half one's friends probably went through the same.

I don't remember there being anything in my diaries except names which were, I believe, deleted in the copies sent with the second half. I suggest you show them to anybody of whom you know I am fond. This should narrow the field considerably. A copy to go to Toby immediately you have one, censor or no censor, blame on me. I am very sorry if you were hurt. All my love and God bless you.

23 March 1942, Western Desert

I am sitting in my revolver and all, with a beflagged staff car outside my tent, waiting to go out as umpire on a brigade scheme. The order has just come out *No beds* – the sort of silly order we used to get right at the beginning of the war when the idea was that if you made yourself really uncomfortable you proved yourself a good soldier. Anyway I am disregarding the order.

I gather Singapore was as much of a scandal as one suspected. The whole picture of British colonial government in the East has been shown up – I think in your papers, but not out here. Alastair Forbes apparently said to Churchill after Singapore, 'The trouble in Malaya was they read too much Maugham and too little Kipling.' The trouble really was we not only did nothing for the natives but we purposely did nothing in order to produce cheap raw materials. In the Philippines the Americans did very differently. You can't really compare conditions in America's only colony and our empire. But there's no doubt the empire is under-staffed, underpopulated, no one takes much pride in it, and the natives are not grateful to us.

There is a plague of ladybirds. The dust storms have been terrible, but I missed the worst two days by being in Cairo, where crossing the Nile is rather like crossing the Thames.

31 March 1942, Western Desert

If Uncle William Temple would take me as chaplain I think it would be worth going into the Church. Not from the point of view of advancement, but it would be so interesting to be with him. Did you mean that seriously? It would be a strain getting ordained as I don't believe in so much of what one would have to study. After that I reckon one could live down a dog collar.

Flash who has been sitting in my tent, with me in bed, has just come back to tell me that Tommy Dugdale is now chairman of the Conservative Party and therefore will be able to get me a seat (Flash is keen on my going into politics and Tommy was very nice to me when he was here). Apparently they are rearranging constituencies and Flash doesn't think his will be a very safe one in future, he has no particular connection with Birmingham. However everything is so indefinite one can't really consider such things seriously for the present.

Your cable 'so thrilled and proud everyone sends congratulations' arrived today and if it had come tomorrow I should have thought it was an April fool, but as it is, it is a mystery. I am divided between supposing I am now Lord Le Scrope, Capt. Hildyard VC, a proud father or possibly in an absent-minded moment engaged. Time no doubt will show. [Michael Parish and I were awarded MCs for the Cretan escape in March 1942.]

6 April 1942, Western Desert: Letter to Toby

You can imagine how little I liked the news of the air raid on Colombo last night, and how I hope to get news of you. If *only* you were here. We have been on our fringe of desert almost six weeks now and I have been happier and more alive than for a long time, partly because I must have been very run down and my two months' convalescing after Christmas did me good, partly because somehow in the bare desert army life seems more natural and comes easier, mainly because I spend every Saturday and Sunday in

173

Cairo and particularly with Robin [Maugham] and it is very enlivening mentally. I am madly socially minded, très très snob, and becoming more and more politically minded. It seems perhaps that this is the time to form a new party. Not to launch it, not even to formulate a programme, but to prepare for a fight for power. One is out of touch here with affairs, for even though there are many important people who pass through and many here with important connections, one is out of touch with the feeling in England. I say out of touch, of course I was never in touch, but war has changed my sense of values, made me appreciate the obvious. Robin says a war mentality is almost as unreal as a degenerate peacetime one. And it is certain that though it is the upper class who show up so well now, they are incapable of using the opportunity which war has given back to them, except a few, but I believe those few could get almost anywhere with a little self-confidence. The only self-confident young man I know is Randolph [Churchill], on his way back here now after a debacle in England which showed up his utter lack of control and understanding.

Finally last weekend, having received an enthusiastic but vague telegram from Flintham a week before, it was reported to me after church that someone in GHQ had remarked on my MC. It appears I have been gonged. I consider this satisfactory, it has a certain social value, I can live my own life with greater impunity. One slight snag is that I always said that if I got it I would have the courage to find a job on the staff, and I still haven't. Robin is dead keen now on getting a good job, I'm trying to place him with the Minister of State. But I am not of Robin's calibre.

Tell me how you think the war is going. Not too good. I think Churchill's position is dicky. How dicky is Madagascar?

4 May 1942, Western Desert

I came back to the Regiment last night, getting bogged in the desert on the way. It is really impossible in the dark to see bad patches. I stayed in Cairo again with Billy Maclean, played tennis with

174

Dawyck Haig, went to church, bathed each day and both Billy and I got very sunburnt. When I got back here Flash told me that in my absence he had more or less accepted for me the job of intelligence officer to our division. I am in a big way trying to make up my mind about it. It's not a very good job – I could aim higher. On the other hand Flash absolutely swears that I can come back any time I like, and keep my present seniority, and that if in my turn a squadron becomes vacant I can step right into it. I believe the Divisional General and staff are unusually intelligent and nice. I really want to get away from the Regiment, but just today after three weeks away and seeing things at last moving and my squadron fully equipped I feel I want to stay. I think I shall go on approval.

10 May 1942, Western Desert

I am now a staff officer. I have sat all today and all yesterday by the telephone as duty officer, but just as well as I am broke. I went out with the General in his car the other day, he is a most charming man. Gatehouse. We are in the middle of the battle of the Coral Sea – very exciting – and he impels me to beg you to begin preparing for my return. I really don't see why the actual war should last more than another 18 months. But however long it lasts it will be followed by at least a two years' occupation all round. Whether we shall be relieved by troops from England or merely given leave by plane I don't know. I think the troops will mutiny and I tell everybody I shall desert.

We had six new officers come to the Regiment the day before I left. Not an impressive collection and I told Flash that I considered only one to be possible – a tough but nice-looking former trooper in the Skins. Next day my Panzer boy had his new troop on parade and said, 'Everybody gets on with me, but if I don't get on with them, they're sorry. You've got to smarten yourselves up. It doesn't surprise me when I look at you that Rommel walks through you out here. You are wearing berets, the insignia of the Royal Tank Corps, and you've got to live up to the Tank Corps.'

175

Another letter from Michael P saying he hopes to be back soon as his job is dying on him and he will come to the Regiment. Last summer is a complete dream.

8 June 1942, Western Desert

My course on aerial photography finished on Saturday. We had done a good many tests and wound up with an annotation and report-making by syndicates lasting one and a half days. I took two WAAFs out to a sweet shop and everybody else played cards with bits of paper, it was a casual kind of course. Billy B says his girl Ann Clitheroe gets very annoyed because he enjoys himself over here without her, and I feel you must at times feel that I concentrate too much on enjoying myself. The truth is that I am not a good worker, and anyway cannot tell you anything about what little is interesting in my work, and therefore write only about my leisure in which admittedly I take far more interest. We are of course now in the middle of a battle, but know very little more about it than you do. It is impossible to get information. Great care is being taken not to make extravagant claims and one might think it was going badly, but really I think it is going very well. No news of casualties. One of the Indian brigades from here, which was under this division, was reduced to ten officers and 28 men the first day. We missed going up fairly narrowly – instead we sent up a large number of men and stuff [tanks].

15 June 1942, Western Desert

Air-raid sirens are going faintly all around, most likely the Coptic monks of the Wadi Natrun practising on whistles. Robin Maugham has been wounded at Tobruk and is in hospital. I went into Cairo on Saturday to see him. He was first wounded in the chest with spent shrapnel and next day he was sitting by an open truck and they were attacked by an RAF plane, which fired at them very low level killing his batman, badly wounding others and Robin was wounded in the head. He was shipped back from Tobruk and on the way his arm went septic. His wounds are now completely healed but his arm has been really bad and he hasn't been able to sleep at all. Consequently he looks very run down. I took him a lot of books, cakes, scent and hairwash, and hopped on a lorry on my way back. Halfway the lorry began to groan and looking round I saw a river of oil and a bonfire about 100 yards back. The bonfire turned out to be a large part of the engine with big interlocking cogs burning merrily. I then got a lift in a staff car full of very important people rushing down via GHQ from Syria. The Cairenes are full of rumours of parachute landings in Syria because passage with Palestine has been forbidden for three days.

I have just been dining with my regiment and been rude to the padre because actually I care quite a lot about it. Hughes, our divisional padre rector of Mansfield who was with the SRY at the start of the war, told me he went to Alex last week where there are 11 padres and one was once his curate in London and an excellent young man. He said to him 'How are things here?' and they all said 'Splendid! Nothing to do at all.' Hughes said 'What do the chaps do?' and they said 'Oh they bathe and go to the cinema and chase the girls.' 'And what do you do?' 'We chase the girls too.' So Hughes called a meeting of the divisional padres and told them this story and said they mustn't get like that and they should decide once for all what they were working for. After one and a half hours' conference 40 per cent still wouldn't agree that it made the least difference to the Almighty whether we won the war or not. After two hours with all the pangs of childbirth they conceived: 'We are working that the war be won by godly men, so that the Almighty may direct the peace', or some such. I said with insults that they were two and a half years late and why do they wear captain's or major's pips if the army's objectives are nothing to them.

I agree we have outgrown war, I certainly continue to find it absurd. Flash left today on a course for future brigadiers.

21 June 1942, Western Desert

Yesterday I went into the town which begins with the same letter as Miss Hume and her house [Margery, The Mount: Mersa Matruh], mainly to get maps. The place was stacked with maps from here to Tripoli, ready for our advance! I got in a bathe of course. It seemed absurd that in peacetime people should have come so far across the desert for a bathing resort, but it is a lovely bay, circular and blue and gold. There were a certain number of soldiers bathing and I envied the ones with guns by the sea. I walked round two sides of the bay and watched some foreign soldiers playing in the water, Czechs or Poles or perhaps more likely Yugoslavs with extraordinarily beautiful bodies. Mostly our men are not much to look at without their clothes, nor were the Australians in Crete. When he heard of our moves my servant said, 'You must take a bathing dress, sir.' They are like snails without their shells on the seashore – or at least those funny crabs. I think the German and Central European physical culture craze is strengthening to the spirit as well.

The General and his ADC were just off to bathe yesterday morning when they met a sailor who said he was moored off the mole of Tobruk when the German tanks came on to it. This news was a surprise to us. How the Germans have managed it or we mismanaged it no one knows, but I think they do it by their speed and drive, which comes from the top. The situation looks dangerous but no one at Army HQ is fussing. I only hope they aren't depending on us!

6 July 1942, Western Desert

Yesterday I wangled leave to go to Cairo, ostensibly to go to GHQ but really to get away, buy a few things and find where Robin was. I went straight to the Russells'. There I learnt what a panic Cairo had been and still was in. As I discovered for myself later, GHQ had been burning its papers for days and evacuating all the English families to South Africa – also Jews and known pro-Allies, and of course the Greek-Levantine population was in a stew. The ordinary Egyptian led by Nahas Pasha had been behaving very well. I did my best to reassure Lady Russell, who wanted to stay with Russell as long as he was in Egypt but not to be in his way if he had to bolt for it. There are only two roads out, personally I think if the Germans had broken straight through they would have caught practically everybody. The situation is critical presumably. The Germans' extraordinary successes make further successes conceivable though his men must be very tired. Equally our extraordinary failures make further failure conceivable. [We had just surrendered Tobruk.]

The Germans call the war in Africa a gentleman's war, and if it lacks savagery it also lacks on our side much feeling for Death or Glory. The climate, boredom, lack of tangible successes in desert warfare, most of all the muddling which goes on from the top and makes the history of other units beside ourselves fantastic, are to blame for this. There is no feeling of all out effort, and none of the confidence in a general which the Germans have in Rommel. It is no longer satisfactory to know that incapable generals have been bowler-hatted, one wishes they needn't be proved incapable. I reckon we are all right here, but if there had been trouble in the Far East or through the Caucasus at the same time, we'd have been sunk.

24 July 1942, Cairo

We moved last week. We are on sand again. An enormous camp, where the Regiment has been all the time since Matruh. I am alone in missing the Delta.

Yesterday afternoon I came down again for the 48 hours' leave we have all been given in turn – staying with the Russells. It's too hot to go to Luxor, and I spend a lot of time with Robin [Maugham], so it's very pleasant. Flash and I sat up till midnight when I dined with him. He wants me to go back to the Regiment. He is tired of Kurt Gottlieb. He has asked Division for me but it's in abeyance till our general comes back, who I think will let me go. I am afraid you will be very disappointed if I do. But as you can see Division isn't necessarily safe. Robin's colonel has been killed. Anyway I can't refuse Flash, of whom I am very fond. There isn't enough work for two intelligence officers at Division. I have put in order the whole filing system and now there's nothing left to do. And divisional IO isn't a very important job, though of course it is on the ladder to staff success. I think I am quite well suited to being a staff officer. Admittedly regimental IO is even less important and I don't particularly want it to lead me back into a squadron. However I think Flash wants to see a battle and then either be given a brigade or go home, which he can do as an MP, and I could break away possibly with him. Intelligence at GHQ is really most unsatisfactory as a career, practically all the officers do clerks' jobs, keeping files. The sort of political work Robin is angling for is most interesting, but I don't think I am bright enough for it.

25 July 1942, Western Desert

Uncle William wrote me a most wonderful letter, at least in its ending, which was 'We must get some good talks when the state of the world allows it again. I wonder if I could help you at all about religion and sacraments or the like. Probably not – I am of another generation. But I would like to try. Write when you can. You are, I think, the best letter writer I know. Much love, yours very affectionately William Cantuar.' Such from an archbishop and the most brilliant man possibly in England!

How annoyed you must be to read in my letters only of bathing at Matruh when you were imagining me sweating in a tank. I'm glad you are proud of our stand at El Alamein, I only hope we don't stand there much longer. Anyway there's nothing to worry about there, everything depends on Russia. If she's beat it really would be rather tiresome, not that I think she is going to be, but we are in such a good position compared to other years that we can afford to take a good look and appreciate the dangers and the good chances too.

31 July 1942, Western Desert

Mummy's mention of transportable trees in the forest has of course appealed to all my passion for moving things to positions where they hurriedly turn themselves into last year's pea sticks. Before giving my invaluable advice on this most important problem, however, I must have a promise that the work is done at the nation's and war effort's expense and not by you. I may say I still suffer from a creaking back from trying to move full-grown trees. Furthermore your war effort is *most* important and I suspect gravely that you overwork. Daddy, when he comes back from judging, should mooch around and *not* dig up nettles which are also God's creatures and happy in their simple way awaiting myself. Mummy, who is liable to make a fool of herself listening to the wireless if given half a chance, should sit several minutes each day knitting socks and counting mercies. When, if ever, I get a chance I shall spend whole days doing so, but not if you refuse ever to sit quiet in the opposite corner.

The mercy I suggest for first consideration is that if there had been no war your eldest son would have been very miserably ensconced in 23 Lansdowne Crescent, returning for disgruntled weekends and disgracing his father's reputation in Lincoln's Inn, your second son would have been providing the yellow press with something quite sensational in the way of viscountesses, and I've no doubt John would have sent you whitehaired to the grave somehow. How much nicer to see your children only through their own glistening eyes, earning salaries, never late for breakfast, ready any moment to join the Cabinet.

2 August 1942, Western Desert

My clerks are all out drawing the Hildyard coat of arms, and I am hoping to get a bookplate reproduced by the machine we use for our summaries etc. We produce now two summaries a week and distribute 60-odd copies; I wish I could send you one but they are secret. They give the latest news about the battle, identification of enemy units, notes on enemy methods, tactics, equipment etc., and translations of captured documents particularly diaries, some of which are most entertaining and interesting.

No, Tobruk made very little impression, on me anyway. We only learnt slowly what a disgrace it was (our bombers are still trying to destroy the installations we left untouched). I had understood for ages that the navy would not stand for another siege and up till the last I did not think we should hold it. Nor I imagine did the S. Africans who apparently thought the whole scheme a silly one. The English Guards and even some RAMC who were surrendered by the General (S. African) nevertheless fought their way out. I read this today in the *Spectator*, by the military correspondent: 'I am not sure whether they [Cairo correspondents] were aware of the new German 88 mm antitank gun which has proved devastating in its fire (and which may possibly be a converted anti-aircraft gun).' The 88 mm has been here as long as the Germans, everybody has known about it, it is anti-aircraft and only subordinately used as anti-tank; its only novelty is its numbers, and we know the supply was very good. Yet in England it is a surprise! There is a gap somewhere, or you are being purposely fooled.

8 August 1942, Western Desert

I have just been photographing Randolph's father inspecting my regiment in a topee and a long cigar. I hope they come out. Flash, who was on leave in Palestine, flew down yesterday to dine with him and the most select company imaginable. He was very outspoken and we all have great hopes of this visit. I heard this morning that Dawyck Haig is thought to have been killed as his tank had 16 hits. I am very sad as I liked him so much.

On Friday morning I went to Gezira where I found Adam Watson [on British Embassy staff in Cairo], just back from meeting de Gaulle and the Russian general on a desert aerodrome. De Gaulle is wonderfully pompous. I saw him at Shepheards later actually, very white-faced, unhealthy looking. Adam was completely knocked out by the Russians. As soon as they landed the Russian general said 'What are those buildings over there – workshops?' 'No, messes' 'Are there workshops?' 'Yes, somewhere behind' 'Have we time to go and see them now?' 'No, the party is just leaving.' There was a few minutes' delay getting off, and as they left a Russian colonel came up to Adam and said 'The General says we could easily have seen the workshops.'

On the road the catechism continued – 'Very good road, how often is it repaired? How tall are the pyramids? How much stone? How old? Really, almost 50 centuries, what do you use them for now? What is the mental outlook of Egypt? So the Fellahin have no mental outlook? That is like our citizens of Turkistan, they are not *vocal* either. How many water buffaloes are there in the country? Are all these officers wounded? All Russian staff officers are wounded. How many planes have you available in Cairo? Well, can the General have a plane to take him to Moscow? Well, how long will it take you to find out, five minutes?'

I read in today's *Egyptian Mail* that the citizens of Bristol, after an impressive parade, have shipped to Russia two old captured Crimean siege guns 'to help the war effort' and 'in token of . . .'. The Russians think we are inefficient. They very likely think we are unheroic, they think in terms of divisions when we think in 'token forces' of platoons, they are fighting for their lives, and we burden a ship with some useless old junk to show how we long to help them.

21 August 1942, Western Desert

We started off for the desert in the dark, and the sun rose as we drove along the sweet water canal. Pied kingfishers hung upright with flapping wings looking down into the water, men dusky or glistening, and every shade from cream to nigger brown, were washing and bathing along the bank. The women washing clothes but hardly ever themselves, and then only fully dressed up to their middles in water. Once or twice we passed boats building on the bank, great skeletons of curved timber, a fine sight. Then we ran into a thick wet fog and everybody in open vehicles was blackened by the damp and the dust from the road. Our new home is a flat bit of desert, sand and bits of scrub. When it came to making a meal I found that Whitaker had lost my kettle and never bothered to tell me. Also two army blankets. I get very cross with him and it is a nuisance having such an ass, but I don't think I should do any better if I got rid of him as you can't spare good men to be batmen.

I haven't yet answered the letter I had from Uncle William some time ago as I wanted to read his book you sent first, and having been disappointed by it, this new one. So far as I have got, it does convince me that the church has a duty to take a part in public affairs at least by announcing general principles and approbation and disapprobation. It is a book dealing with home affairs and I think it is easy to overlook housing conditions, education, etc, partly because these have been much improved, partly because Utopian dreams of Europe and Empire are far more colourful. But in fact one cannot appeal to people who think they have been done down, or who are embittered by conditions which are no fault of their own, or expect them to see things in their minds as we see them. If you say to a soldier 'Lord Nuffield may have money and Rolls Royces but he hasn't got a family and there's no reason why he should be as happy as you', they say 'Just you give us the chance to be Lord N, that's all.' They don't care about empires except in the most abstract way, and they never will do, so long as they spend this time ceaselessly (if good humouredly) grumbling about their own lives, with very good reason because they have been dumped into lives which are drab, meaningless and often squalid.

My operator has just admitted he doesn't know the General's name. Another, yesterday, asked whether Ceylon was under British rule. How packed full of interest the ordinary man is. I was reading at lunch an article of Harold Nicolson's from the *Spectator* of how he sat with two intelligent friends recalling their undergraduate ideas in Fabian days, and how the answer to all difficulties was to have been found in education and not capitalism. He questions democracy but refuses fascist tyranny, trusting in British political genius and leaving the decisions to the electorate. I don't think the electorate either deserves *or* desires this responsibility.

29 August 1942, Western Desert

All quiet on the Western front here and it looks as if intelligence have made fools of themselves, although it's still too early to say. We have moved again, but one part of the desert is very like another. I have been too busy to do any reading, let alone sleeping or bathing in the afternoons, but I like the work. I visited today the brigade IO whose job was offered to Robin, it's a pity he isn't here. We are important people now. Alexander was here yesterday and Montgomery today wearing no medals and a slouch hat and collecting everybody's cap badges like Louis XI.

Big barrage last night, the first I ever heard I think, followed by a great display of incendiary bombs dropped by the Germans. Made in 1936. Not quite so effective here as in London. I drove back with an unexploded one in the back of my truck tonight. Much as I hate my ACV [Armoured Command Vehicle] on the move, it is a godsend at night as it has three or four strong reading lamps. The sides let down to make sort of cabins where we sleep in great luxury, however this morning I was sitting on my bed shaving when I was almost asphyxiated by diesel engine fumes and had to dress in short bursts from outside holding my breath. The flies are extremely bad, though individually I have met worse. What people do about them out here in peacetime I can't think, but I believe they have always been worse in the desert than anywhere.

Night, 2 September 1942, Western Desert

Well, intelligence saved its face at the last moment and the enemy attacked during the night of the 30th. Everything has gone to date much as expected and well, I think. Here at Division it has been tiring and confusing; absorbing endless messages and trying to make a picture. But it is very difficult to realise that one's friends are fighting; one feels very impersonal. The first day in the evening we were shelled – which was pretty amazing. We had our vehicle's side down and it takes ages to put it up as it rolls and is stiff with camouflage paint and we have far too much luggage and our servants weren't much help. Consequently we moved off last and didn't know where the others had gone. Fortunately I knew and stopped the driver who was heading straight for the enemy. Everything was thrown on board in confusion, and then it got dark. We had a small convoy of other lost souls and we moved round in the dark till almost morning without finding the rest of the Division.

Yesterday nothing much except a heavy bombing attack. Today lots of Stukas; my tummy has fallen out to make it easier. I went in my little jeep behind the General in his tank this morning to visit the brigades, led by the ADC as navigator, who took us through everything, including the front line, on to a small knoll clearly marked on the map and behind which our guns were firing. We sat on top of the knoll looking rather obvious with the depression in front of us milling with German tanks and shells bursting, fortunately behind us. I brought back a very important map and saw it handed to the C-in-C [Monty], who was still wearing his ridiculous hat. Tonight Peter Solley Flood borrowed my jeep and took it with all my clothes and bedding on it and now midnight is not back nor likely to be. The Regiment has had one officer killed, no one you know, and a difficult time.

This was the Battle of Alam el Halfa. On 31 August the Germans had attacked across the Quattara Depression at the south end of the Alamein line. The 8 Armoured Brigade – SRY (Sherwood Rangers Yeomanry), Staffordshire Yeomanry, 3 RTR (Royal Tank Regiment), 385 Battery RHA (Robin Hood Gunners) – were in action against German tanks of 15 Armoured Division which was heavily shelled and bombed. On 1 September the SRY were ordered to attack tanks hull down on the ridge above the depression. On 2 September SRY attacked again. Seven of their tanks were hit and exploded in flames and four more were disabled. The Germans began to retreat, after great losses.

4 September 1942, Western Desert

Yesterday morning the news was that the enemy had withdrawn some miles from our front, and I drove out to my own brigade HQ, which in fact was as far from the battle line as ourselves. When I woke up it was to hear that the enemy was withdrawing through our minefield which he crossed the first day. I drove all over the battlefield today and on to a side which the enemy's rearguard was still shelling spasmodically. Whatever comes (if anything does) it has been a complete victory for us, to date, in every way, and very satisfactory. One can only suppose that Rommel was completely misinformed about our strength and disposition, and for once we stuck to the battleground we had chosen and didn't let ourselves be decoyed off it.

We are swamped in captured paper – every German soldier carries around all the letter postcards and photographs he has ever received. Tanks were full of British rations and stuffed with soap! They have lots of cards 'to an unknown soldier'. Lots of photographs of country places. Religious weeklies. Their newspapers make interesting reading, quite reasonable mostly. They have games – one is the *Fight for Colonies* game, all in Africa. Two officers in the Regiment were killed, one squadron got into awful trouble, their tanks a dreadful sight today.

8 September 1942, Western Desert: Letter to Toby

Here we are sitting back for the moment after the enemy's attack on 2nd September. It was quite a short though full-scale affair and went very well indeed, so we are well pleased with ourselves. The very first evening Divisional HQ to its great surprise was shelled. When the General went out to visit a brigade HQ in his tank I followed in my jeep and by mistake we drove right through our line of tanks into the depression where the enemy were. The desert round here is strange, with depressions where the land has apparently sunk, quite level but with steep sides. I did a good deal of driving about the battlefield as the enemy withdrew, learning my way around, looking at derelict tanks, and watching the battle – now only an artillery duel – from two miles off. A gun off the latest tank is the first seen and is flying back to England. Two officers in my regiment were killed.

I interrogated several prisoners, all quite willing to talk, young and undistinguished. One can't help seeing when one talks to Germans what very ordinary people they are. And these are crack troops here or supposed to be. I am sure that in England, too, people can be made less apathetic. Either one can get their support by taking an interest in their comfort, and then let them sit half asleep till one has established oneself sitting on their heads, or better of course carry them with one.

I think you are right about the Japs sitting on what they've got and I wouldn't be at all surprised if they didn't keep it either. We don't seem to do much good in the eastern climates except for a few people's pockets. I dare say two years is about right for the war, I've given up thinking about it but if Russia holds I think Germany will be very exhausted. With a rest however she might go on much longer, she doesn't seem any shorter of necessaries than ourselves, and we are still far behind in effort, generalship and equipment.

Our air force had great superiority in our battle here last week and was most effective. We have had journalists buzzing round saying there is a story all over Cairo that an American crew in an American tank knocked out six German tanks. We were rude to them. It is maddening that invariably the publicity goes to every dominion or Allied troop to hand and never to our own. Which is bad for morale, and creates a bad impression outside as people think all the fighting is done by others, which is absolutely untrue. As for the colonials they are told so often how marvellous they are that they think they can behave as they please, *vide* Tobruk. Actually you know the air force can't stop tanks, but it is a terrific help against supply columns.

188

We hope for good things from our new army commander [Monty] who has begun well. He is a strange-looking little man, wearing no medals or red tab but a South African slouch hat and dozens of hat badges. He is most optimistic at the moment which is always a mistake. However, judging by this last battle we have learnt something from past mistakes, at least not to charge 88 mm guns.

One could hardly describe this country as a 'political arena'. Here at this HQ I never talk politics or anything much interesting, still I know I can find people to talk about such things if I want. I continue to live my own life. I agree you can never legislate for happiness. Two things I believe necessary – a new ideal for life to give people something worth living for, and possibly living not in the greatest comfort – and a strong government. Democracy I consider a bum institution and pure *faute de mieux* and if I ever belonged to a party in power I would present the country with a five-year plan and no nonsense once it was launched.

I got a proper letter from home yesterday, from Mummy. It was dated 18th July, and she said, 'We had an airgraph this morning from Toby to our greatest joy and relief, dated 23rd June. Chou also wrote to say she had had two airgraphs and a letter.' They are always asking what the form is nowadays about Chou; naturally I don't know, but always hope that, as it took me three years to recover from l'affaire Hugh Chisholm [a friend before the war], you may have quietened down a little before you are greyhaired. However, the only thing that worried me about you was that you didn't seem happy. Mummy probably wants a nice girl about the place to hitch the family lace to and talk about babies. I hear frequently from Beryl; the last letter sounded so dangerously affectionate that I haven't answered it.

12 September 1942, Western Desert

It is getting cold early and late with a heavy dew sometimes at night and a lot of wind. Even a little rain in the air this morning. I went off before lunch with three men in my jeep to bathe, a wonderful

189

moment when we topped a ridge and saw before us instead of yellow sand, very white sand and fig trees and the crystal blue sea. It was very rough, enormous breakers and a strong current parallel to the shore. It was impossible to get through the breakers, but most joyous and invigorating attempting to. We picnicked on the beach, I slept naked and pleasantly full of sardines, biscuits, gingerbreads and honey, and bathed again. Back here again through a duststorm and up to the mess to see whether there were any letters. There was – yours of 17th August with the news of the requisitioning of the ponies' field and potato field. You can imagine it is very bad news for me and that I long to send cables and shoot myself. Instead I must sit quiet and wait to hear what your charming contractors have in mind.

Montgomery has told us that if we can clear out Rommel this winter we will go home for the spring offensive. That is a big 'if', though by *no* means an impossible one and many things might intervene; still it is a great thing to fight for. I wonder if you met Myrtie Kellett and how you liked her. I did not know her very well; she has great character and charm. I sent off about two dozen Christmas cards yesterday which will probably infuriate the recipients as they were all captured German postcards and my book plate, either singly or combined!

I'm afraid I shall wait impatiently for your next letters, but till I hear the worst I shall pray that nothing permanent will be put up. It is fortunate that I never pretended I was fighting for England and Democracy, for both are absolute sods.

27 September 1942, Western Desert

Flash has sacked the padre of the Regiment because as I said repeatedly he was quite useless before battle and when there was a job on hand he was capable of, i.e. burying people, he just didn't turn up. Instead he has got Hales, son of the Archdeacon. I haven't met him yet. Our departing padre Hughes in his last sermon told us how he was hawking books round the Brigade and a chap chose an expensive one on St Francis of Assisi. Hughes said, 'Do you really want it, it's a bit expensive and looks rather heavy?' The chap hesitated a long time, then he said, 'I'll have it. I want to see whether St Francis suffered like I have.' The ordinary soldier really is fantastic! So small-minded and self-centred and yet steady and confident for all his incessant grumbling.

Today I took a German pilot to Corps and on the way saw three gazelle to which we gave chase, me firing with a revolver at great speed. I think he must think me peculiar. All yesterday I was out watching the Regiment do battle practice. I took with me two sergeant photographers who have been attached to us and they had a field day as we had whole squadrons firing together for their benefit, the General climbing in and out of tanks, and all sorts of guns cooperating. Flash hadn't expected the General, all the same we had an excellent lunch on a clean checked tablecloth, and he was so beautifully dressed that I have shaken my servant by demanding my shirts and shorts should be properly starched and ironed. The Brigadier never turned up, which was hardly surprising as he foolishly rang me up to ask where they'd be and I gave the wrong place. My main sergeant photographer retired to hospital today, suffering from over excitement probably.

Dawyck Haig is POW in Italy, great relief.

23 October 1942, Alamein: Christmas Letter Card

Isn't this gay? The meet of the season is tonight [Battle of El Alamein]. I haven't had time to consider the implications but if all goes well this may be the last time we have to send our Christmas [from the Middle East].

28 October 1942, Alamein: Letter to Toby

I think this is the first time I have been able to sit down to anything but work and now I am tired and it is not very restful with a hell of a lot of guns firing all round, each one of which resounds inside one's head. Our approach march, beautifully worked out, was impressive, in clear moonlight and the whole sky lit by gunfire. It was the army commander's order that the plan should be explained to every man and now I have to write a news sheet and don't quite know how to word it as the original plan was very optimistic. We have done great damage and are advancing, if slowly. There is a big bombardment going on: as we have chosen to sit down in the middle of a lot of gun positions we naturally share their trials and are bombed and shelled during the day. And no doubt if one wasn't so tired when one gets to bed they would keep one awake all night.

The last few days have been very tiring, as I bring out an intelligence summary which isn't finished generally till about 1.30. My most important job as far as people up above Division are concerned – counting enemy knocked-out equipment – is going very badly, which is natural when everybody is far too busy to stop and take notes after knocking out a target and too tired to go creeping round at night checking up. As long as one is busy one doesn't notice much else and I have been very busy. I'm not quite sure where it has got anybody, however. I feel ashamed of being here while my regiment is having a bloody time and I avoid going to see them. I was too busy up to the last moment to realise that we were on the verge of a great battle. So far, we are not in Benghazi but I think we mean to get there. Our barrages have been terrific; we have hit the enemy very hard and one prisoner said he had never met such artillery fire in Russia. But the Germans are pretty tough and very good soldiers and they don't make anything easy.

I found a nice Italian diary: 'We suffer very much, no sufficient food. One bar of chocolate. Very little wine. Half a tin of sardines. I am waiting for death because we cannot resist any more.' This from a sergeant major. I have had quite a lot of prisoners, all German. Some awfully nice officers who had been in Russia and Crete and were very complimentary to us but complained that while they fought for their existence we fought for sport! I have had a certain number of papers, nothing terrific. I have now a good German and another good Italian translator working for me. German prisoners today said they had arrived ten days ago in Africa and only came forward the night before they were captured when they were immediately sent out into the line with machine guns. They had no idea till we told them that there was an offensive on.

I was putting on my trousers and something dropped – out of them, I thought. It was a bit of shrapnel! This morning I opened a little round cotton bag which was given to me as Italian hard rations all sewn up. It was full of thin square wafers which didn't taste of much though quite sweet, so instead of giving it to Whitaker to cook as I'd intended, I took the bag across to my Italian man to have an inscription on it translated. It was gelignite.

31 October 1942, Alamein

Flash came to see me and I lunched with the Regiment which is out for a short rest. He is enjoying his battle and everybody is in very good spirits. Patrick was wounded and sent back, hit in the back by shrapnel but not badly. I have been enquiring after Michael M as his battalion was overrun (at night after a terrific fight all day and after knocking out 56 tanks). I think he's all right. Flash lost four officers, all killed.

Now at three o'clock in the morning I am sitting in the General's tank at tactical headquarters. Our bombardment in support of a night attack is terrific and thumps the ground. The enemy is replying with his heavies, 210 mm, which I think are going overhead. Here after a trying day with shelling and bombing everybody is digging trenches. The General says it is like France. Twice on the way up I had to get out of the car, once they were shelling the car and the other time the famous 88 mms were doing airbursts. The General [Gatehouse, who was sacked soon after] never puts on a tin hat and whatever happens just goes on talking in his very quiet voice sitting by his tank. Today a shell landed about 15 yards away and ricocheted but did not explode. I have never known a man give a stronger feeling of confidence than he does. He is a big genial man, entirely unflustered, and knows what he's about. Unfortunately it's

193

very rare for a general to understand armour. So far as I am concerned I wish my general were C-in-C.

I have just been handed a bouquet from Corps for my summaries while Teddy Boulton was away. He is now back and I am mostly in a bad temper as a result, as I am a hopeless collaborator, particularly with anyone slow. So I leave him and rush about in my jeep. I have written an appreciation of the battle so far, i.e. down to the end of the first phase. I found it difficult to start as I disapproved of the whole thing, so I made it very general. No papers arrive during a battle and practically no one has the faintest idea what is going on, so the General told me to write something less intellectual than my summary.

I am reading tonight – the first reading I have done for ten days or more – Tolstoy's *What I Believe* by the light of a torch. Not reading much really as it gets me thinking. He rides through Spasskoe Wood, 'fresh grass underfoot, stars in the sky, the scent of blossoming willows and dead birch leaves, the nightingale's notes, the sound of cockchafers and cuckoos – and physical health. And I thought, as I constantly do, of death.' It seems one only thinks of death when it is not very probable; I always thought the saddest things when I was walking at Flintham.

1 November 1942, Alamein: Letter to Toby

I have had two bathes in the last three days which isn't bad in a battle. The sand and dunes and rocks here are all extraordinarily white, as white as Persil you'd think till you watch the breakers on the beach and they are far whiter, and the sea a very pale blue. I ran and wandered along the coast and found a monument on a little cliff – the most beautiful lovely concrete latrine you ever saw and I sat there for hours in the sun looking at the waves. The last two days there have been a lull marking the end of one phase and the opening of another. I have written an appreciation of the battle to date and been handed a bouquet by Corps for my daily summaries, but my impressions of battle are nil. I visit my regiment when they come out of the mire for a moment and learn their deeds, our headquarters is bombed or shelled, I live at tactical HQ round the General's tank and sit around but it is all wireless and messages and trying to make a picture and worthless papers and prisoners and losing things and no room to move and getting cross and lovely sunrises and clouds to which we are not used here and our thunderous artillery screaming tearing and thumping the ground and the incredible dust of the tracks two foot deep and powdered so that people's faces are white masks and goggles – but I couldn't draw a picture of it and make it resemble a battle, visibly or emotionally. Typical staff officer, in fact.

7 November 1942, Alamein

I believe today General Montgomery has cabled Churchill that the battle is won. I should think it was 3rd November, but maybe earlier, that I drove off for the afternoon to Corps and another armoured division and returned convinced that the battle was won. I have not been so excited for a long time. Probably, when I last wrote, the first phase of the battle was just over. It had been nothing like the immediate and overwhelming success which for some unknown reason it was expected to be. This HQ was expected to be right through the German lines the very first night. In fact, although we broke through and lifted mines to make a gap for the armour, the infantry did not form a bridgehead the other side, and as the armour came into the last gaps it was heavily engaged by guns beyond. By then it was getting light and the gaps through the enemy mine fields and no man's land were so packed with vehicles that it was hardly possible for a shell not to make a hit. Our tactical HQ was in enemy minefields.

For a week we remained in this position. Our artillery gave the enemy, who were still in the line or who had formed a new line outside and their guns behind, absolute hell. Our infantry took further forts and gun positions by night and with the armour repelled the enemy armoured counter-attacks with the very heaviest losses to the enemy and very considerable loss to ourselves when we in our turn tried to advance. There was some very unpleasant shelling and bombing, though nothing like we gave them.

That was the first phase. We then launched another attack exactly in the manner of the first, but this time everything was concentrated on the same gap and the enemy line was much narrower. The attack was successful and the armour was at last outside the enemy minefields. It was still hemmed in by an anti-tank gun and tank screen which was broken next day. We moved up then after the tanks and I found my regiment and its brigade sitting in the line where the antitank guns had been. Actually they were still there and very many of them intact, and piles of stores clothes and equipment.

That afternoon I saw General von Thoma brought in as a prisoner. He commanded German Afrika Korps and was caught out in a recce in his tank. Before I could talk to my regiment the hunt was up and I stood and watched them pass in single file headed by Flash in smart peaked hat. They went off south and next day we followed with our infantry, the General very impatient, for a change. We had a stop of about an hour and all round us were Italian tanks which had been knocked out and which the REs [Royal Engineers] were blowing up and, as they were full of ammunition, things came whizzing past exactly like a battle. Fifteen hundred prisoners were taken on the spot and the amount of papers etc. taken was horrifying. I saw Flash driving round in an open German touring car in his element. But he said the whole thing had been spoilt for him because just before the final breakthrough Derek Warwick had been hit in the forehead by shrapnel from one of our own guns falling short, while he lay asleep by his tank. He went off to hospital in good spirits but Geoffrey Brooks says his chances are only 50–50. I don't think I ever told you to look out for articles by Macrae McLennan, maybe I did. He is official observer with us and writes articles and is amazingly brave, going forward everywhere in the battle. With him three days ago was Edward Ardizzone, the artist who had first come on to us from the rifle brigade and Ardizzone told me that in their attack on the last enemy

196

line of resistance Michael Mosley was killed. I suppose he must know. I find it difficult to realise, which is as well as I was very fond of him.

We had no sooner got rid of the 1,500 prisoners than we had 1,500 more. Among them was a squadron leader in the Italian Armoured Division Ariete who was delighted to help and I spent all yesterday with him. Among other things we collected 15 Italian drivers and went down to a cove by the sea where we found hundreds of big diesel lorries. I gave them an hour to find a lorry each and bring it to me and they ran off in the best of spirits. Almost immediately however there were despairing cries and I found that they were all being arrested by English patrols. I spent my time rushing round freeing them, but got my 15 lorries in the end and drove them back to the prisoner-of-war camp. We were a fine sight going down the road, headed by myself and Carlucci in my jeep, then 15 enormous lorries all driven by Italians in uniform, and one full of German prisoners we picked up, and no guard at all! The lorries were full of arms and ammunition, they could easily have shot me, I'm sure it never occurred to them. Last night we had 22,000 prisoners.

This morning we moved a bit and then halted by the sea. It would be wonderful, only unfortunately both yesterday and today there have been torrents of rain and clouds all day. Even here we have had prisoners who have walked along the shore and one lot who had got off in a boat and been swamped. I gave the officer, a very nice boy, my clothes to wear while his dried, he had been all night out on the dunes in soaking clothes and was chattering. I also gave him Homer's *Odyssey* in German which seemed suitable and he gave me his parole for the day so I kept him by me instead of under guard. He had the Iron Cross first class from France. This afternoon we had bullets whistling past and some of us rushed out to look for snipers, but all we found was two signallers shooting at a bottle, now under close arrest. My German is improving very much with use. The other good thing is that, very much to my surprise, I find I am not frightened, or not much. It is obviously almost all a matter of getting used to noise. I hope we really have won.

197

13 November 1942, Matruh

Padre Hughes of Mansfield, now Assistant Chaplain General, tells me Michael Mosley is definitely dead, which I still hoped was not true. You will be getting some extremely good photographs of him I hope, taken on my last leave, and two particularly I want enlarged and sent to Mrs Mosley. I shall tell her to expect them. We have had very good news of Derek Warwick, who was wounded at roughly the same time, from Patrick, who is in the same hospital.

Personally I have found the relaxation of tension, so suddenly, has made a complete victory feel like an anti-climax, and wish we were chasing the enemy across Cyrenaica. We were the people the PM mentioned at Fuka, since when we have fallen back. I have never seen anything like the roads, vehicles nose to tail and two deep for miles and miles as though there never was an aeroplane. Today we hear Tobruk is ours and it looks as though everything is over.

Matruh definitely smells, I'm not sure of what, and there isn't much left of it. Nobody has found much loot except me and I found a sort of camp which had been deserted in a hurry – full cupboard of tea left standing and lots of tinned food and things which I hope to get tomorrow. Also millions of fleas and I feel or imagine them all over me now. Fleas are definitely Axis, our soldiers don't have them. They had tins of delousing stuff too in every tent.

P.S. I've caught one flea.

15 November 1942, Western Desert

We had a good church service this morning and both the Divisional General and the Brigadier came. After it and again after dinner tonight I heard on the wireless the bells ringing for victory in England and wished I could hear St Augustine's, and how you felt about it. Within a few days' halt this place is turning into a gypsy encampment with the men building chalets against their tanks. We only don't move because there seems nothing to move against.

George Hales the padre is a very good man indeed. I am still taken with the idea of going into the Church, but Flash has decided I shall live quietly at Flintham and write the Regimental History and that would be more fun. Flash has put the most handsome crosses on the graves of the two men who were killed in his tank with wreaths made from the modest little flowering shrubs which grow here if one looks for them. They are buried at the entrance to Matruh. This is typical Flash effort combining publicity and sentiment. How long Flash will stay I don't know, he is sure to be promoted and if he isn't I think he will go home for a command there or politics. He has done wonders for this regiment and it is delightful to be with him. Unfortunately he has a very great affection for Derek Warwick, so if he gets a brigade and wants a staff officer of that rank, he would be sure to take him rather than me. However he talks himself of my going to the Staff College which would suit me very well. Geoffrey Brooks has gone off to hospital and I don't think we shall ever see him again, as he is a delicate person and once he is in doctors' hands will never be allowed out to these conditions. He did wonderfully in the battle.

Brigade has just telephoned 'air raid warning red', the wireless gives the football news, and someone killed in a car crash: it might be peace time. Why do you think the Russians have been a revelation? No one ever doubted they were brave and patriotic. I hope you aren't going Bolshevik. I have just seen an English pound note printed by the Germans with on the back in Arabic a note saying it would be made good by the British Government after the war. I don't think you will be 'very alarmed of your cosmopolitan son' when you do see him, but you will hardly be able to see him for fur coats as at the slightest breeze now I shiver. The temperature changes so much during the day, and I get up in Iceland and lunch in Africa, which means dressing for Africa.

23 November 1942, Western Desert

My application to go to the Staff College has gone in. The next course is just starting so it will not be for five months but it is a good moment to apply as I left Division in very good repute and if I am alive in a few months I may be less well thought of. I like being adjutant and Flash received me like a bride, with the bridal suite in an American tank. Actually we share a fine tent for a day or two, with a lorry alongside to run electric light off and I shall travel across Cyrenaica with him by car and go ahead I hope to see Tobruk, the ruins at Cyrene and Benghazi.

I was in bed yesterday. I think it was from eating gazelle – run down by Donny after a ten-mile chase and killed, poor pet, with a stone but delicious. We even had redcurrant jelly. Today Monty came and gave everybody medals in our area and he couldn't be a sweeter little thing, rather like Aunt Muriel. I think our role should be a very nice one too; he told us his plans. The first is that we should do no training or fighting on Christmas Day – Boxing Day we move. He only drinks lemonade. Our maps are quite hopeless.

3 December 1942, Near El Egheila, Desert: Letter to Toby

Your marvellous long letter of 12th October arrived tonight, having been sent on by the people I was last with on 23rd November [10 Armoured Division], so it hadn't done badly at all. The people who forwarded it are now crowned with laurels in the drawing rooms of Cairo and the annoying thing is that everybody thinks the war in Africa is won so that we can only do badly from now on unless we do splendidly. In fact, though we had a great victory at El Alamein we did not break straight through and the Germans had time to get a very large proportion of their men out. I always thought so. Till today it had been officially stated that there were only 1,500 Germans at Agheila. Today they say 25,000! We did destroy almost all the Italians at El Alamein; the ones now facing us are troops who have not been in action before. The Germans have some tanks, but I don't think they got any back from Alamein, these were behind or new. There would be nothing to stop us here but the Agheila position is naturally an extremely strong one, with marshes and more or less impassable sand. Our supply problems as you can imagine are considerable.

I remain fatalistic, by which I mean I take things as they come. I thought the tank in which I was travelling down the main road today, leading the Regiment and expecting to be Stukaed, was going to run off over an embankment and I felt nothing at all. Perhaps Michael Mosley was right, all soldiers grow like the Duke of Gloucester. Actually people are not more intelligent at Division than at a regiment necessarily – my mess had some quite intelligent staff captains like Charlie Brocklehurst aged about 40, director of Christie's and England's greatest expert on old silver, but none of them in the same street as Flash Kellett here, with whom I spend my time. He is the only reason for my coming back here. He is a great friend of Alexander [Earl Alexander of Tunis], as they are both Welsh Guardees. I believe that both Alexander and Montgomery are in favour of people only being out here a year, and that when Africa is cleared up quite a lot of people may get back. In that case Flash would very likely help me. We now only have 90 men left of those we brought out from England; you only get home on fairly rigorous compassionate grounds. Still, we have been out longer than most people.

I find myself an awful crosspatch and very unfunny, and I think that though I soon get bored with being with my regiment, as I don't like tanks or fighting, it is still the place where people are doing the best work and where they are least pompous and most companionable, and at the same time efficient. It is true, I think, that the first to be fully trained is the soldier – then the troop, the squadron – the regiment – and Divisional Corps, Army, GHQ are the last. But I can't go swanning off bathing here when I want; I must stay by Flash and we talk of it and then something crops up. If I don't bathe I take no exercise and that probably makes me gloomy. Today I put up a tent and had it dug in as I thought that we were here for a week or so, but we move again tomorrow. I suppose we do make ourselves fairly comfortable, but only in a very comparative way.

4 December 1942, near El Egheila, Desert

Bread and butter for dinner, such a treat as you never did – bread made by our cook without yeast and more like cake, and butter from Benghazi.

Temporarily we are at the end of our journey, being 12 miles from the Germans. Yesterday (and again today) I travelled in a tank for the first time. The worst was when I jumped off over the back and put my hand over the exhaust! I now have some leather gloves and I mean always to wear them to guard against such things, which are inevitable in a machine one knows so little about. I also have a new scarf from Cairo, green with white spots and a silk fringe, most frightfully delicious. While the people I was with till lately are the toast of Cairo, we find ourselves up against a very considerable remnant of Rommel's army which jolly well ought to have been cut off before reaching this very strong position. Whatever we do we shall get no reclame as it has been publicised as non-existent.

I have found this by Arthur Bryant which I like. 'War is like a fever: a violent disease which has to run its course. Physicians can prescribe, nurses watch and toil, and in their devoted ceaseless labours future life and death may, and does, depend. But nothing they can do can alter the violence of the disease, its fluctuations, its recurring crises. They have to be borne patiently and treated as they arise. Anxiety on the part of onlookers when things go wrong – as go wrong they will – can do no good: in certain circumstances it can do great harm. The only proper course is to do all one humanely can, and remain calm and cheerful. That is also the proper course in war.'

17 December 1942, Desert

Last time I wrote we had just taken Agheila. After Agheila the road runs between the sea and a salt marsh and the Germans have a strong gun position across the bottleneck at the end. On our map the road was marked as a causeway across impassable country but we advanced across the marsh. Halfway across the tanks began sticking and we sat there the rest of the day, heavily shelled at moments, and our guns in action behind us. I read a great deal of Virginia Woolf during the battle and when Flash wants to fire I load the gun holding up a cushion to catch the shell cases which bounce back.

During the night the enemy went, whether because he was surprised at our taking on the marsh at all, or more likely as part of a prearranged scheme. We got a message like this: 'Bernard VC (Freyberg) has more enemy forces than he can cope with to his East. All ranks will therefore understand that no effort must be spared to push forward and complete the destruction of the enemy forces.' After Alamein Flash met some friends who were then coming back from serving under Bernard and said, What have you been up to! Oh, they said, we've been on a TEWT (which is a dull thing 'Tactical Exercise Without Troops' we often have in training). How do you mean TEWT? Oh, they said, 'Terrible Experience Without Tactics.'

We went all out all day without a sign of enemy (nor any signs of a hurried withdrawal either) and captured Marble Arch – I didn't actually go under it or even very near because it was mined round, but it is a real and impressive modern arch which you can see almost 20 miles off, standing alone except for an airfield, and perhaps marking the boundaries of Tripolitania and Cyrenaica. Last night, just as it got dark, vehicles could be seen some miles away and this morning we met them and it was part of Freyberg's force. Alas, the pincers cracked an empty nut. Tonight on the air we hear London announcing that we have cut off a big part of Rommel's army!

Flash has the DSO, Derek and Geoffrey the MC from Alamein. The news came in after dinner when I was in my office and it was raining. I started off on the 200-yard trek to tell Flash and arrived an hour later soaked through, having made one complete circle and passed right through our forward line. Thank goodness there is now a moon – even if it also has its disadvantages.

25 December 1942, Desert

I am sitting on my bed waiting for the King's speech, writing on your *Old England* by Mottram. I have only looked at the pictures. They are delightful and new to me. Your parcel arrived yesterday and I put it by my bed to open in the morning.

Flash and I drove over 20 miles visiting our squadron and echelon dinners, feeding ourselves on port and cake first. We had 26 turkeys, 20 big cakes with icing, 18 big plum puddings, nuts, 600 bottles of beer, 30,000 cigarettes, rum. Generally each vehicle cooks for itself, 'brew up' they call it – with petrol and sand in a petrol tin. We have an officers' dinner tonight, generally an officer lives with his crew, in peaceful times in a squadron mess, but never in a regimental mess. We had cards filling the great Bedouin encampment of a tent we put up and which must come down and be packed away after dinner as we move at dawn. In the middle of the morning we had a parade service. The Brigadier came over to wish us a happy Christmas. Everyone seems to think the Germans will not seriously try to hold Tripoli, although the country from Sirte to Tripoli is superb for rearguard actions with impassable wadis running from the sea 100 miles south and then marshes and cultivated ground with dykes and even a forest they say, which will be nice.

Patrick sends the following message to you: Myles is *very* well and a frightfully efficient adjutant. It's Christmas day and it's just starting to rain and it's horribly cold.*

(*Quite untrue.) Hope you are well and are having a happy Christmas.

29 December 1942, Sirte, Desert

Flash, Patrick and I walked today the flagstoned streets of Sirte like Christopher Robin, with Pat excitedly pointing out possible mines. It must have been quite a nice village straggling on a hillside along the sea, with little tree-lined arcaded streets and piazzas, all now

204

entirely in ruins, and booby-trapped to hell. I do hope Tripoli isn't like that, we want a nice flat and a lorryload of Chianti, Pat wants a piano too. A tune on the wireless tonight made him tell us how when he was working in London, I think for Sandhurst, he was mad about some lady on the stage and managed to get into her show as chorus boy for a week!

If you see me in 1943 I at least shall die with excitement, don't dream of it being in the New Year.

5 January 1943, Libyan Desert: Letter to Toby

'What is Libya like for sightseeing?' Where shall I begin? The orchids, my dear, the horses *devour* them. And the ruins! How do you think we could navigate if it weren't for the minarets? On a map of five miles to one inch you mark 'British grave' – it's a landmark. Not that our maps are as good as that. Actually, I believe the ruins at Cyrene have been very well done by the Italians, and though in photographs they look a crowded hotchpotch of pillars on the side of a hill, they are very worth seeing. Unfortunately I crossed the desert south of them. I have an idea that Carthage was near Homs (Leptis Magna), halfway between Misurata and Tripoli, but so far as I know it has not been excavated. My idea is that when we get to Tripoli we shall sit around for quite a bit so I shall go out with my spade.

I don't really know who there was in Libya for the Italians to pacify. We have been a long way and you could count the Arabs we have seen on two hands. But that proves nothing in war time. I believe in the last war we had a large force tied down in Libya, defending Egypt from 30,000 Senussi, but after the war (and one action when the Duke of Westminster charged some Arabs in armoured cars) it was discovered that the Senussi were a myth. There are a few oases of which Siwa is the most famous – for its date palms, whose feet grow in heaven and heads in hell, and its inhabitants who are degenerate beyond a joke. The Italians treated the Arabs very badly and are very unpopular with those that remain. They like us and the Germans equally. The Italians built forts against the Arabs and their little towns are very well done in the provincial exhibition style. Benghazi, which was pretty well complete in 1940 with its hotels working etc., is now ruined and deserted.

11 January 1943, Libyan Desert

Flash preached last Sunday and I got one of my clerks to take it down in shorthand. He didn't prepare it so it's not much as prose:

'I like, at the beginning of each year, to have the chance of saying a few words to you, because I think one line of thought is a good thing to have in any body of men who live, move and have their being together, and the Padre has given me this opportunity of putting that thought into your minds.

'After one of the worst periods in the history of the Jews, after they had had what we call heavy casualties among their people and their cities had been laid waste, we read this, "In Ramah we heard the voice of lamentation, Rachel weeping for her children and she would not be comforted because they are not." Now Rachel, whose tomb many of you have seen on the outskirts of Bethlehem on the Jerusalem road, is taken to be the type of all Jewish womanhood of the time, mother, wife and sister. I want you to think of the Rachels of London, of Nottingham and of all the great cities throughout England, of little lonely shacks in the Canadian prairies and of the great sheep stations of Australia. We, living together, have a man sitting next to us in our tank one day, and he is not there the next. We miss him, and miss him terribly when we have time to think, but we do go through the same feelings as those people who sit at home.

'I want you to get a clear picture in your minds for one moment, of the horrors, and what those Rachels of today have to put up with. Think of Poland, of Russia, think of the frightful atrocities that have been committed there, and think also of Germany and Italy – and whose fault is it? It is not the fault of Hitler, or Mussolini, or any one of our statesmen in the years immediately preceding the war, but it is the fault of your fathers and mine, the very men who went out and fought and won the last war; they are the reason why there are Rachels today, the reason why so many of our friends are dead is their fault and theirs alone. Because nobody had learned to think during the last war what they were going to do when it was over. The only thing they thought of was getting out of a khaki suit – they thought of nothing and nobody else but themselves – there was no planning for the future.

'It is no good you and I sitting here, winning these battles, and leaving it to someone else to plan for the future, because they won't do it. It is you who have got to make these plans. It is you who have got to say, "What are we going back to – what do we want the world to be like when we go back to it?" Are we going to throw ourselves on to the world with all sorts of promises, like Lloyd George gave after the last war – "A country fit for heroes to live in?" After six months it was not a land fit for anybody to live in except for people with unearned incomes or vested interest and after six years we had one and a half million unemployables who were a disgrace to the whole country. That was the fault of our fathers and nobody else.

'In the lesson which has just been read, we heard of the Prophet Elijah going away into the desert, running away from his enemies and there he was visited by many of the great manifestations of nature, earthquakes, storms and lightning. But he did not get the power to think things out from any of these – it was when he sat down by himself that he began to think things out. Nor will you and I get really useful thoughts during the storm of battle, but when quite alone, we sit down and think things out.

'We have plenty of time these days, we fight perhaps for a fortnight and then there follows some weeks with plenty of time to think. I want you to think it out. You are young, most of you, and the greater part of life lies before you. We live in a democracy, and it is your vote, and your thoughts which can make post-war England something worth having. I am convinced that the British Empire will never get another chance if it fails this Peace – it is not in the nature of things, it is not in keeping with life and history for that to

207

happen. Think of all that England has done to see that her work continues. To do this, you must think and plan for the future.

'As I speak to you in the middle of this church service, it seems a proper time for me to remind you that no greater plan was ever conceived than the plan for Jesus Christ coming down to earth under most humble circumstances. It would have appeared at first sight that the best thing to have done would have been for him to come in the shape of an Emperor of Rome, but it would have fizzled out in a very short time and his name and what he stood for would have been lost in mists of ancient history. Without successful planning, nothing of any value can possibly be achieved, and as we look ahead into this New Year we see a different prospect than was the case last year. Then I told you that you had hard fights ahead of you and there was a great deal to be overcome. Now you are all veteran fighters and have seen the best and worst of war.

'In the words of the Prime Minister, "We are not at the end, we are only at the end of the beginning," and so what you have got to do is carry on as you are doing, nobody could do better than that and remember to plan – plan for the future, sanely and sensibly, so that when that great day comes when peace is declared, you do not find yourselves floating about like rudderless ships. And now, looking forward into the New Year, I feel I cannot do better than to quote you the words which His Majesty the King gave us two years ago in his Christmas broadcast: "And I said to the man who stood at the gate of the year, give me a light that I may go out safely into the unknown, and he said unto me, go out boldly and put your hand into the hand of God, that shall be to you better than light, and safer than a known way."'

Patrick who likes to sit and listen to the men says that his friends got quite the wrong end of the stick and thought they were being urged to make quite sure of a job at the pit against their return. Flash very nearly missed the service as he had gone to a conference a long way off with General Montgomery. They told him there he'd never be back in time and then he had a puncture, but he arrived halfway through the service. Though I can't pretend to think it is representative, I should like to show it to Uncle William sometime

208

because he would be interested that shortly before a battle such a sermon should be preached here in the desert.

18 January 1943, Desert near Tripoli, Libya

So weit so gut, and I saw some trees this afternoon. All morning we crossed frightful rocks and wadis and then down into a most precipitous valley with proper old wintry trees scattered about and cultivation, colourless at this time of year. We started this party with two night marches, moving in column. The dust is fearful and I was in such a bad temper after the first that the next night I went in a jeep alongside; that brought us to within a mile of the enemy line and next morning we moved before it was light and were soon entangled with them. There was a battle all day. All afternoon Flash and I sat separately in a slight fold with delicious goldfish swimming past [armour-piercing shells]. It was a very successful and expensive day, and we played the major part in it. The enemy withdrew in the night, we passed the relics of the battle as dawn broke and crossed the wadi ZemZem. [This was the offensive leading to the capture of Tripoli by the Eighth Army.]

All that morning we chased a fugitive enemy column. The column seemed too fast for us, but we had hardly moved on before we ran into trouble on a bare flat plain without any dips in it. After a while much of the enemy who were dug in surrendered and we swept down on their line, but had to back slowly out of it again as it was a veritable bowl of goldfish.

At the moment we are within a couple of miles of a road which he is holding and within a day of Tripoli. Donny, who went out to reconnoitre our route before Christmas, got back a few days ago to an agreed rendezvous with three armoured cars. Unfortunately the armoured cars waiting for him were German and he was captured. I'm afraid he will make a terrible prisoner and it will be bad with his asthma. Patrick got a direct bomb hit on his truck and lost everything in it (and some things of mine). We were very glad today to see our planes had got up with us, but unfortunately they didn't recognise us. They are doing wonderfully and have hardly any trouble from the air.

20 January 1943, Desert near Tripoli

Flash is sitting back in a little dry runnel writing. The ground creamy and faintly green runs away from us to a plain, and then hills and mountains to the west tumble into the distance. I cannot see the north; if I could I could see Tripoli perhaps, and the enemy who are firing could see me. Flash got a direct from an HE [high explosive] very large shell yesterday. Bits went through his map case but he popped his head down in time. We handed over our position yesterday afternoon and when we moved out my tank crawled at about 1 mph, which annoyed me very much as we have had to cross several skylines. In the end I abandoned it and borrowed a jeep. I then went out to find it by moonlight and ran into a kind of Sahara, billowing soft sand into which I eventually subsided.

My main incentive actually had been to recover my bed, though naturally after this long chase every tank is priceless. I slept in my bed all right. However, I had a new tank today; an officer was killed in it yesterday by a bit of splinter, very unlucky. Anyway, I always sit well inside and read a book. It's the armour-piercing shells we aren't keen on, though of course they either hit you sock or miss you and they are rather pretty and you can watch them. You can't see a HE shell, you only hear it coming long after it has burst. I always remember you saying it was very wrong of PC Bourchier to write home and tell his papa [Vicar of Flintham] that someone had got shot near him, so I hope you haven't carried Mummy upstairs on hearing there are two kinds of shells. I am getting quite an expert and know the sizes by name, and one day I actually fired my big gun but it went in such a funny direction that I was baffled how to correct it, and anyway I don't consider that my business so I haven't tried again. I am merely a telephone exchange. It really is too lovely here.

Later

Terrific news tonight – Donny has escaped!

We had my photographer friend over to see us. He gave us gin and tonic (he had produced Turkish delight last time) and begged for a picture of a tank firing at night. So we laid it on, and after he had photographed it from every angle with three cameras for the Russian and American papers, an indignant message arrived on my set to say someone was shooting the neighbouring regiment. They didn't know it was us. We were delighted as, after we had done all the heavy fighting, they have jockeyed themselves in front of us for the advance on Tripoli tonight or tomorrow.

Flash says we'll take a house outside Tripoli with an Italian cook and send officers in parties. Tripoli is sure to be bombed so nobody is going to be allowed to live there, also it's fatal once people settle down anywhere in a town. Our regiment has been in every battle since 30th August. Flash is the only one who has been with it all that time and never been back; most have been wounded at one time or another. I wonder if your letters will still have to come via Cairo. We are nearer you than Cairo now, I think.

21 January 1943, Desert near Tripoli

This morning the sun rose (long after we rose under the stars) and flooded the hilltops, but the valleys were inland seas of mist in which swam the little white houses. The enemy guns still covering the road through the hills (but moving right out now – midday), the sun getting warmer and warmer, I wash and sunbathe with my shirt off for the first time for a week, and send a jeep scouting for red wine and write to Tony Fillingham about a caterpillar. And the jeep comes back with three dozen bottles and cheese and tinned butter and the firing is far away and nothing that comes over the air seems to concern us very much. I have a new tank this morning that is the fourth since the battle started a week ago. General Montgomery said we'd be in Tripoli on the 21st. He is slightly uncanny. The battle is over bar the shouting. We found a way round over the mountains and could have moved on Tripoli last night, but for political reasons they want the New Zealanders to get there first. It doesn't matter, it is lovely in the sun and we have played our part, three officers killed and 11 heavies knocked out in one day, and three days fighting out of six, I wish I could cable you that I am all right, but I expect I shall be able to soon. I should have told you that if you are wounded at all, even a scratch, and go to the first aid post you are automatically reported and your next of kin informed, which is often unnecessarily worrying for them. Also only the wounded can cable home, so nobody else can send reassuring messages.

It is bliss here. I think we shall move soon, we've been held up by a man and a boy but we'd outrun everybody else and it was no job for tanks. We are too new to this sort of country, but my goodness glad to see it.

22 January 1943, near Tripoli

We are sitting on the side of the road lined with blue gum trees south of Tripoli, with people walking on ahead. We could have moved on Tripoli, but for political reasons they want the New Zealanders to get there first. General Montgomery said we'd be in Tripoli on the 21st. He is slightly uncanny. The battle was over yesterday, bar the shouting.

Last night Donny returned. We dined in our tent and Donny, Flash and I went to bed luxuriously in it. Donny is extremely well. He was a prisoner three days, escaped near Tripoli and walked 200 miles by night without a compass. The Arabs were extremely good to him. He was taken as you know by an armoured-car patrol, sent back to Afrika Corps HQ and lodged in a tent next to Rommel's. He asked to see Rommel but he was away. He had a big talk to his Chief of Staff and was extremely impressed not only by the smartness of the Germans but by their kindness and charm. He was then handed over to the Italians who drove him up the coast road, potting at Arabs like rabbits as they went. They were extremely ill mannered and gave him no food and a stone floor to sleep on. However, he demanded some wine and made his guards fairly tiddly and bunked. He said the German food was superb and the intelligence people all charmers who had been at Oxford or Cambridge. They don't like Russia and they said, why on earth were we two people fighting? They hoped they'd meet in London after the war and Donny (of all people) gave them the name of his club.

25 January 1943, near Tripoli

Yesterday midday I was watching the flower beds being tidied up round the palazzo, Flash and the squadron leaders being out on a recce, when I was called to the wireless and told to move immediately with or without him. So much for the rest and the roof over our heads. We went through what appears on the map to be the largest colonisation scheme round Tripoli and which must in fact be the largest as it consisted almost entirely of very new houses scattered over 100 square miles of virgin and broken desert. The labour of levelling this alone must be heartbreaking.

Last night we were in touch with the enemy again and leaguered the night with Toby Horsford. His regiment [11th Hussars] is the most famous in the Middle East and their only complaint working with us was that we moved too fast to allow them to do their work. Now they've left us today to rest, but we go on, to make Tripoli safe for those behind. I hope you are pleased about Tripoli, it is a great feat. Officers who have come up from Cairo say that we have a terrific reputation now. We also have chocolate which is more important.

I hope before they leave to see more of the actresses than I have yet, but at first sight Vivien Leigh is disappointing, no longer very young, rather hard and affected, vain and no great humour. Dorothy Dickson has an attractive throaty laugh and looks amazingly young still. Bea Lillie as ever in a black tarbush. Leslie Henson

213

is mostly tight. I had my first bath since 10th October the other day passing through Tripoli. I saw sister Binnie who is now in Tripoli, poor dear she got separated from her baggage coming up by sea, and in it were a cake, a huge box of fudge and 53 bars of chocolate all for me. Isn't it frightful?

5 February 1943, Tripoli

I wrote to you the day before yesterday when Randolph [Churchill] came to see us, intending that Flash should give our letters to Randolph's papa next day. However, he hadn't the opportunity; no great matter as my letters sent you by such means never seem to reach you. I didn't see the review in Tripoli, we sent a party and it was apparently marvellously well done. When Flash went to the rehearsal he was told he mustn't miss the real show as someone he knew would be there – and this really was the first we'd heard of Churchill coming since our parade for him on the road was cancelled. When Flash got back to our farm he was greeted by the Italians with, 'Good day sir, we are so very excited that Mr C is coming to Tripoli. You know he was at Sirte yesterday and tonight.' So much for security.

7 February 1943, Tripoli

Yesterday was a lovely day, and I walked down to the sea. I had just had a bath and covered myself with Flash's latest, Reve d'Or, but it was worth wasting. I lay in the sun in my little cove, and after an hour of Shakespeare's sonnets, dived from a rocky ledge into clear cold blue water, but not impossibly cold and great fun. When I'd climbed the cliffs again I met Flash and we walked back to the sea and lay on the sand. When we first arrived here the Italians locked themselves into their houses at night because the Germans used to come along and take a girl like an orange. They are very surprised at us, but I guess in a week or two they'll just think us wet. So I cannot find myself looking at this as conquered country.

Churchill said that our march to Tripoli was one of the great achievements of history, but one can't look at it like that yet, not till one has forgotten 'the facts' and re-read them in history books. As it is raining this morning I went into Tripoli for high mass at the cathedral, with Micky Gold. To our amazement we found it absolutely impossible to get in, the church was so full. However, we made desperate and separate efforts and I did eventually reach a position where with one foot on a confessional I could see a corner of the altar. Most of the men were Scotsmen with a large number of New Zealanders, about 4,000 in all. I was very surprised at so many Scots being Catholic.

Tripoli is absolutely nothing compared to Tel Aviv or Haifa. It is a modern town and quite small, with only two decent streets and a few dirty-coloured plastered buildings. We wandered around the Arab quarter which is more fun, narrow streets frequently arched, the usual little Arab shops but not smelly and all whitewashed, and living houses with doors on the street very nondescript to look at but in fact hiding attractive little pillared courtyards.

We are delighted to hear from our old Padre Hughes, now Assistant Chaplain General, that two American generals dining with Montgomery each tipped his ADC £1 when they left!

10 February 1943, Tripoli: Letter to Toby

This morning I lectured on Algeria and Tunisia. Starting at 1500 BC and ending yesterday after putting into the picture Phoenicians, Troy, Pious Aeneas, Dido, Cato, Hannibal, Scipio, the Vandals, Belisarius, Mohammed, Ferdinand and Isabella, Charles V, the Turks and the 150 cm concrete emplacement of the Mareth Line. I would very much like to know something about Algeria and Tunisia, actually. Everyone said it was a first-class lecture. Next we had a discussion on what to do with the chaps between armistice and demobilisation. The chaps who spoke were (if you expected them to do nothing but gulp) surprisingly sensible. I am not even quite sure that they thought the government had taken their jobs and forced them into the army, and must give them back, but I expect they did. One said emigration wanted looking into as in South Africa they'd had a great welcome, so Flash tried out on them his scheme of making use of a going concern (the army unit) by marching off somewhere to settle plus wives and families. But a unit includes so many diverse types thrown together, and I expect most of them will have seen enough of each other by the end of the war. But somehow or other something has got to be done. I thought the army might offer vacancies on jobs as it offers vacancies on courses.

I hear Gandhi is fasting. You may blame our government of India but if it hadn't treated the Indians generously to our ideas of nationalism and freedom we should be having none of this tiresomeness. I am going to act in a play in front of Monty and more important people still, first rehearsal tomorrow. Monty spoke to the officers of the three divisions in a theatre in Tripoli yesterday – he is a cocky, conceited, witty little man, but a genius at his job. He was so complimentary that we feel sure he is going to ask us to do something frightful. He said the Germans made a grave error in not going all out to destroy the Russian armies in 1942 and now they never would. But they were still formidable, if tinged for the first time with doubt.

16 February 1943, Tripoli: Letter to Toby

We have had an interesting two days. Monty had a conference attended by 100 generals from England, Tunisia and here, and each of the three divisions which took Tripoli put on a demonstration. Those taking part were given seats for the whole conference, and captains were definitely chic, there being practically nobody but generals and all the rest colonels. Monty talked all the first morning; he is a priceless little man. He told them how to win battles. Then Freyberg and his New Zealanders did a demonstration, and this morning the Highlanders did theirs, in each case a big sand table in the middle of the theatre with the generals sitting round in a circle. But this afternoon we went a long way better. Instead of being done by generals and brigadiers it was done by Flash and another most excellent colonel and about eight of us, and we were on the stage in dummy tanks, with proper scenery, curtains etc. We did the whole thing talking on the wireless as you do in a battle and the pieces were moved on the sand table as we went along. When we knocked out a tank it was set alight on the sand table. Flash is only rivalled by Monty as a showman. I'm told it was most exciting, and at the end Monty stood up and said, 'I have nothing to add to a completely superb demonstration, the best I have ever seen.'

After us Cunningham [Air Marshal Sir Arthur] spoke, very well, on how the Eighth Army and the RAF worked together and how in England there was a kind of 'petulance' between them, and in Tunisia the non-cooperation had meant that instead of sailing home from Tripoli we have to face hard fighting and win their battles for them. I reckon all the boys went home hating the Eighth Army. England's C-in-C is Paget, a puce-coloured stiff. The Americans look like dear old doctors or as white as sheets; I never saw such a collection.

18 February 1943, Tripoli

Yesterday in answer to Flash's 'regret urgently require Hildyard as Adjutant', we had a most peremptory signal from Division that Hildyard report there by the 19th. This infuriated everybody. Copies were sent to Brigade and Corps, and they thought it cheeky too. So we are keeping quiet, knowing we come out of command of that division on the 19th! Meanwhile everything is looking very bright for me, and with only one or two fences more to clear I may get a job I like very much. It is a captain's job, but if I get it I shall stop my Staff College application. The Staff College has dangers as one may be sent as G2 sewage at Tewfik or somewhere where the society is not high class.

When after dinner everybody sits and drinks and shouts, I always either read or write or walk in the moonlight, and last night I went to the cliffs (you could see the bottom of the sea by moonlight) and on the way back hunted a heffalump and caught it, and brought it back in my fur coat. It smelt, but I don't think it was a skunk. Unfortunately during the night it escaped, whether before or after I covered it with my rug to keep it warm I don't know. My fur coat is now laid out in the sun, covered in eau de cologne. But he was a charming fellow, with long fur in black and white stripes and a bushy tail and a head like a nice ferret, perhaps a lemur.

4 March 1943, Tunisian Desert: Letter to Toby

Do you get the BBC where you are and a wonderful something called *Front Line Family*? It is going on now, a staggering performance to which the Regiment used to listen in Tobruk in spring 1941 and which continues daily if not twice daily, about a family called Robinson – fascinating in its masochistic portrayal of an English middle-class *famille*. This morning at dawn we moved out as for battle and all day I have sat in a little walled field in which there are two palm trees, three very old olives and many figs, a bit of barley and a mass of wild flowers. You can sit on the ground and count 20 different kinds of flower.

Just now two planes shot down, one definitely German, one I think so, the pilot is still swinging about on his parachute. Rommel is doing the obvious thing, hitting out at each of us in turn, and it is our turn now. The retreat in front of the Americans I feel sure was part of the plan and far from the victory they claimed. The Germans seem able to bring all their available tanks from in front of both the First Army and the Americans down against us. We are hoping Rommel *will* attack (they tell me).

Yesterday like a thunderbolt we are told to march to war, whether because the First Army is doing well or badly we honestly don't know, but certainly blame *them*! Early this morning we left, on two roads, one up to the sea, the other a bit inland. To my annoyance I am on the inland one. When I drove off to report just now that we had made six miles by evening having got heavily bogged in salt marshes, I heard that the lucky people by the sea were now lighting fires to dry their clothes.

5 March 1943, Tunisian Desert

Another peaceful day among the flowers, Monty came and was very pleasant this afternoon, he said he thought Rommel would attack just where we are tomorrow. I think there are great advantages about being attacked as against attacking viz you can keep your paraphernalia just behind and fall back on them for dinner.

Next morning. Well, Monty's always right. When I woke up of my own accord this morning I thought, That's good, and by the time I'd had a leisurely breakfast I thought, Another nice day. Unfortunately it got a bit noisy and we heard that the Germans had attacked – though not exactly against us. However, we moved from our garden to meet them a bit nearer the mountains. It has been noisy all day and in the air too, but not too dangerously close so far, and we have given the Germans a nasty knock they say, 24 tanks claimed. Includes Mark VIs. Getting darker and noisier! [Battle of Medenine]

7 March 1943, Tunisian Desert

The total claim last night was 35 tanks and the enemy had nothing to show for it. Patrick McCraith, out in front observing with Mark Strutt, had an exciting time when after being heavily shelled they suddenly saw 100 infantry attacking them followed by tanks. They stayed firing themselves and directing our guns, and remained master of the field. Patrick who goes round in circles about nothing is quite unperturbed by explosions. Leaguers are always tiresome even after a peaceful day. One isn't in till it's dark and if there's no moon you put your bed down and can't find it and if it's raining it's funnier still. It was a noisy night and my pillow got wetter and wetter. Now the sun is well out and we are sitting still, so thank goodness we can dry blankets.

Flash and the Brigadier are just back from a scout round with the back of their jeep full of loot out of German tanks, *all* American and including a new pair of blue bathing pants, two bucks fifty from California! And the Germans are definitely off, having made fools of themselves.

Later

Twenty-seven tanks found on the ground so far. I have been having a long talk with a prisoner, a Pole, who was in the Polish army and was forced to fight for Germany. When they entered his village they hung two of his friends on trees. There were English prisoners working in mines near his village and he said they were OK and gave him cigarettes from their parcels, but of 500 Russian prisoners working on a road through the village, 450 died of hunger in two months. He said there were 30 Poles in his company and they all wanted to desert. Before their attack here they were paraded and told that if they failed to take the hill and cemetery on either side of us the Afrika Corps was finished in Africa. They were pulled out at three o'clock this morning having failed dismally, he hid and deserted. He was a nice boy, good looking, not very brave when we were shelled.

Monty will be even more conceited. When he came to see us he said, 'I'm famous now. I've had four proposals in my fan mail. One was from a widow of 42 who said she felt like 28.' He is a very odd little man with a terrific histrionic sense, and a great soldier. His order of the day for the battle yesterday must have been printed a week ago to reach us in time.

10 March 1943, Tunisian Desert

Monty says that when Churchill came to Tripoli Monty said to him, 'I have taken Tripoli for you, and I want in return direct air-mail service.' This is now running twice weekly and taking two days from London! You want to put 'Eighth Army' as I told you in my cable. Flash has gone to Brigade at last, as a full colonel and Brigade 2 i/c. We have been very lucky to keep him so long. Donny Player reigns in his stead. For a long time it was doubtful whether he would succeed, but we got a new brigadier and then he made a good impression by escaping from the Germans. I like Donny very much, he is good tempered, a good organiser and very fond of country things.

I think Monty did very well last week, he only came up to Mareth to create a diversion to save the First Army and with all our rush we were absolutely ready and lost no guns and no tanks in the battle. The First Army is exactly what I'd expect in my lugubrious way when other people talked of a march on Berlin. All soldiers from England are paralytic; in fact, they seem exactly like we were when we first came out here. I don't see how anybody can stay like that for three years and be sane. Thank God for the Russians.

12 March 1943, Tunisian Desert: Letter to Toby

You say, 'Do squadron leaders lead the charge or only go occasionally as with us?' And in another letter, arrived today, 'Someone tells me casualties are not high.' The latter is true, we have had about 50 men killed in the campaign, this winter. About ten were officers. At Alamein most officers were killed or wounded. Since we gave up having charges we have won tank battles. In the days when we had very bad tanks we had to do it because we could only fire at very short range and had no artillery support. We advance with our light squadron leading, the Colonel and I lead the remainder but in action we are spread out across the front. The idea of small groups (Jock columns) has been entirely debunked and we keep consolidated, though individual troops or squadrons may be sent out during an action with a specific role. Of course a very large proportion of the Regiment are not in tanks at all. I have never seen a Churchill; there were three at Alamein. The Sherman is a

221

first-class tank, frightfully cold the only time I went in one. I have never been in a light tank! Crusaders are the most attractive to look at but very unreliable. Grants are much too good a target but the most comfortable, which is all I think of.

18 March 1943, Tunisian Desert

Flash in a letter which he made me promise to burn, said of his life's plan, 'The primary point in the plan is never to take up anything without succeeding, and in that I have been greatly helped by a strong religious sense, by which I am utterly convinced that if you work hard and keep your eyes on the object, all the rest will be added to you.'

I am casting about a little for an object in life, for I am sure that for happiness one must possess two credentials – a firm base (family, or in my case Flintham) and an object. I believe intellectuals are the most ineffective and disappointing people because they despise material objectives but cannot generally replace them. I have said for some time that anyone with my opportunities who set his mind on any one achievement must almost inevitably gain it. Actually there are very few ambitious people and I shall never swell the number. But I wish I could assess my own possibilities as well as I can those of others. I am afraid it is sure I was not born a man of action.

Flash wrote on leaving the Regiment, 'My chief pleasure was being in your society, yet such a state of blissful contentment and ease destroyed Rome, let me remind you.' To whom was it Baldwin once said in the House, 'You (the right hon. member) have all the attributes of the courtesan – without the responsibilities?' One's reading tends to make one unworldly, slow to appreciate the present which moves so rapidly while one sits indoors. I suppose it is strange to say this the day before we move to battle but battles are not on my visiting list. I never ate better chocolates.

23 March 1943, Battle of Mareth, Tunisian Desert

There are moments when I wish I were a little intelligence officer at GHQ sitting at a table all day instead of in a tank. Yesterday I was woken at 2 a.m., told to get us moving by a quarter to five. We moved by moonlight, were under heavy fire as soon as it was light and it was after eight at night and a bright moon again before we began to pull back for the night, having been fighting all day. At the moment there is a slight lull and we have had some breakfast (which we didn't yesterday, nor other meals), enlivened by shells whistling past which have just set on fire a tank behind us. Yesterday morning Donny and I went out via Flash, who appeared in the frigid dawn, looking chic and cheerful and blew me a kiss. An hour or two later standing shaving on his tank, he was killed outright by a shell burst. Patrick was with him. Enemy planes attacked at very low level, dropping bombs at about 20 feet.

Again this morning we moved out by moonlight, and a day of bursts and bangs, of smelly diesel engines running, and earphones on all day crackling, and mountains on both sides and guns all round. We were a fine sight in nine lines of tanks followed forever by endless lines of guns and vehicles. We drove till about ten o'clock, losing most of our wheeled vehicles however, stuck en route. The Free French had taken a wadi crossing for us and during the night I contacted General Leclerc on a hill surrounded by black troops and shell holes. He was very nice indeed though he spoke no English. He led the French forces all the way from Chad.

26 March 1943

Life doesn't improve, we have a free morning back from the front waiting for a big attack tonight and it has to be a khamsin, hot and muggy beyond words. I slept last night from two till six which was something, though I felt *worse* after it. Now this afternoon we make a great effort – we are being used as infantry tanks, i.e. going at walking pace before the infantry which we have never done before as it is not our role. Mareth has not been a success and everything hinges on us now. It will be real gangster fighting this afternoon. Robin Hood [one of the Regiment's tanks] was knocked out two days ago by a shell slap on the back which covered everything in diesel oil. Luckily it wasn't a petrol tank. I have never felt so squalidly dirty. I will tell you more when less busy and exhausted.

Poor Myrtie.

27 March 1943, Tunisian Desert

Writing by a torch. We were pulled out for a rest this afternoon and promised 24 hours. Fifty per cent of the officers don't make sense at all. Now we move again at 1 a.m. which means practically no sleep. Last night again only two hours. But we have been victorious and I have been quite excited. I didn't look much yesterday afternoon, particularly as I'd invented a new way of doing my work by listening to two wirelesses at once and speaking on both, not including a sort of private wireless, complicated the first time, I don't think anybody else does it. It must have been a genuine battle because today there are dead men and derelict tanks and guns everywhere. We advanced in two lines right across the valley behind a barrage followed by infantry on their feet. We have knocked out 30 tanks and innumerable guns and taken thousands of prisoners. But the evening before, watching an attack of this kind on a small scale was really fine. At 5.30 our tank-buster aeroplanes armed with cannon came over and were directed on to the enemy positions by us, talking to them on the wireless and shelling to show them the way. They gave the Germans absolute hell, flying at ground level behind the hill again and again. Fifteen minutes later a terrific barrage came down on the hill, and after five minutes under a smoke screen our tanks advanced. I watched for some time on a hill before coming down to join in. We took the hill but just as we were settling on it for the night a fresh battle started in the dark and we never got to bed at all – that was rather amusing and pretty seeing tracer shot flying around. People get quite excited but I felt sure the

224

Germans were much more excited than us and thought we were attacking him where he had gone to sleep half a mile away, while actually we only woke him putting our guard out. Tonight we move to take Gabes and cut Rommel off.

31 March 1943, en route to Gabes, Tunisian Desert

Sitting peacefully in the sun behind a small green ridge in Robin Hood (who like the King never dies). On my left the right-hand regiment of another armoured brigade is withdrawing for the second time after being heavily shelled. This is charming, to listen to 205 mms meandering past like a goods train and exploding on somebody else. We are cocky and contemptuous of our friends on the left, a brigade comprised of the most famous cavalry tank regiments. Our little ridge and barley field is open to the public today and we have had all the corps and divisional commanders, loosed by our efforts from Mareth, peering over the top, having heard obviously that this is a place where a general can get some idea of what is going on. Freyberg delighted with us and told us he said to Monty 'This is the best bloody brigade in the British army,' and Monty said, 'You're telling me what I know already.'

We have had two good nights' sleep, particularly last night, and we look like sitting here all day as we have outrun everybody except our friends on the left who go in the wrong direction anyway. What we did was to go right round the mountains which run down west of Mareth parallel to the sea, and broke through a pass between mountains, just south of the salt lakes and west of Gabes. There is a Roman wall 1,500 years old right across this valley, against earlier invasions. The Roman-wall position was held by Italians backed by German tanks and the position further back, which we took on the 26th, was held by Germans some of whom had only just been rushed up from the Mareth line.

225

1 April 1943, Gabes, Tunisia: Letter to Toby

I'm afraid it's some time since I wrote but there's been no means of posting letters. We have taken the Mareth line. We began our move by night on 14th March, and for a fortnight we had practically no rest. On the 22nd Flash was killed, he was a man of whom I was intensely fond and the only person I have ever been influenced by.

My regiment destroyed six German tanks, took the enemy position and had three officers killed. On the 28th, after meeting some screens of tanks and guns, we passed Gabes and arrived first at the Gabes Gap – so we sat down and waited for everybody else. The Germans pulled their whole force out of the Mareth Line in one night and got away, but the ones we had met had had a good pasting. We have sat observing the Gabes Gap but it is very difficult to say how seriously they mean to defend it; the Americans are only 50 miles away on the other side. There are a good many possible lines of defence between here and Tunis.

It is charming here, with mountains in front of us and a valley of dark green barley flecked with waves of marigold, we get shelled a certain amount. My tank Robin Hood (it is always called Robin Hood) was knocked out when it got a direct hit in the engine from a 105 mm. We had several very near misses including one bomb which was dropped from about 50 feet and just missed my head. Our tank-buster planes are quite terrific and I'm getting out of tanks before the Germans invent one of their own. We have been much praised by everyone except the BBC but as one commentator speaks from Cairo and the other from Algiers they are not wildly informed.

Have you anything to live for? I feel I have very little. Flintham was to make up for a solitary old age and is being wrecked, but more than that I feel I have completed myself. I am no longer shy. I am no longer very frightened, I can make friends when I want to, I have no ambitions, practically no one interests me and no one attracts me much or for long. I am uninterested in the war and I suppose at last reasonably efficient at it. I am quite willing to finish with it all, which is the right frame of mind for a soldier. The thing our family lacks is *joie de vivre*.

We are building up to attack the Gabes Gap; it looks as though the Eighth Army will have to do the whole thing. We discount the First Army and the Americans altogether of course; if by some miracle they revived it might make a difference. Certainly this Gabes Gap would be quite untenable if the Americans did anything. Montgomery spoke to us today, I'm afraid we are like the favourite hunter now, and likely to be taken out four days a week. We are attacking tonight, but only likely to get into trouble later tomorrow, as the infantry are making the gap. The country here is very faintly green with patches of barley and some proper mountains and near us are two Arab villages which differ from those further east in that they have dazzling white square towers instead of minarets, about the size of an English church tower, with a little clocher on top. Each has a large oasis of palms and olives round it and walled homesteads. The Arabs sit and watch us rushing around and no doubt think us bloody fools.

6 April 1943, Gabes

Our infantry attacked the Gabes Gap before dawn this morning, and our green and gold valley became a dustbowl. We were to break through as soon as the infantry had taken the hills. But the exits from the mountain defiles were covered by enemy tanks and guns and we failed to get through. We were reserve regiment and so had an easy time, the others had rather an unpleasant one with many pockets of resistance still left in the hills all round them. A party of Hugh's friends very kindly bombed us and killed the crew commander of the tank behind mine, two German big bombers were brought down just by us in the afternoon at the same moment as I was handed a huge mail, I don't know which was the more exciting. Look out any photographs of Flash for Myrtie, will you?

13 April 1943, Sfax

The last time I lay in bed under an olive tree looking dreamily up at the silver and blue I also had a sick tummy, but things were rather different [in Crete]. It is blissful here. There are no noisome crickets, only masses of pale olives and flowering banks. Corporal Waite, Flash's wonderful servant and now mine, is ironing my shirts, the orderly room is typing copies of Freyberg's cable to the NZ premier after the Mareth battle, the mess is definitely working on something delicious, and even if we up sticks I shall remain feigning and feeling rather sick. On Robin Hood the wireless reports the leading regiment now very close to Enfidaville and not at all certain the enemy means to hold it. There is no doubt the speed of our advance has rattled him.

I last wrote to you from north of Sfax. We moved that afternoon, stopping for a little by an Arab hovel whose owner told me in very good French that he had been to Paris and with his brothers owned some ten hectares of land. It was almost dark when we passed through El Djem, a little village clustered round a colossal Roman theatre which appeared to be almost complete and unrestored. The country between Sfax and Sousse was flat, meadow and olive groves, rather like Palestine, but NW of Sousse we hit hilly country, very difficult to manoeuvre in as it was all olives surrounded by big cactus hedges and ditches, and narrow lanes. We were fired on by what I think was the eight-barrelled 150 mm mortar we have heard so much about and never met. Frenchmen came running up very anxious to help us to get round the back of this and we let them guide us. We were led into quite a town on a hill where the streets were very narrow and the turnings impossible for tanks. The population, part Arab in turbans, part French, were jostling and shouting with excitement and clapping all the way which was fun and I hear it was the same in Sousse. It didn't further our aggression against the Germans as we were leading Eighth Army. We reached the hills overlooking the plain in front of Enfidaville and were heavily shelled, but this morning another regiment has taken up the lead.

Reference the Mareth line, I can definitely tell you that I have never been as frightened in battle as I have often been in a motorcar with someone driving too fast. The other day a shell went past my head so close that its blast knocked out Donny and the driver. The tank went on quite nicely with no one driving.

14 April 1943, Tunisian Desert: Letter to Toby

It was almost dark as we went through El Djem. I was rather drunk on wine from Sfax, and considering the implications of a letter from you which had just been handed me, which contained the sentence, 'How do you feel about marriage, any urge?' I don't think Billy Maclean could take Hughie's place [Chisholm]. I suppose you know what Hughie's place was (he wanted me to tell you before we went to Obersdorf, and I wouldn't). What made you think of Bill in the same light? I like Bill very much, though nothing like so much as Billy B [Brooksbank]. Actually I heard from Michael P today; he writes very often, though I haven't seen him for 18 months. He wrote to say he was probably getting married, to a Greek girl, Minette. My, Clem will be mad. Michael's work has centred round the sea we both sailed on and the town we first arrived in, helping others to do the same and having many adventures. His eye and arm are still wrong. He often comes back but we invariably miss one another.

As far as marriage, I think if I intended to live in London some smart and strong-minded widow would probably marry me, but as I intend to live a life of squalor and am unlikely to get entangled with the house maid I don't really see much hope. The main trouble of course is that I only like to be admired and not to admire and am consequently a disappointment (though perfectly courteous). As for the house, personally I'd far rather pull it down.

19 April 1943, Enfidaville: Letter to Toby

We almost started the new battle yesterday but found we had got the day of the week wrong so it is tonight instead. What sort of cissy party do you think this is? Fifty killed in the Regiment of course, not the *Division*, more now.

My house is a Grant [tank], obviously it's no use trying to be secure. It's the only one and therefore very conspicuous. They have their big guns very low so that you have to expose several feet of tank before you can shoot. They are quite unmanoeuvrable but fast (35 mph we did the other day down the road chasing towards Sousse). If we stop for any length of time at all my office comes up, and I don't go near the tank, except for the wireless. Also the mess. We generally manage to keep a truck with my servant and the Colonel's almost right up with us to come into leaguer at night, during action. I've never been in a Valentine, they are infantry tanks and quite US. Personally I think the day of tanks is over but both sides go on building bigger ones.

Yes, I am all for Nazi feudalism; I think England is going to be pretty bloody for toffs like you and me.

21 April 1943, Enfidaville

There has been heavy shelling all today but we had a good sleep. There are so many shells going both ways over my head at the moment I am quite dizzy. I have just been looking at some German trenches and picked up a very disreputable walking stick which to my delight turned out to be a homemade sword stick.

Thank you so much for your cable about Flash (and letters now). I find that I take such things quietly, so long as I don't feel I missed the opportunity to give friends like him or Michael M [Mosley] pleasure while they were alive. The photographs you have just had sound like the men I took at Matruh. I have sent more of Flash since.

I'm trying not to notice bombs, nor to attend to other people's reactions to them. I have never seen any bit of country so pitted with shell holes as this.

22 April 1943, Enfidaville: Letter to Toby

The BBC says this is purely an infantry battle and that was our idea too before it started. We leaguered the night the infantry attacked by the gun line and a Roman wall, and what with the screaming of guns and the mosquitoes got no sleep before moving up to help the infantry at three in the morning. We attacked a bit left of Enfidaville, a very strong position indeed in the mountains. The NZ did very well to get through it, and we moved into the mountains at dawn to protect them against counter attack. Everything was very confused and it was a long time before we realised there was still a lot of enemy behind us, particularly in a village called Takrouna which nestles amongst magnificent crags on a mountain top commanding the pass.

All yesterday and this morning we sat looking on this place and were shelled like hell. This afternoon with a sigh of relief we were relieved and moved back into the plain to do repairs. I don't know what it is about my tank but the moment we moved our new position became the centre of interest. Fortunately I have a deep hole I am sitting in, but it isn't very restful. The Germans and Italians are quite remarkable diggers, wherever they have been you find wonderful dugouts and trenches. We more or less cleared up Takrouna last night when about 300 men surrendered to us; the Italians were parachutists and unusually tough. After the Maoris had established themselves on the top some Italians made their way up again and began throwing grenades into the houses. Two Maoris caught eight of them and threw them down over the crags.

I sat this afternoon in the front of Donny's truck for shade and went through some papers with my orderly room sergeant. The windscreen was holed by a shell earlier. Then I got out and while I was out a particularly unpleasant shell tore a hole in the seat and three in my hat, which it is very questionable whether Corporal Waite will be able to mend as I wasn't wearing it and the shell tore great chunks out of it.

Easter Day, 25 April 1943, Enfidaville

When early this morning they told me Donny had died I remembered how we drove through Enfidaville a few nights ago by moonlight and I looked over a wall into a little churchyard and thought it was almost a pity I hadn't arranged matters so as to land up there. Last night before dark Donny and I drove in the jeep back into Enfidaville to reconnoitre a night move and look at the bronze cock I had noticed [Hildyard family crest]. Just as we got into the town a shell fell in front of us and then another and Donny stopped the car and jumped out saying they were starting to shell the place again. He lay down in the ditch by the side of the road, I got behind a sort of great mobile crane which was standing there. An awful lot of shells came down, on the road and over the hedge all round us and then Donny cried out, hit by what was in fact almost the last shell. He was in a bad way but I could see no wound and when I got from him that it was his legs, no sign there. So I got into the jeep which had suffered a bit and had a flat tyre, and drove back to get a doctor.

By what seemed an extraordinary bit of luck I met our own doctor in someone's car and sent him on while I went for an ambulance, and that reached Donny within quarter of an hour. By the time the doctor reached him he was already delirious. The doctor himself had difficulty in finding the wound which was a small one in the shoulder but the only one. The shrapnel must have turned down after striking his shoulder. He was very soon in hospital and died during the night. It was a great shock to me because I never dreamt he was so bad at all. We buried him in my churchyard with shells whistling gently by overhead, a charming churchyard full of flowers and even a rose bush, surrounded by trees and a wall and distant mountain tops. You, I am afraid, will again be greatly worried about me; it was an unlucky affair, and did me no harm at all. Donny was an extraordinarily nice person whom I greatly enjoyed being with and looked forward to having as a neighbour and I am very sorry. He is a great loss to us here as he had done very well indeed, far better than I'd ever expected, as I thought he was much too rash. Actually he was wise and sensible.

Michael Laycock commands for the present. Whether he will become colonel I don't yet know.

26 April 1943, Enfidaville: Letter to Toby

I can't tell you what the mosquitoes are like here. I should think we are all certain to get malaria. You say you are convinced the Hildyards are fated to survive. I on the other hand thank God every day that contrary to chance so far they have done so. There is only one thing would upset me when a friend was killed – if I felt one might have made better use of one's friendship. For us brothers it has often frightened me a little to see Daddy and his brothers so little anxious to meet, and in the days before I could cope with the situation I could still see that we were likely to grow up and part with the barriers of family not entirely broken. I felt this strongly too about Mummy and Daddy, which is why I have made every effort during the war to repay them by letters for the adolescent pains I most certainly have caused them. We are an unemotional family, too much so. I don't think many brothers could have lived more closely or fondly than you or I, and there was never any question of the place you have always had in my heart, but in a way you were too much part of myself to be seen as a separate person and I believe if we live we can carry our love for one another ever further. I am glad time has toned down your feelings for Chou slightly because I don't think you would find lasting happiness there.

30 April 1943, Hergla, Tunisia

A move and battle tonight have been postponed. We have a new colonel. He knew as little about it as us till yesterday, but Monty wouldn't approve either Michael Laycock or Lawrence Biddle (a Sherwood Ranger who is Brigade Major), so this chap was called for from Robin Maugham's regiment. He is a Viscount Cranley and seems quite nice, young and not impressive to look at, and not popular at school I'm told, but that means nothing. I think he will be OK. We had a French colonel arrive almost at the same time, who only left France six weeks ago, rescued from Clermont Ferrand in a RAF plane. He's a tank expert in their ministry who in 1939 inspected Mareth's potentialities against tank; and he won't speak English. He said he wanted to go away and come back, and asked Michael when he should return – '*Demain or après demain . . . ?*' '*Je suis,*' replied Michael L. On this note of firm understanding they parted.

9 May 1943, Enfidaville

I have so little to do that I frequently listen in to the other regiments on the telephone (they are busy night and day and it drives them mad when I say come and bathe, old boy) and this morning I heard the Brigadier ask another regiment for an officer to go to England to instruct on the Sherman tank! No one knows what is going on, 'we' are in Tunis, the breakthrough of Eighth Army troops on the First Army front has been a complete success, but here the Germans sit on their hill tops and at Pont du Fahs they are still fighting hard.

We now call ourselves the Sherwood Rangers (Notts) Yeomanry, I'm not quite sure why except it's good to move with the times and give other people something to talk about. You said once we weren't so modest, and my you're right. But it is good for the men to think they're in a good regiment, and at the beginning of the war they *couldn't* think that. We consider ourselves superior to the Blues, the Horse Guards or the Greys as soldiers and in smartness. If you could see Cpl Waite starching my clothes for church parade and my three tin boxes and two suitcases full of more clothes and my dressing table covered in bottles and pots – you would honestly think we NEVER fought battles, which is what we want you to think till you notice our medals, all obtained by Flash's and my unusual literary powers.

12 May 1943, Enfidaville

The BBC news has been amazingly up to date lately and you have known everything as fast as ourselves. This afternoon General von Arnem was captured and the Chief of Staff of the General commanding the forces still resisting here at Enfidaville has come down to see General Freyberg. Both before and after the breakthrough to Tunis we have tried to get on here, the last time with a new division and it was very expensive. For two days we have sat back and shelled them all day long with the First Army reporting on the fall of shot from the other side.

The 90 Light Division, our oldest and finest foes, have put up a superb finish and I hope they are allowed to march out with the honours of war. The Italians have in places tried to surrender before and been fired upon by the Germans. Elsewhere, while we have sat here, everyone has rushed around collecting German divisions and to our astonishment there has been no resistance, no evacuation, nothing but complete chaos apparently. I cannot discover any necessity for this complete collapse. The day before yesterday we sent a German into the hills here with the terms of surrender; he was recaptured next morning by some stragglers of ours, sent out again yesterday and returned with a 'last man, last round' message; it really looked like going on for ever. We are permanently on an hour's notice to move which means I can't go bathing. I hope it'll all be over tonight.

And what do you think is the talk in the market places? Of victory after three years, of home and one's dear ones? Oh no, oh dear no, of a coming offensive, of training, of refitting. Let's get on with the job boys . . .

14 May 1943, Enfidaville

This afternoon I climbed Takrouna. There are gun positions among the rocks all the way up and you can see for miles, over every inch that we fought. It seems unassailable. General Freyberg came to say goodbye to us today, and said again that the heights were taken by a Maori sergeant and eight men. There is not much left of the Arab houses, only a mass of telephone wires among mines, the headquarters was cut deep into the rock. We thought there were some 30,000 Germans and Italians in these mountains here; it looks as if we shall take 80,000 prisoners out of them. I do not think anybody understands the collapse. When we broke through to Tunis our general on that front thought it was a trap. The enemy guns surrendered without firing. While we have been continuously fighting we have not had time to meet our reinforcements, they came up and were absorbed automatically.

Our French colonel has left us and we miss him very much. He said many interesting things. We agreed about the Germans, that they are charming. But he said, 'One wolf only has to bark and the pack howls. You must listen always for the bark.' And he said, 'In the morning they are charming to my old mother, midday they get their orders, at night they burn down the house and everybody in it, without hesitation or remorse.' Their efficiency and formality made the ruin of France more unbearable. A woman he said went to a German officer to report that her bicycle had been stolen by one of his men. 'It is not possible,' he said. 'Yes', she said, 'I know where it is.' 'It is not possible, it is against orders,' he said. 'Let me show you,' she said. She took him to a yard, the bicycle was there and five soldiers, the officer said, 'One of you stole this bicycle, which was it?' Four soldiers all pointed to the fifth. Drawing his revolver the officer shot him dead. The woman covered her face in her hands saying, 'If I knew, I would have let him steal everything I had, and said nothing.' My French friend says that we must treat the Germans with the same simplicity, and not cover our faces. When he was asked which was the worst day of the war, he said 11th November 1942 – when Laval and Pétain betrayed to Germany the whole organisation of a new army of 500,000 men which they had allowed to form and arm.

I drove yesterday with some others through Hallouf and Bou Ficha to picnic by the sea below Hammamet. After lunch we slept in the sun. As I stood up to bathe I saw some men on the beach pointing out to sea and looking through my binoculars I saw there was something floating there. It was a drowned man. I walked down to the soldiers by the sea and said, 'Get your officer and spades and arrange to pull out this man who is obviously some poor German, and bury him.' 'Oh no,' they said, 'he is one of ours, he was only drowned quarter of an hour ago.' So I went in and swam back with him. They were all Guards. He was very young. We did artificial respiration for an hour, when a doctor came. We left but it seemed hopeless. It was rather shocking to see his comrades so casual, probably he could easily have been saved. That is the effect of war.

26 May 1943, Hergla, Tunisia

Reading your letters, so practical about wild-cat schemes for rebuilding Flintham, I smile to myself at phrases like, 'covered yourself in glory', 'saved us and the world'. We have set one's hands to the plough and this war must be won or lost, therefore won. But glory. Poof. In a hundred years they will call this a regrettable, an unnecessary, brutal, discreditable war. If we are honourable, we have strange bedfellows. Here at least there is no excitement, we thank God it is over, and make ready for the next. Leave those words to the populace. In this war only individual deeds are glorious.

It is everything to know that one has people who mind how one is. You quite frighten me though, and get me wondering how far I have been affected by all this out here. I am very well, very happy. One lives in the present; that is inevitable when the present is a matter of life and death. I accept things easily, perhaps that is a pity. I care mainly about simple physical things, sunshine, trees, bathing, my own appearance. I am tolerant of other people and though I recognise people of my own outlook when I see them, I am not really anxious to talk to them.

All in all perhaps I have become commonplace. But at the beginning of the war I saw that the solid and the sensible were the salt of the earth and I have recognised that the friends I loved were the Michael Mosleys and Billy Brooksbanks, rather than the Robins and Hughs. To be out of the ordinary is a youthful complaint, tiresome to all and sundry, not making for happiness or success. And really by out of the ordinary I only mean intelligent, and to appear intelligent always was an effort. I am explaining to you that I no longer *have* a language of my own! Nor have I ever had any ambitions or ties very much, nor belief in the future, for myself or for humanity. Therefore war suits me. You need not disturb yourself. Indeed I am sure that I shall never be so contented again. After the war there must be all the struggle which I hate, for money, the decisions which I loathe, the personal contacts which I mismanage.

28 May 1943, Hergla: Letter to Toby

Hey, I take a bloody poor view of that base censor. I can't recall any letter to you which wouldn't lead straight to a concentration camp. It appals me to think of describing the past week on a letter card, so I will answer your letters first. We had rather your idea about tanks to start with, at least we imagined hard shot just bouncing off the armour. The first time the Regiment went into action, on 1st September 1942, against Rommel's 'reconnaissance in strength', it had a rude awakening; a squadron was written off in ten minutes, of which seven tanks blew sky high. Why this happened nobody understood and it has never happened since. But practically speaking if you are hit by hard shot it goes through and it is not a nice thing to have whizzing about inside. German tanks work closed down while we keep our heads out and though generally a tank can only be disabled by HE [high explosives] we do get a lot of casualties from it. For instance when I was hit at El Hamma, Mark Strutt in another tank very close was wounded in the head by a bit of the same shell.

Do you think marriage keeps you young? I never heard that before. There are persistent rumours that Michael P has married his

Ninette and I also hear Charles Parish is missing, believed killed over Germany. We are the last of Eighth Army left up here. I heard someone say today I was terrifically brown. Someone else said I had no stomach at all and as my chest gets bigger and bigger I get more and more vain.

3 June 1943, Hergla

We have a brigade camp up by Tunis which the Colonel and I went to see the other day. As I've told you we like him extremely and he has told me quite a lot about himself, which we can supplement from outside sources. He has done extremely well out here, but before the war was it seems no mean rake. At 17 he ran away from home and went to Australia as fireman on a ship. His father seems a charming old-world person and when our colonel married wrote to him, 'This last and greatest impudence – the decision to people the world with beings as base as yourself.' He married a Dillon, of Ditchley.

Earlier his father wrote, 'Your mother and I hear with the greatest displeasure how your life is spent in a round of dissipations, moving only from restaurants to theatres, and theatres to coffee houses, and coffee houses to brothels, to the utter disgrace of your family.' Our colonel kept these letters in an album and certainly lacks respect for the aged peer. He lived in London with a velvet cage hung from his bedroom ceiling full of doves, with aquariums built into the walls of his dining room framed in old carved picture frames, and with book cases in the library replaced by cages containing live toucans and other strange birds. Our colonel is in fact individual, which is in the tradition of the Regiment.

I took a girl bathing, but the sad thing is that if you do you have to wear a bathing dress and no one can appreciate the *pêche* which I have triumphantly attained all over (to the furious envy of all rivals). It is quite out of the ordinary to take girls bathing and it happened as follows. A few days ago Brigade Headquarters gave a

239

party and I went dressed as usual to kill. I knew the girls from Lady Spear's hospital were going to be there and I wanted to meet one who was a friend of Toby's, but when I heard she had left for England, I refused to be dragged up to any of the others and proceeded to guzzle toffees and rum cocktails in a corner. However eventually the Brigadier absolutely forced me up to one of these girls, and who do you think it was – Biddy Pattinson! So that was rather fun. She is also a great friend (and admirer) of Toby Horsford's. These girls have done most extraordinary things, first they were in Syria, then at Bir Hacheim and Tobruk, and now have followed us up here and mostly they are car drivers who do all the maintenance.

7 June 1943, Hergla: Letter to Toby

Without the pressing possibility of being killed before imparting the latest gossip I am relapsing into a lazy correspondent. I get a great many letters and many of them from you and I answer none of them. I am at the moment debating my answer to Uncle William's latest. I think I told you about Biddy Pattinson. On Sunday when I was out she brought over six bars of chocolate!! There's sex appeal. Last Sunday we had a dance for the men with 100 local beauties laid on, it was dreadfully hot but rather fun and we had a brawl with some South African gate crashers and the Regiment sergeant major got a black eye and I fell for a young American air-force man and brought him in.

Did I suggest people are revolutionary? I don't really think so, they are grumblers at most. Discontented people (and why should soldiers be discontented?) are revolutionary, and over-intelligent people. I am very aristocratic and I know that my position is not threatened by the common people, therefore I am quite in favour of dispossessing the middle classes. I don't know why one's desire to live should decline as danger increases, but I think it does in so far as one comes to accept the inevitability of things. I live in the present with vast enjoyment but I have no real desire to live. I didn't feel flat at all, it was different after Alamein when I knew there had only been half a victory and we were still in the beastly desert. There may still be much ahead but at least the weather is good!

I don't know the Bible at all (Flash knew it by heart). Does it say civilization is a farce? How can one forget the war in five years? I forget battles in five days, but in five years our lives must still be affected by the war. I have not made up my mind yet to a real bid to leave the Regiment, hating decisions as I do. The way to get on in the army is to be very good or very bad; both bring good jobs. I arrange the most beautiful jobs for people we don't want, with promotion and every allowance for the expenses entailed by living in Cairo or New York. Actually, here there is an acute shortage of people who can do the job well.

18 June 1943, Zavia, near Army HQ

We have settled down not far from where we first stopped after Tripoli. This is not our destination but it is where the person Admiral Brom I believe pays court to is going to inspect us. [This was a reference to George VI.] Therefore the rush to get us down here. Michael Laycock is busy practising saluting and bowing at the same time and Patrick is to be cheer-leader. We are distressed because we look like losing Cranley. About the time Flash was killed another regiment with us lost their 2 i/c and their colonel was wounded, now he is on his way back and to their great annoyance and ours there is to be a reshuffle. It is a great pity as C wants to stay and we want him to very much. We have to send in recommendations for promotion every now and again and have just had to do so and I got him to put me in again for the Staff. He wrote after something about Crete, 'He has great character and initiative and has for the last seven months been a first-class adjutant to three successive COs. He is very hard working and would make a very fine squadron leader and with experience CO. He would also do well on the Staff, having previously held the appointment of G3 (1) . . .' You can of course see the drift of this, we are short of decent officers. We actually lost more officers and men than any other armoured unit since Alamein.

23 June 1943, Tripoli

The King got back from Malta on Monday morning and inspected us in the afternoon. We lined the road where we stopped outside Tripoli, he inspected two armoured brigades before our brigade. I stood on Arthur Cranley's right and got a very good view as the car stopped for the King to talk to each colonel. He looked very smart, white and agonised, and asked Cranley the same question twice, after a pause during which he failed to think of another one, and looked miserably at me for help. I discovered later that whenever he got a chance to get out of the car he made straight for the end of the passage, disregarding marquees, flowers and refreshments. He had *very* bad gippy tummy. Poor man. He asked everybody how long they'd been out here and of course Cranley only came out 18 months ago, but to Basil Ringrose when he heard he'd been out three and a half years he said, 'Oh *dear*! Take a note of that, General Montgomery!' Monty was sitting next the driver looking as sour as a quince because nobody was looking at him.

I took Flash's despatch case over to the C-in-C's camp where the King slept the night and his equerry took it back for Myrtie in their plane. Monday was packed with excitement. The same evening I went to a party given to welcome to Tripoli Vivien Leigh, Beatrice Lillie, Dorothy Dickson, Leslie Henson and other personages. It was a fairly grand party and Patrick and I waited till all the generals were merry and then began fearful intrigues to get Cranley left with us. It is still too early to say whether anything will come of our efforts but Cranley meanwhile has gone, and been succeeded by Ian Spence, to our great annoyance. The whole thing is too complicated to be worth explaining. There are some delicious rumours in high circles about returning home. They make it even more difficult for me to know how to plan my own future. The fact is that if you sent home the few remaining original officers the Regiment would cease to function.

9 July 1943, Tripoli: Letter to Toby

I was very relieved to hear from you again as I was afraid you had fallen from a precipice. Your letter arrived just as I was leaving for a night in Tripoli. It was the hottest day I've ever known. Toby Horsford and I shared a bathroom where we sat and drank gin and at the end of dinner when they turned the lights out the dining room turned over once and settled down on its side. I spent the rest of the evening sitting at the feet of Bee Lillie, only to see her give her green snake-skin tarbrush at the end to Toby. Next morning I took Vivien Leigh bathing – she looked cute sitting in the front seat of my 15 cwt truck! In Tripoli I went to the market to buy sweetcorn and melons and bought instead a tiny gazelle called Bambino which is completely tame and very beautiful and sits under a bush all day by my truck. It is theoretically a good life at the moment but I find myself only medianly cheerful – which is quite normal really in wartime.

Toby and I collected a lot of marble lapis lazuli mosaic stones from the shingle near Leptis to make a bracelet for Bee Lillie, who wrote him a farewell letter saying she adored him. Vivien Leigh blubbed all night before leaving and asked me to write a poem for her to recite in Gib. Some ass had told her I was a poet.

21 August 1943, Tripoli: Letter to Toby

I am what is called G3(1) i.e. Staff Officer Grade Three Intelligence, which is the head intelligence officer in a division. I have an IO with me who is Martin Lindsay and a photograph interpreter, both captains. After turning over various possibilities for my future for a long time I was suddenly asked for here, which settled it quite satisfactorily. When it came to it I was extremely sad to leave the Regiment. Life was dull there and was going to go on being so, but I had a big position, and I hate changes. Becoming G3(1) meant going to the same job as I had at 10 Armoured Division. last November when I left them at Matruh, i.e. losing all the way I had made in the fighting, and starting again, as a staff officer. However, I am enjoying my work enormously. G3(1) is a good job because you are entirely your own master. At the moment there is a very great deal of work which I find intensely interesting and I sit all day inside a wire fence with a guard on.

I have however one great misery which is that Corporal Waite my famous batman hates it and I shall only keep him while we are here. For one thing his being a corporal makes it very difficult to take him, and for another he doesn't really want to leave the Regiment where he never has to do anything so *infra dig* as guards or driving or anything rough and tumble. I try and cheer myself up by saying it will be good practice for after the armistice, and that soon I shall be wearing a fur coat and no one will see if my shirts aren't clean (at present I have everything cleaned and starched twice a day). It is very sad. All in all I think it is a good move, I am excited about it all.

7 September 1943, Tripoli

As you say, one can't put off invasion hoping Italy will collapse. Maisky was in Cairo when Pat McCraith was there, saying that if we could draw off 60 divisions the war would be over by Christmas. But if Italy were to give up, Germany would probably still fight there, so they have very little to gain by annoying Germany and very little to lose by remaining nominally in the war.

Myrtie has written saying she is selling all Flash's clothes that I don't want. It is difficult to say what I might want not seeing them and I have suggested but only half seriously that she has them valued and I buy everything except riding boots. His things fit me extremely well and of course he had very beautiful things always. It may be a matter of Mummy going to look if she could ever get to London; it is all rather uncomfortable, though it shouldn't be, as I expect Flash would have preferred his friends to have them. But I'd want to pay for anything.

13 September 1943, Tripoli

I dined with Arthur Cranley last night, he has a madness for 'nigger parties' and at the sound of distant merry-making flies out into the night, falling down wells. Last night there was a great moon and a party quite close, outside an Arab tent, it was a party celebrating a wedding which had taken place four days before. The men sat on the ground in a circle just away from a fire of palm fronds, every now a poke at it sent up a flame which flood lit some incredible figure, immobile, toga like, stick in hand, or cringing, in rags. Over the fire they heated their tambourines and they sang long songs to these and their plaintive pipes, double horns. A man Arthur called a 'Sidiman', a holy man, began swaying in the circle, they brought a brazier of charcoal and some herbs and everyone smelt it, first he and then the others began dancing drunkenly on one foot and the other, flinging their arms around, wrapped in their white cloaks. Meanwhile a small sickle had been heated red hot in the fire, one of the dancers took it and put it in his mouth, dancing with it red hot between his teeth. Others did this and others bared their bellies and stuck the sickle through folds of their flesh, I think, but it was hard to see as they crumpled on the ground as they did so. It seemed a painful operation and the brazier was held to their nostrils to encourage them. And where blood has been drawn in this way another would clasp the man and suck it. A father led a boy up to the sidiman and the sidiman sat on him. Afterwards the boy lay on his face and the sidiman kneaded him and lay on him either intoning into his ear or biting it. Then the boy got up and returned to his father and later it was done to three grown men at once. It was all beautifully fantastic under the palms in the moonlight. It is thought that these men are dervishes and nothing to do with Mohammed, they mention the names of saints, some sound Jewish, 'sidi Jacob', it is thought also that the Italians probably forbade the

245

practice and it is only just starting up again, and that it is only old men mostly because the young have been taught to despise it. At midnight they went to bed. The bints, the women, stayed all the time inside the tent.

13 September 1943, Tripoli: Letter to Father

I got your letter yesterday telling me you had put in to resign, and I do think that is extremely wise, though of course I don't like to hear Dr Kinmont thinks so too. I do hope it is allowed before the winter. I hope the news is doing you good. It is a bit confusing in Italy still but all in all very satisfactory and I really think we should be in a position to get home on leave at least next spring.

If after this war I settle down at Flintham and live an exemplary bucolic life, and there is another war (as appears inevitable), I should certainly say that I was severely to blame for it. That would not prevent my taking no part in affairs, which is a question of weighing personal contentment against certain disappointment, but I would admit that I could have done more and that since I didn't and left it to a few men in whom I had no great confidence, they now have the right to send me or my children to be killed. That our Foreign Office before the war was absolutely useless I have never heard denied by anyone who knew Europe at all. However, after this war things are going to be so much worse, there will be so much hatred, distress, misunderstanding, disagreement, that I can only see high-handed action by the major powers leading to eventual war between those powers, or immediate chaos. In the next war with luck I shall be in the home guard.

16 September 1943, Tripoli

In the end I gave Bambino [the gazelle] to the Mucktah of Souk-el-Khameis. He is a nice man who brought him food regularly every evening, and swore he didn't want to eat Bambino but keep him like

246

a son in memory of me, and I should bring my soldiers back next year in order that I might see how Bambino would be flourishing.

Our area was spotless – and typical of a good regiment that they should leave a bit of sand dune without a hole or a bit of paper, the joke being that as soon as you go the Arabs dig up every one of your buried dumps; and in fact next morning when Division left our area, far from equally clean, an army of Arabs swept down on it as though the legions had withdrawn. My last night there I went to see George Formby at Leptis, he is a man very popular with the troops, a rather Edwardian banjo-strumming figure but he makes them roar. Half an hour before it started the theatre was full, over 6,000, and soldiers were being turned away. I sat on a column behind the stage with a 20-foot drop and looked up at the half circle thick with soldiers. There was a girl first who played for the men to sing and it sounded very fine and Hollywood, with the footlights lighting up the ruins behind us and the moon rising over the capitals, and a thousand little cigarette ends glowing in the towering black mass.

21 September 1943, At Sea

It is eleven in the morning and I have just put on a pullover, which is an unusual thing to do, and a sign of my change of address. There is a bluish white sky, quite killed by the sea and, in very faint outline only one shade darker than the misty horizon but very large indeed, Mt Etna. It is absolutely calm and the news is fine and I have quite a good American book and won 50/- at poker last night. We are incredibly comfortable. The first day on board in the harbour I of course stayed off till the last possible minute, bathing and lunching on shore and thinking it would be dreadful on board. When I did go on in time for dinner we had roast chicken with bread sauce and potatoes in their skins, followed by sponge cake, strawberries and ice-cream, and coffee and *all* the crew of 75 had the same. The British soldiers had bully beef.

The American officers are very nice and friendly and very quiet. None of them were in the navy before the war but so far as one can judge, and one never can judge outside one's own country, they are of a better type than one would find of ours in this sort of ship. We have nice cabins, there are very good washrooms, the only stupid thing is that no room has a porthole so that all the ventilation is internal and not very good. All the jugs and things are very heavy and nice-looking silver; they make delicious bread rolls and there's butter!

The mountains in Sicily seemed terrific as we got into the straits of Messina, the sea dark blue and silver, the toe of Italy rather tawny. It is very beautiful going through, the mountains a mossy colour. With glasses you can see they are cultivated high up and there are enchanting grey villages, one with a baroque church and ruined castle on the mountain side, lost in a mist as we passed. The toe became more mountainous and Sicily less so as we went on but both are all mountains, the mainland less rugged, a bluish high plateau and red-roofed houses along the sea, Reggio all pink and Messina grey with churches and towers. It seemed to get greener, and on the mainland very broad, steep, dry river beds ran down to the sea. We passed Scylla and Charybdis, and the sun set behind Stromboli and the Sirens, Stromboli a strange volcanic peak rising out of the sea.

26 September 1943, Salerno, Italy

The Sirens did not let us pass scot-free. At four in the morning smoke was seen coming up a hatchway, something was burning down below. Of course it was my ACV [armoured command vehicle]. It was directly under a hatch and they pumped water over it until the hold was three feet deep. The fire was put out before the petrol and oil caught, if they had burst and spread over the water there would have been a fine blaze. As it was, the inside of the ACV, all cased in steel, pretty well burnt itself out. On the roof was my tin box full of winter clothes and a big leather saddle bag which had one side burnt off it. Inside were all my business things and my books and my small attaché case. The books in a wooden box were only singed and soaked, those loose were destroyed.

The bay was packed with cruisers, destroyers and assault ships and we ran on to the beach at Salerno and were driving off in no time. I went almost straight to a conference on the next day's operation. However it was an optimistic conference and next afternoon I was able to go to Paestum. Salerno was the most completely wrecked town I ever saw. All German prisoners say that our artillery is far more devastating than anything at Stalingrad, heavier and more accurate.

27 September 1943, Amalfi

After a magnificent display of molten gold behind purple clouds and mountains, the sun has set a furious red, and I am cross too because I stayed in all day expecting a battle instead of exploring. Yesterday the noise of the guns was enough to drive anyone crackers and we fled north under shells. It is a wonderful coast, mountains falling all the way steeply to the sea with ravines, stone walls and narrow terraces carrying pergolas of vines and oranges and enormous lemons and heavenly villages above little coves, and the road never runs straight for 50 yards. Our bridge had been under shellfire which has knocked the parapet away both sides, a cruiser lying off in the bay was firing over our heads still.

Amalfi is a small place and no hotels or modernities to spoil it, just a small bay and houses running inland up a gorge and crags up both sides. In the centre is a square with a fountain of St Andrew holding wooden fish and fresh flowers in his arms. A steep broad flight of steps leads up to the cathedral which has a lovely square campanile topped by five cupolas but a rather ugly façade in the 19th-century Florentine style. In a crypt, whose walls were entirely covered with marble and under an altar terrifically embellished by Philip II, are the bones of St Andrew brought there from Constantinople. The people are poor and short of food, they have an attractive line in blue trousers. Only the very young are attractive but some of them are beautiful. When we left the sea was a cloudy pink and every spur dark against silver. It gets dark very early now. Tonight it is pouring which is rather distressing as I burnt my tents.

2 October 1943, near Naples

We moved up the coast this morning. All the way the streets were lined with cheering people who believe that we carry lorries loaded not with petrol and shells but with bread. The Germans demolished everything systematically as they withdrew, destroying village water supplies, electricity etc., and blocking streets with blown houses. Coupled with the effects of our bombing, Italy is not prosperous. It makes our progress abominably slow as side roads are mere tracks and sticky from the rain and it is all very different from the desert. I am a little ashamed of myself moving from village to village while my friends sleep in ditches in the rain.

Here tonight we are in a hamlet with a pilgrimage church with a very holy and miraculous picture of the Virgin and child, much older than the church and covered except for the faces in gold. Everyone has given pictures of their cures and these cover the walls up to the vaulting and even the pillars. It is a big church with a Benedictine monastery and splendid monks in black and white who asked in Latin whether we were 7 Armoured Division and have erected an altar covered in damask in their large theatre (which reeks of wine) for our services tomorrow. I joined in a choir practice there tonight by candlelight.

I may go into Naples to see if the museum is open but I am told the town is very disappointing. There was quite a lot of street fighting, Italians versus Germans, before we arrived. The Germans are killing women after they have already suffered a fate worse than death; I dare say they are fairly browned off with the Italians. Yesterday we brought down one church tower and put a shell straight through another, suspected enemy observation points. Splendid war.

24 October 1943, near Naples

Life has been made tedious lately by two interpreters sent to me, one a marchese air pilot who spoke very little English, the other a middle-aged duke. My marchese is Carlo Capece Minutulo, Marchese di Buguano. His family also refaced the façade of the cathedral which has his coat of arms on the bronze doors. The duke gave me a small picture from his flat. This is really rather nice and they are trying to help, but dumped on one in natty suits rather a liability, and not popular among some of my bone-headed companions in the mess.

My duke was thrilled when the ice creamers declared war. Personally I consider it the final degradation and I don't see how it helps us, though no doubt by the end of the war we shall have forgotten they ever kept us four years in the desert.

27 October 1943, near Naples

I never told you about Pompeii. From the road you climb a bit up to it. You never get the impression that it has been excavated. It is a walled town, with gates, the main one the sea gate towards the bay. This with the museum alongside and practically every building in the place had had direct hits by bombs. As a result the place has rather a natural ruinous appearance, increased by the weeds in the pavements and grass in open places. After Africa the main monuments are unimportant though together they are very interesting, and some very early, Greek. The streets are very straight, lined with roofless buildings. Mostly the buildings are of brick and rubble, plastered over, even columns, though this applies more to the later Roman buildings which must have been the ideal of Mr Nash. Vesuvius with its plume looks down on the town, which is itself above the plain.

All this is interesting, but the paintings are astonishing. Their preservation is quite extraordinary. Many of the best villas have been re-roofed and it is impossible to believe that they are earlier

251

than the 17th century AD. Their plan is always the same, an atrium, sometimes very large and high, with a roof sloping inwards and open in the centre with a pool to catch the rain water below. There are rooms round this then the peristylium, a colonnaded garden with rooms off it. These rooms are all painted, not in thin wash like medieval frescoes, but in thick brushwork, and often the walls are as polished as marble, so that it has the effect of lacquer, with its rich colours, frequently black or crimson. The feeling for perspective and spacing is extraordinary, there are delicious little amorini, Egyptian gods, birds, flowers, parakeets, walnuts, poles wreathed in ivy, all so 18th century it is amazing. Outside the wall with its square towers are villas still surrounded by vines, and oleanders, and very complete down to the wine presses, exactly the same as the Arabs use in North Africa today – a huge tree trunk levered up and down and the juice runs from the floor into great amphora outside.

Actually, though one might not think it at the rate things go here, I really believe the war will be over next year. It is about this time of year I become optimistic and decide I may be with you for my birthday [December]. I went yesterday to the Elysian fields, which are very middling, and to the mouth of Hell. West of Naples is a peninsula entirely made up of extinct volcanic craters, many of them filled with water, and the coast line the same, extremely broken. Lake Lucrinus, which was then famous for its oysters, is only separated from the sea by a strip of land and the road runs from it to Lake Avernus down a canal which Agrippa built to turn Avernus into an inland harbour. Up till the time of Augustus Avernus was regarded as the mouth of Hell. It has a steep crater rim all round it which was covered in trees then and the story was no bird could fly across. Very likely it was still faintly volcanic and bubbled. Agrippa also built a tunnel a mile long from the lake to Cumae which we drove into but it was blocked by oil drums.

The main base of the Roman fleet was Miseno Bay, also joined by a canal to an inland sea called Mare Morto, all old craters. Cape Miseno which is a very high spit was the Elysian fields. We had an exhausting but superb climb over it, you could see both Ischia Capua and Sorrento, but it's not much of a playground as there's not a level bit on it and the mosquitoes were bad. Cumae was the first Greek colony of all; Odysseus of course spent some time in these parts and Aeneas consulted the Sibyl there and it is certainly a curious part of the world and very attractive. What a war.

25 November 1943, Sorrento: Letter to Toby

I am afraid our letter writing has fallen off, which I take to be a good sign on both sides. I am behaving very badly and writing daily to something pretty staggering in Toby's outfit [11th Hussars]. However that is quite interesting as it really is very staggering indeed, and not only not at all out of hand but really I think platonic, a change after Chisholm. It is a double blue, 21, extremely good on books and art and quite fantastic to look at and I am certain you would like it as much as I do.

I forget whether I have written since we moved to the most beautiful country probably in Europe. We have actually taken over a small hotel on a cliff above the sea with mountains all round and the vines and trees the most beautiful colour. I haven't been to Capua yet as I have waited for Toby and others in that outfit to be free, but I hope to go soon for several nights. Unfortunately the Americans have taken over all the islands and good hotels here, adding insult to the injury which prevents my lying with my hair on Greta's chest at the moment.

Of course I don't charge around in a tank. HQ is the safest place alive. We sit in byres and barns well behind. However I am already wishing I was with a regiment again as I think it rather undignified to be so safe. In any case, if I could be sure of a nice clean job I am in favour of dying for King and Country as the future seems so tiresomely complicated. Arthur Cranley wants me to try and get into parliament with him. Anglo-Italian relations are really very interesting and not at all satisfactory, particularly with all Europe watching. My Neapolitan friends are very smooth, nice really with lustrous names, but very woppish. I still can't talk one word which is a handicap but I feel tuned in to begin.

I am extremely glad that things are brightening socially your end. We have a dance next week here, I am doing the decor. Forty nurses are laid on and will obviously get their great hoofs entangled in my trailing vines.

3 December 1943, Sorrento

I did something which I haven't heard of anyone else doing since we've been here, which was climb the cone and look down into the volcano. The whole thing is exciting and the greatest fun. You can drive up as far as the base of the crater, which is Mount Vesuvius, the rest being Mount Somma, and you climb up loose shingly sort of stuff with some lava streams overflowing from the crater lip in great writhing black masses. Over the lip of the crater it is flat with lava like gollops of copper-coloured frozen treacle, and in the middle is a great slag heap, all smoking, which is the final cone. The whole thing is vastly hellish. The lava round the cone is piled up in great writhing masses and in a few places which change every day it is hot in the cracks and there are Italians there who make things out of the lava, ashtrays etc., but the rest is cool but pouring out smoke.

From the country, the volcano seems to smoke all the time, but in fact it throws up about every half minute red hot lumps most of which fall back again inside the cone and the rest on to the cone which is how it is formed. Yesterday a great puff of smoke went up at intervals in a great pillar, and ended up in a wreath which cleared like a St Catherine's wheel, till a ring as clean and bright as an electric sign was left up in the sky. Quite by chance we hit on an Italian who said we could climb right up so long as we watched the stuff thrown up and side stepped, the guides wouldn't go, so we went up with him. It is very cloudy near the top and you suddenly find yourself on the edge and there is the inside of the volcano all red hot. It is quite narrow, only about 20 feet across at most. One big bit very nearly hit us but it was worth it.

The day before yesterday we had our dance, and I was frightfully busy doing the decorations which were very successful in the end. The *pièce de résistance* was the staircase where I had in a window embrasure a black column with a black bowl of marigolds on it and on a platform in the middle of the staircase, a jungle of branches and some red autumn ones hanging over – found in the mountains with great difficulty. The dance was a success, not quite enough girls arrived and of my two guests one got hopelessly drunk. I danced with one girl only, she was really quite pretty and said I looked like some Australian which was poor taste. I am worse with girls than you'd think possible and enquire with elaborate charm after their old parents and how they like the countryside, it must be dreadful for them. Far from *grande toilette de bal* they were in battledress trousers, being from Nanny's part of the world [Canada] and had to swim for it recently.

The autumn colours are startlingly lovely here and the light effects often wonderful. On a dark day you suddenly get gold clouds pouring over and down a blacker mountain top, or Vesuvius across the sea all in sunshine. When it all is sunny it is merely paradise. Not that one is often really happy, my nicest friends less than most people, human nature being what it is and very muddle headed.

After this, I had a month's leave at home for the first time since I left England with the horses in January 1940. 7 Armoured Division Headquarters was at Didlington Hall in Norfolk, but I was sent to work in London on planning the invasion.

11 February 1944, 47 Morpeth Mansions, London SW1

I have just had a colossal lunch at Claridge's given by Robin for this most awful man in very secret intelligence. Billy [Maclean] was late and I went up to rescue him from Mrs Maclean who was sitting in a fireless drawing room in her suite looking furious. When we left her, lunch laid for one was wheeled in. In between times she was boring and tiresome, and we asked one another as we went downstairs whether she was mad or why she was so awful.

Billy goes back to Cairo in ten days, to his misery, but also I think to further success and importance. I don't know anybody who has had such a sudden success since I went off for Alamein leaving him a jobless lieutenant. Last night I had dinner with Myrtie at Boulestin's which wasn't very good and hell to get away from. And in the end I boarded an underground at Paddington which bedded down at South Kensington, a most out of the way place. I can walk from here to Claridge's which is a great thing, but South Kensington is too much!

18 February 1944, London

Apparently I had a very great success with Harold Nicolson, who has asked me to dinner, but I'm not sure he isn't rather a silly man. On Tuesday night I dined at Lambeth. Uncle William and Frances [his wife and my second cousin] were alone and were quite as nice as ever. They asked about everything and everybody during dinner, and afterwards I sat in Uncle William's study and he talked about politics and things, which was what I wanted so as to get an idea how he felt. As I should like to keep well in with them and as I am bad at judging how well I have gone down with people, I think you might write and say you hear I'd been there and been very grateful to Uncle William for giving up an entire evening, and see what they answer.

24 February 1944, London

Mr de Courcy lives with his mother, and the only other guest was the Swedish minister, a charming man and ex-international industrialist, who came on from the Soviet Embassy party. He said everybody was there and Monty was holding court with lovely girls fingering his medals and ADCs holding back the throng. The Soviets were wearing their new uniforms for the first time, covered in gold braid while everyone else wore ordinary clothes. Mrs de

Courcy is very religious and started dinner with a terrific grace, there was a butler and footman and excellent burgundy and port. The house was quite crowded with black spaniels, everything in it the most expensive sort of furniture – tapestries and portraits by Lely – they have seven servants there and a house in Leicestershire they find too small which sends up butter etc. They seemed to be rolling and I'd like to know how! But I liked de Courcy very much and stayed talking with him till one o'clock this morning, long after the minister had gone in the middle of an air raid which scared his chauffeur into fits.

The two of them said a lot of very interesting things, de Courcy for instance thinks that historically we shall be criticised for our pledges to Europe which we couldn't carry out, so bringing unnecessary misery to various countries. He compares the 1938–9 situation to Walsingham and Burghley when Walsingham wanted us to fight in Europe and instead we waited to be attacked, and again with Marlborough where we did fight in Europe and failed to achieve our aims. He thinks we could have let Germany overrun Europe and stood on the Middle East and that Germany would have found Europe insufficient and had to fight us on our own ground and been beaten off, and then forced by us to review the situation inside Europe. There is something in this but I'm not sure they would have failed, after five years building up in Europe. The Minister said that Eden told him personally later, and that it was a conviction of the government, that our entry into Greece saved Russia.

I think de Courcy's honest and I agreed with his ideas, but I must find out more about him. He doesn't think much of Uncle William, who he thinks needs a Salvation Army conversion; he approves of the Bishop of Chichester; he loathes Harold Nicolson!

26 February 1944, London

Myrtie has just asked me whether you might know of anyone in the village who would take in the two small girls (nine and seven) of a

SRY soldier from Battersea. I believe a lot of people are evacuating London; at least, you can get seats at the theatres. Most people seem to be minding it much more, they say, than the real Blitz, but I expect they'll get used to it. Lady Maugham's cook for instance can't face it this time, which is sad as she makes such good pud. Lady Maugham loves it and insisted on going out last night after dinner to see the square all lit up by a fire in Pont Street. Both Spinks and Partridges, the antique shops, are flat and God knows what in them. I haven't been to see the damage in that part of the world, or indeed anywhere, but you hardly hear any bombs come down. It is not at all terrifying so far.

At dinner last night the Maughams had Bertrand Thomas, the Arabian explorer, who has just been appointed head of the 'Arab Centre' which is to be started in Jerusalem and of which Robin was one of the originators. He didn't think you'd ever get an Arab Federation further than an offensive combination on points of foreign policy.

Lady Maugham wants a photograph of me but I don't think I've got a tolerable one, have I?

29 February 1944, London

I dined with Harold Nicolson last night at Boulestin's and he also had a very recherché-looking man called Jim Lees-Milne, who is secretary to the National Trust. He had spent the day salvaging books at the London Library where the new wing had been destroyed and he thought some 15,000 books lost. Near where he lived in Chelsea he had helped clear some ruins and he said he found the women much tougher. They'd say, 'Now don't be such an ass, anyone can see that hand doesn't belong to that arm over there, why look at the index finger, you see, it's long and *that* one's short . . .'

Harold N told us what Proust used to say to him, and what George Moore and Henry James said when they met for the first time at a house party, and about Virginia Woolf. Lees-Milne has been to lunch and tea this week with Bernard Shaw who wants to leave his awful villa to the nation which does contain all his manuscripts, but all he pointed out were fake Queen Anne bureaux and how much he paid for them. He said Shaw must be rather mad because he has quite a bit of money and he proposes to leave it all to start a new alphabet of 140 letters which he says will certainly be very popular in this country because in a generation its use will save the country sufficient money to finance three international wars. Then this Lees-Milne turned to me and said, 'I read and was very impressed with something of yours.' Of course I said I'm afraid you're making a mistake, but funnily enough he had read my diary.

After dinner we went to Harold N's rooms in the Temple, King's Bench Walk. It was moonlight and most beautiful and we looked at the old bomb damage – which of course looked rather good in that light, but is frightful. He, Harold, is a governor of the BBC. He said that at the last meeting there was quite an attack on the National Trust for protecting mouldering manor houses of the mildewed landed gentry. Stupid, but one of them, the blind Sir Ian Fraser, tried to describe Byron to the board – talking of artists whose private lives need not prevent an interest in their work – as 'that peer who was eaten by sharks off the coast of Italy about 50 years ago'.

25 March 1944, Didlington, Norfolk: Letter to Toby

Six weeks ago I finished my month's leave at Flintham, and have been in London ever since, till today when I am in Norfolk for two nights. One of the other things I did was to take from Chris [Hildyard] the picture he painted of you all in brown and put it in my office. This I thought would guarantee my writing to you as I'd so shamelessly failed to do from Flintham. Far from it. I dined out every night and generally lunched out too, and I never wrote letters or stuck in my photographs which I took to Chris's for a quiet evening that never came. I am sorry though that I haven't written, because if you are like me, which you aren't fortunately, you would give great meaning to it and think that I was not thinking of you, which would be very far from true.

I adored being in London, I have never felt so well, and I'm afraid it did me far more good than being at Flintham. Because, of course, what one needs after the isolation of soldiering abroad is gaiety and talk and I was no end depressed when I got back. It's the awful periods of sitting doing nothing which get one down, which we did after Tunis, and I was gloomier and gloomier in Italy even though I was amusing myself very well, and quite suicidal by the time we got home. Very silly, anyway I feel very different now. At first in London I was very idle, but lately I have worked very hard in office hours, though I have still been dining out always. I am completely my own master, which is the great point of a job which I am beginning to feel is rather a disgrace when all my friends are colonels. I do think you've done well [Toby had been appointed Wing Commander]. But really you *should* come home. I think it is a mistake to stay out there and hell what your rank is.

Really England is extremely unaltered by the war. There were air raids while I was in London and I'm sure they weren't anything to compare with the Blitz, but they disturbed people quite a lot. You never heard a bomb only our own rockets going up. Billy Maclean was staying at Claridge's till a week ago when he went back to Cairo to be a colonel. He had been seven months in Albania and now in London was living a most exhausting gay life, getting up in time for lunch and going to bed at five o'clock, very immersed in girls and eating with royalty and visiting Mr Eden and the Bag o' Nails [a brothel]. He is as fresh and unspoilt as ever and very intelligent.

I asked Spenny's wife, the Polish Maria, to Claridge's for a drink and she was very pretty and attractive, but I'm afraid I never did anything more about it as I never took girls out and don't know how to. I did give Dotty Groome dinner once and was quite ill with boredom though she's a nice girl and as for Beryl Bruce she rings up perpetually and sends me Mars Bars and I am perfectly bloody. I see Myrtie, Flash Kellett's widow, quite a lot, but she is much older of course and no trouble. I am lunching with Virginia Brett when I go down to London for a night in a couple of days' time, which will be interesting.

I like playing round with politicians and dine sometimes with the very curious Kenneth de Courcy who lives surrounded by footmen in Eaton Place and generally asks one other person only, an ambassador or Lord Londonderry once or a Field Marshal last time, a very old one, and I've dined several times with Harold Nicholson who knows intelligent young men. I didn't do half the things I meant to, go to Eton or to stay with the Mosleys or the Parishes. I went to Lambeth twice and they were as sweet as ever but Uncle William is not good at talking religion, which I always want to ask about.

Tell you a good joke, I've had myself put up for The Cavalry Club.

6 May 1944, Didlington: Letter to Toby, RAF Ceylon

In the middle of April I went to London for an investiture and induced Mummy to stay with me at Flemings Hotel in Half Moon Street, where she had her first air raid. The investiture was a deadly show except the beefeaters were rather nice, however Mummy enjoyed it. Before we filed in Admiral Bromley told us how to conduct ourselves on approaching the Presence, who stood on a dais in the middle of a long room crowded with friends and relatives. One moved along in a long line gazing nonchalantly at the pictures while a band played sacrificially. As I arrived on the dais old ankipops [Ancaster, Lord Great Chamberlain], John Willoughby's pa, whispered in the sovereign's ear and so when I'd made a bow and taken a step smartly forward to bring me within one inch of the Presence (in order not to exhaust his arm) he said mumble, mumble, mumble, mumble. Just as I was wondering what the hell to do he said 'Where were you made a prisoner?' So that was splendid and we got the whole thing properly straightened out before I'd gone.

This has been a most glorious spring; I don't remember anything like it before. I have been most frightfully lucky in this place in Norfolk. I was at Flintham for a week over Easter; Jimmy Burridge came to stay just for Easter. This place is I am afraid more beautiful than Flintham and one of the nicest things is a green lane whose hedges are all great bushes of blossoming trees and shrubs. The lake comes within 100 yards of the house and is broken up into many pools and stretches overhung by magnificent beeches and the birds are quite astonishing. Thirty-six different kinds have been recognised, not by me as I can't tell one song from another, and by the time I've taken off my glasses and organised my binoculars the tiny sweet has generally flogged on. There are little dykes everywhere here as it is boggy sort of country; there is no real park, only poor pasture between woods; but it's all rough and wild and most attractive. I had quite the wrong idea of Norfolk, which I had always imagined flat and arable like Lincolnshire. Instead it is rolling with a lot of trees and little streams and very winding roads and old churches often with round towers.

I am busy but in my own way, which in London meant three hours for lunch and dinner out, and here means reading very secret papers with my back to a tree and going to sleep. I am beginning to wonder whether reading isn't a dangerous and idle habit and a dope which instead of sharpening my intelligence allows me not to think for myself at all. I get very depressed about myself. I have just been mentioned in despatches which means you wear a bronze oak leaf after your medals, but as I recommended myself for it a year ago after Tunis when I was adjutant it's a wee bit bogus! I do enjoy the country quite enormously and I regard the invasion with the greatest equanimity and even with pleasure as another sightseeing tour. I shouldn't though if I was still in a tank. You seem a bit hazy about what I am doing; it's the same as Italy, in the headquarters, running the intelligence which is a very free and pleasant job though not very responsible. I went up in a Mosquito just before I cabled to you for your birthday, they fly very low and turn sideways in a nasty way and I was sick three times, too shaming.

*   *   *

There follow extracts from the journal I kept, leading up to, through and following the D Day Landings, interspersed with the few letters I wrote at this time.

19 April 1944

When I drive in a taxi through the streets or when I walk across the park and old men smile approvingly at me, thinking no doubt 'well set up young officer', I do realise what a wretched fellow I am to find respite from incessant self torture only in sunshine and nature, when these people work all day in electric light and only get out to go home to untidy, uncomfortable houses, not Half Moon Street. But then what do I want? Do I want to be sensitive or don't I, or do I curse myself for being both. I could not write poetry, for a dozen reasons. I am a whirlpool, I dream and turn out nothing.

Look at this railway carriage which is making writing difficult, two other men and three women, all sitting, silent, looking out of the window at factory yards. They must be thinking something, God knows what. I find it difficult to think. Therefore, searching for ready-made conclusions, I read. Have they any doubts, these five poorly favoured folk who have no business in a first-class carriage? No. No – because they are unimaginative, fulfilled, happy, stupid, resigned – what? I am in a miserable state. I have excellent health, a happy and stable family, a sufficiency of money, some good friends including Jimmy, who has the added charm of novelty and I must add uncertainty. I am treated as worth entertaining by intelligent men like Harold N and Kenneth de Courcy, I am Robin's greatest friend. I might easily say that I have an excellent job, a job which has given one six weeks in London, and so much freedom, idleness, comparative safety, but it may be a root of trouble. I am free but without responsibility, unconvinced of its importance, inactive. It suits me too well. I like bustle and orders and short periods of great busyness. I have no interest in women. Toby Horsford is already longing to escape to France and I really don't want to be indulging in such complications, nor to be married, but that supplies a vital interest, coupled with his belief that sooner or later round the corner there lurks something really good. I have no hopes. This obvious sequence to homosexuality could have been foreseen by anybody who thought at all.

Jimmy in his diary, which he has left with me and which is a most revealing work, notes exactly and reviles his own weaknesses. It is years now since in a slough of inferiority complexity I drew up a list of the good and bad points in my character. Now I should have to think carefully in order to list them. Quite wrongly I feel I am formed. Wrongly because I am unhappy and therefore can only be mis-formed and that wants correcting.

4 June 1944

Wrote to Michael Parish, Micky Riviere, Sidney Morse, Dawyck Haig, all POW and on my conscience for months. Windy, and heard that operation postponed 24 hours, however no alteration in move down to ships. We left Warley Barracks after tea. Long stream of lorries on the road, a few children waving. At Tilbury nothing out of the ordinary, ferryboats were taking civilians on normal trips from the same pier and shiploads of soldiers out to the MT Ships lying off in the river. At the entrance we were asked for our tickets!

Dined on 'assorted cold meats' in the first-class dining room, which was empty and quiet, as all our money is in francs and we have difficulty in raking up enough. Wind only increasing. Got on board [*Liberty Ship*] about ten o'clock. My ACV is on deck which is a great thing and gives me a comfortable place to sit, as the ship is hell. You go down steps into a hold crowded with men lying on the floor and very noisy and across this is a bit with hammocks in four tiers.

5 June 1944

The assault should have been at seven this morning. The wind is if anything stronger, and though it was sunny early it soon clouded over.

We didn't know whether there has been another 24 hours' postponement. At 12.30 we moved up the river to Southend and anchored in the middle of a host of shipping of all sorts. Rome has fallen to the Allies and the wireless describes the enthusiasm of the populace.

6 June 1944

The invasion was launched at seven o'clock this morning. The Germans announced parachute landings at various points, and then sea landings, with emphasis on Caen. SHAEF [Supreme HQ Allied Expeditionary Force] made a short announcement and Eisenhower spoke. The BBC was excellent in the evening, with the King, Monty, de Gaulle, Uncle William and some very good front-line reports. No mention of Bayeux nor of the Cherbourg peninsula, but fighting in Caen (may be parachutists only) and anyway a decent bridgehead. It was rough and they had more trouble from the mined obstacles when landing than from the enemy. Here tonight it is raining and I have a headache. We expect to sail at six tomorrow morning and reach the beach at midnight.

7 June 1944

Passed Goodwin Sands with three or four wrecks and the French coast visible. English coast like an aquatint with cardboard buildings on the shore and strips of wood and pasture behind. Opposite Dover Germans sent six shells at us (on BBC later) which straddled us about three ships back from ours, but no more. After 'windy corner' we went very slow, because we'd taken it at about 16 knots and were ahead of schedule. Very little news on the wireless. Tony Pepys tripped over the cable holding my ACV and fell on the deck, dislocating his shoulder. Put in again after some difficulty and chloroform. Ordered to sleep in our clothes; I didn't of course. Another convoy being bombed, which kept the Americans up but they forgot to tell us.

8 June 1944

Up at six o'clock, early news announced Bayeux in our hands and Caen-Bayeux road too in places. Caen apparently not, reports of tank attacks beaten off sound the same as the one early yesterday. By ten o'clock off Normandy, shipping at anchor over a large area, very peaceful but a little distant gunfire, coast recognisable through glasses, cliffs west of Arromanches and La Riviere. One corvette wreck. Nearer in, the ships packed together against a hazy background of villages from which church spires alone stood out. Might have been some busy port. We intercepted a message of tanks south of Bayeux, and enemy just south of the Bayeux-Caen road and infiltrating across it. There are some enormous floating forts or future docks being towed around, and every kind of ship from battleship down.

It is sunny, such a good thing for the first day of the holidays. After lunch I went to sleep on the floor of the ACV. Nothing more happened. We recognised the boat carrying the advance party of 131 Brigade just unloading; it should have landed yesterday. Wireless reports fierce tank and infantry fighting. Caen has been bombed so obviously we are not there. Action Stations about two in the morning. Tony Pepys said the Americans panicked about E-boats and are as windy as hell. They are incredibly civilian. I have not recognised an officer yet. The chief mate looks exactly like a sailor. The decks are always dirty. However they don't object to me using their lavatories etc. and that's a great thing.

9–12 June 1944

Roughly this is what has happened. At ten o'clock on the 9th there was an air-raid alarm and ships put down smoke in the harbour. At the same time an LCT [a landing craft for tanks] came alongside. It was getting dark and half hidden in smoke; on it were four English sailors, no dockers to help unload. So it was decided to start at six next morning. My ACV was the first off and it took an hour to get it into the LCT and then it was facing away from the end of the drive off. The whole LCT was loaded by about one o'clock, and there were then three or four more waiting empty alongside. The ship had six derricks but no one to man them. All over the place were other ships longing for one LCT. We reached shore at two o'clock and plunged for depth – about five feet. The tide was about half tide and coming in, not many boats were unloading, and there seemed nowhere particular to go and no sign from the shore. An LCT started unloading on each side of us and we saw several vehicles get ashore, about one quarter of a mile drive in the sea.

An RAF lorry pulling a trailer stuck and the crew got out on to the roof. Two lorries put off simultaneously from an LCT which immediately deserted them, both stuck and their crews also got on their roofs. All three lots were taken off by a launch and within half an hour the tide had entirely covered the lorries and only the RAF trailer (a radar van of great value) remained floating. We tried to unhitch it from the launch but the tide was too strong. Our LCT was British and nice chaps. No orders, so we cruised up to Le Hamel and waited for high tide and grounded there, but they said from the shore it was boggy so we put off again and eventually fetched up at Mont Fleury our other beach, on the high-tide rush. It rained while I was trying to take photos of a quite invasion-like scene. We were only a few yards from the beach but it remained too deep for some time, and even then the first ACV stuck. Mine had to be winched off and the two lorries which followed me were both drowned, one my map lorry. A lot of 49 Div. Inf. were landing so not everybody was as behind schedule as myself.

We found our way to the Division location which was near Ryes north of Bayeux. Corps were near and 11th Hussars. Found Martin [Lindsay] asleep in a ditch after several sleepless nights, went down to our Tac HQ [Tactical Headquarters] with GI in two Dingos [armoured vehicles], warned snipers very bad. Ate in mess which is in a building with an avenue, quite nice, washed and went over to 11th Hussars and found Jimmy. He had been in my convoy and almost hit when we were shelled going through Dover, he'd landed yesterday, after 11th Hussars' main body. He left the 11th in

England in order to get the form before they arrived and his troop is still with B Squadron. Silly ass was at Brentwood and never thought of my being there too. We walked back to my ACV and I gave him a map board and talked sitting on a bridge till ten o'clock. The country is green with narrow roads all tree lined and clean cut stone buildings, very pleasant. Signs of battle not so great.

On 11th June we moved at 0500 hrs – I had to get up therefore after three hours in bed. Martin was still in bed in his ditch when we were due to move and I nearly left him. Collected an officer POW on the way and had him up on the roof. Went out to see a Panther tank, it had been immobilised by a near miss from a shell and the crew must have baled out and set light to it. Rifle Brigade having a fight in a wood beyond. Worked hard summarising battle to date. At eight o'clock Colonel Bill came with Jimmy. Jimmy in a state. He is liaising with 8th Hussars for tomorrow's attack, and was under-organised. Tried to help him and gave him some whisky. Our mess is a nice farm, arranged by me; they gave us the biggest pile of butter I ever saw. General had conference for attack tomorrow. I had to open it which I wasn't told by GI and brought map with nothing marked on it. Heard that Michael Laycock was killed this afternoon. Bed after midnight. Fighting flared up in the evening and went on till after eleven o'clock, 8 Armoured Brigade Tac HQ attacked by Tigers and various tank parties suddenly appeared. Attack not going well, opposition in Tilly and lateral road strong. Army Commander came in and I talked to him. Change of plan – switch to US army boundary where very little opposition has been met so far.

12th June a lovely sunny day. Gave a mass of stuff to farm to wash and iron, finished by evening, very nice people and wanted no money. It has a yard in front full of chickens, ducks of all sizes and kinds, a goat, three dogs, nine children, a gun, our mess lorry. We had one deserter today, three yesterday but in general enemy fighting extraordinarily hard. Laurence Biddle wounded yesterday and evacuated home. Went on to Regiment, found them out in position and followed them out into a wood, drew down shell fire. Stanley in command. Stephen there, in all five officers killed –

Michael, George Jones, Head, Keith Douglas, Pepler. Patrick wounded. A shell killed the first three standing by RHQ [Regimental Headquarters] tank. They have had a very exhausting time, fighting for six days and never more than four hours' sleep, but come out tonight. Advance headed by 11th Hussars was most successful and almost reached Caumont. I am duty officer in ACV all night.

13 June 1944

We were in Villers Bocage at 0830, a great success. HQ moved at five o'clock. My wretched ACV broke down on the only diversion where a railway bridge had been blown near Bayeux, and blocked it. We stopped in the road to Balleroy and after breakfast I drove back into Bayeux with Tony Pepys. It is a very attractive little town, there are some very old houses and the cathedral is superb outside, massive towers but the rest perpendicular with wonderful flying buttresses; I like the flamboyant lantern tower. We got back just as HQ moved on again, to La Butte, through Balleroy and then SE. The Tilly road is still strongly held by enemy and we have to go to Villers by Caumont which the Americans now hold. HQ 1 US Infantry Division is in a chateau quite close. I went there twice, the second time to try and get their bombers on to Villers which we had to quit in the evening. We had only a few POW. These were identified as two Grenadier regiments and a Panzer regiment which was good (or bad). In one case a Sgt Davies of 11th Hussars was captured by the Germans and left under guard by two men, one of whom he strangled and the other he brought back, who identified the second Grenadier regiment! 4 CLY [County of London Yeomanry] had a very bad time – a whole squadron was surrounded by Tigers and believed lost. I got a bit of sleep teatime. Up late after midnight doing summary. Brigadier Loony told on the air that the position was hopeless.

14 June 1944

Not much doing today and thought it looked like early bed but it is 12.30 and the summary only half done. Arthur Cranley missing, RHQ all missing, and the Rifle Brigade company. Visited Americans. My friend there is Roosevelt, a grandson of Theodore's. Frank Gillard and other reporters called. We are withdrawing from Villers and forming a line NE from Caumont till the 33 Armoured Brigade and 56 Brigade come under command. In the evening the enemy attacked strongly [the Battle of the Box]. Road back to Caumont cut. Our tanks formed line including Loony with his wooden dummy guns and the 11th Hussars in their cars.

The battle of Villers Bocage was a disaster. 18th Hussars seemed to have made a breakthrough, till their leading tank was knocked out by a panzerfaust (a German anti-tank weapon). They couldn't bypass Villers and a great jam of British armour clogged the narrow road. Early next morning 4 CLY under Arthur Cranley took the lead and ran into five Tigers under Captain Wittman, celebrated on the Eastern front as the greatest panzer ace of the war. He roared along machine-gunning our infantry and destroying our tanks. The survivors were captured, including Arthur. British Infantry support fought among the mined houses. Four German tanks including Wittman's were destroyed. But we were forced to withdraw and Villers Bocage was heavily bombed.

18 June 1944

Went to 11th Hussars with Tony Pepys and talked to Jimmy. He had quite enjoyed the Battle of the Box. [Jimmy's troop was attached to 4 CLY.] Like me it is doing things on his own which he hates. 11th Hussars are near Gueron some way behind us, had to talk to a lot of RHQ in order to locate Jimmy.

Visited 1 US Division. They had had a plane come down near them and explode which they thought was one of the new pilotless planes the Germans started using over England two days ago. These are only propaganda really, to frighten the civilian population, as they are quite inaccurate, but there is no warning. Went on to 11th Hussars, found Jimmy wearing the Jaeger top half of my pyjamas I laid in for a cavalry campaign in Rumania in the winter of 1939 and gave him in Italy. Lay on the grass and looked at Russian poems. He couldn't come into Bayeux.

GOC's conference at six lasted two hours. Several letters, from Flintham and Myrtie and one from Jimmy written in England, saying '. . . your friendship means probably more than you think. The fact that I have got to know you so much better than before is by far my greatest and most worthwhile achievement since I have been back in this country . . .' I am very pleased. The achievement is mine, but it may be I was wrong in thinking we shall never be very great friends. I like to be flattered and made much of and influenced, and Jimmy is inarticulate and shy; it may though be that he is less unfeeling than I thought. We are too alike, at least in lack of self-confidence. He is extraordinarily beautiful and extraordinarily wise but it is nice to think our relationship may become less academic. It was my only achievement in England, outside settling down again more or less, and revelling in the spring.

19 June 1944

Poured all day. Visited by a posse of Civil Affairs, seem fairly agreed that people here are not mainly de Gaulliste. De Gaulle's meeting in Bayeux was not well attended and they ask after Giraud. In general they were comfortably off before the invasion, which has subjected them to bombing and fighting and cost the farmers their markets, the Germans were well behaved and in many cases married to French girls, our soldiers have done some looting – including two military police of this division who held up two old countesses near here in a chateau. The organisation of the Resistance movement, which gave us information before the invasion, still helps and

271

through them I sent out a spy yesterday and two more today. Civilians can go through the lines both ways fairly easily. News of 7 Armoured Division released on BBC and talk by Frank Gillard who was here just before. Plan for attack on 21st June now changed. Cherbourg is considered ours now (it was under some fire today) and we intend to take Caen starting Thursday, but we don't join in till Saturday when it should be taken or almost. High-ups all very optimistic. General told me we'd had 1,000 casualties and 131 Brigade were having a lot of cases of battle neurosis. 7 Armoured Division has a big reputation but neither 22 nor 131 Armoured Brigades are first class and they had too easy a time in Italy.

22 June 1944

Went out late last night with Tony Pepys to Lingevres, a shattered village with five dead Panthers [German tanks], a Sherman, wrecked church, dead cows, a few poor people salvaging. On the way we examined the knocked-out Tiger which destroyed the Corps Commander's two Shermans. It hid up on top of the hill above the Aure and the Corps Commander told his protecting tanks to go home which they did by the wrong road. Officers and crews were all killed. We could see no differences between this Tiger and the Panthers.

Germans not moving divisions yet from Pas de Calais but the diplomatic ban is being lifted and they'll soon know we have no army standing by in England. General talked to G1, G2 and me about what Monty had said to him, complete change so far as we are concerned as Monty doesn't want us to make ground. Satisfied Second Army has drawn all enemy panzer divisions, now wants Caen only on this front and Americans to press on for Brittany ports. So 8 Corps attack goes in but we have very limited objective. Monty reckons he lost the battle of the build-up – five days behind on account of weather.

23 June 1944

GOC's conference at 0900 hours. I talked. American Division HQ heavily shelled last night and all their HQs accurately. 131 Brigade moving because shelled. Probably information from civilians. After lunch to 11th Hussars, took Jimmy to dentist. There wasn't time for me to be seen as ENSA show at 11th Hussars. Extremely bad dinner with Toby and Sandy. Awful photographs of Aunaye-sur-Odon which was entirely obliterated on night of 14th June in error for Villers. G1 saying what a flap they were in at Army Group last November about pilotless planes, preparing cabinet to go out of London. Cherbourg not taken yet.

26 June 1944

Teatime visited Michael Forester with Tony Pepys, in a farm very near Germans near Briquessard. Heard that directly after we left, Michael Forester and Bill Fisher were wounded by a stonk. Very sorry, Michael one of the most charming and attractive people I have ever met, and a fine soldier. In the night John Currie killed by a shell, he has commanded 4 Armoured Brigade a long time. The day's fighting by 49 Division including SRY and 8 Corps went quite well in the end, 1 SS Pz Div. never appeared and enemy forces were small, the AA [anti-aircraft] gun line was overrun (who'd have overrun 88s in Africa?). The GOC and SNO [Senior Naval Officer] Cherbourg have been captured.

27 June 1944

Sunny early. Cherbourg fallen. Mike Carver made Brigadier 4 Armoured Brigade. No armoured regimental or infantry commanders now who commanded six weeks ago in 22 or 131 Armoured Brigades. Went into Bayeux and had a good hot shower at the public baths. Bought Jimmy a tin, very small, of foie gras, 300 Fr, ate it all with him and stayed at 11th Hussars till 8.30. Up late with summary and situation reports. General told me we might have to go round to 8 Corps or even across Orme behind Caen. Monty told him to sleep well in next 24 hours.

1 July 1944

Division moved in the afternoon, to just by the 11th Hussars. Tony Pepys and I went off first to Bayeux, had a bath, room with two tubs, very good. Division has a new leaguer, rather nice but pouring with rain. Battle room made out of ACV 1 and 2 which deprives me of my side. So built a house by my jeep. Awful lot of cowpats, long wet grass. Last night I didn't get into ACV 1 to go on duty till after 1.30 as movement order was being written. Today has I think been a great one. Three enemy armoured divisions attacked and our despised 49 Division claimed 42 tanks destroyed, thus the only armoured reserve will exhaust itself and when the Americans break through there will be nothing to oppose them, little to hold a new line anywhere in France. I am really excited, as I was once at Alamein before the break-through and once somewhere else, I forget where. Bloody Laming came and told me the names of his mistresses in Athens. He said that on the window sill of the cottage he is sleeping in is written in French, English, German, Italian, Latin and ancient Greek 'What am I to do with my Life?'

2 July 1944

General very complimentary about summaries, agrees yesterday comparable to 31st August 1942 (Alam al Halfa) and 6th March 1943 (Medenine). 49 Division can count 37 burnt-out enemy tanks, 15 Scottish are out of contact and advancing through fields piled with dead. Destruction of infantry mainly caused by artillery, of tanks by six-pound shells of our infantry. Bit of intercept (very secret GOC only) 9 SS Div. at twelve o'clock yesterday: 'Abandon hope all ye who enter here.'

3 July 1944

American attack from Brittany opened today with three Divisions. Poured all morning. Draughtsman made a fine map for Monty yesterday, got it set up with some difficulty in big marquee up the road. Tony Pepys went to 1 US Division who said they were miserable because my summary had stopped arriving and they were crazy about my sense of humour! Apparently, they rave about them to everybody, and get hell from their generals for being such bores themselves.

Monty's conference. I slipped in. Arrived in grey Rolls wearing grey pullover with Legion d'Honneur pinned on. Talked very simply, not so flamboyant as he used to be, and very interesting. Spoke first of the battle to date – the five separate landings which had to be joined up – which was completed by 10th June. His second preoccupation had been to keep the initiative, his third that there should be no reverse anywhere on the front. 5 US Corps the first day only made 100 yards, which looked bad. He went to watch from a destroyer, but next day they broke through. Essential to penetrate inland, but cleaning up not completed and many casualties resulted behind [the front].

Tempo of battle had to be reduced while we built up, but at the same time initiative had to be retained. Not too strong in the first days and short of ammunition. Now we have 26 divisions and 3,000 tanks. After the landing the next thing was the building up which had to be pressed at all costs. This was a failure on account of weather, never been such a June in history. Ten days behind now and only 60 per cent up to planned scale. Result – third phase of battle (8 Corps) delayed a week. Next, enemy build-up had to be delayed. Here greater success even than hoped – enemy has had great difficulties from air, deception etc. and even when the head of his new divisions gets here their tail is still in Germany. It took five days for 2 Pz Corps to reach Eastern France from Russia, 14 days to reach battle area from eastern France. Object of British army was to draw enemy and free US forces to west. Succeeded almost too well.

East of the Orne is our only tender spot but the enemy thinks it is his too. We are making the Germans think we're out for Paris while in fact we want Brittany. So tomorrow's attack on Caen opens from West, next day from north-west. Task of Second Army is to keep Germans busy, to avoid a setback, and to get Caen. German POW now 50,000 of which 60 per cent are non-Germans. But they are fighting very well, fantastic allegiance to Führer. Two stories – wounded German in hospital preferred to die rather than take a transfusion of British blood, and a dying German who was offered a priest, said 'The Führer is my priest.'

Big picture – Hitler taken charge. Monty doesn't think he's decided whether to try and annihilate Allies in West and face losses in East, or to try and hold Russians. If he decides to concentrate on us, no bridges over Seine below Paris or on Loire between Orleans and the sea leaves a bottleneck. Hitler would probably go for writing us off here and with effect of buzz-bombs on England, try for peace. Monty says a successful German offensive is impossible against superior air forces.

We were all introduced to Monty. The most memorable thing about his conference was really my map. It was very large and placed so that the only light fell on it. Monty came in with two small map boards which he propped against my map board and spoke from them. When he came to the Big Picture he regretted that Paris, the Loire, the Seine etc. were off his board but pointed to where they would be – Paris here he said pointing to within six inches of PARIS in letters six inches high on my map, the Loire there. I was jumping up and down with rage.

Back via 11th Hussars to collect this diary which I sent Jimmy this morning to read. Jimmy wreathed in smiles, I didn't think he would react particularly one way or the other. He hasn't been like this since London. My God, though, I like him when he's like that.

7 July 1944

After tea went for a walk without my shirt but of course it clouded over. In brief interval of sunshine threw myself in bacchic ecstasy naked in the grass and got stung in the tenderest places by stinging nettles. On the way back it rained. General rather depressed about Americans but I don't think they can fail to break through. If they do, the bridgehead must permanently congeal. Photographs of Villers Bocage make one quite ill. Four hundred heavy bombers went over this evening for Caen. Attack by three divisions goes in tomorrow at 0420, followed later on by another 8 Corps push towards Orne. Tomorrow 50 Division start straightening the line. Opposite us now is 276 Infantry Division [German] from the Spanish frontier; it came on bicycles and foot and sent deserters to tell us all.

9 July 1944

Today we took Caen without opposition, the part of it that is north of the river. The Americans have not advanced much. I heard from poor Lady Laycock. Jimmy and I talked about the chaps in his troop who are very nice and he told me he chose his own crew purely because he liked them, and that since he had been in the 11th Hussars he had never given anybody a rocket. If one can be gentle and get things done it is perfection. I myself flare and rage and truly it is more self-assertion than efficiency. I would never live as Jimmy does in one bivvy on the hay with his crew, partly because it is distasteful to me to live at close quarters with any but a very few people, and I hate other people's untidiness and lack of privacy, but mainly because I'm afraid I like to order and not to lead, and one can't order about one's companions.

15 July 1944

St Swithin's and no sun. Worried whether new plan might interfere with my picnic but it didn't, fetched Jimmy and went to La Tuilene, up into a wood above River Doune, trees and bracken and little tracks but no view, picnicked on tins pinched off the boat and golden syrup and gin and lime, not sure how Jimmy would have reacted if I had tried to stage big seduction scene but didn't anyway.

Civil affairs colonel says 6,000 killed in Caen.

17 July 1944

Reveille 0430, moved 0530. Left convoy to go to 8 Corps. Got there seven o'clock, parked by garden wall, followed it up while breakfast cooking to a fine chateau at Lanthevil, date on sundial 1765, part may be earlier. Explored downstairs, found BBC reporters' mess, Frank Gillard and co. (all still in bed upstairs), moat in front and entrance gates, at back remains of formal garden, statues, donkey and cows browsing, terrace walk and lime walk. Got latest dope from 8 Corps and maps, took them to Brigade. Reached Division at new location near Douvres. After dinner General talked about tomorrow's show. Am very worried about Jimmy, which is unlike me. Going to be a colossal show – all east of Caen. Whole thing turns on unheard-of air support. Over 3,000 bombers, and they depend on good weather. Our address is now BLA = British Liberation Force – can you beat it?

18 July 1944

Reveille ordered 0630, balloon chaps said morning would be foggy, woken 0545 by barrage followed by first planes, flying across sky lit up all in pink like flocks of crows, in incessant din, bombs inaudible. Went on for a long time and a mass of dust and smoke drifted north. Battle went extremely well and almost earlier than

278

seemed possible. 11 Armoured Division reported themselves half to the objective and at 1130 pretty well on it. They left many enemy behind them and the Guards Armoured Brigade following up had to fight its own battle and couldn't get on without its infantry who were behind 22 Armoured Brigade. Bridgehead so packed no one else could cross bridge. Frank Gillard says big row because BBC published a private recording of Monty, consequently another two are off – Howard Marshall closeted and Chester Beattie sent home. Also says Caen Cathedral hit by German artillery. 11 Armoured Division have lost 100 tanks which is appalling and Guards 50. Enemy has less than 50 on the front.

21 July 1944

GOC's conference at seven, it poured off and on all day and we were shelled all round but not in the leaguer. The field is quite impossible, clay and like a byre. We are now under 2 Canadian Corps, after a good deal of rowing with 8 Corps who are considered very inefficient. The mosquitoes here are incredible. Next operation with Canadians would be tomorrow but now we need 48 hours after it stops raining to dry out. Amazing news of attempt on Hitler's life by various generals on his staff. The army is now to be under Himmler and all questions referred direct to him or Goering or Raeder, apparently there was an effort to form a new government. Jimmy came to tea. Big bomb quite close. On duty and slept in ACV 1, four inches deep in mud.

22 July 1944

Plane shot down over us breakfast time. Jimmy and I read together Logan Pearsall-Smith's *Trivia*, which John Verney sent me, and laughed very much. After tea to Canadian Corps with GI. Went into Caen, never saw anything like it, huge area both sides of the river either completely demolished or in ruins. Crossed by Winston

Bridge named in honour of Winston who crossed by one bridge and returned by the other this morning. Said very impressively, 'These bridges are the gateway to liberty and a better world.' About one quarter of a mile further on plane came across over us from Ove and it was a buzzbomb, spurting flame but looking quite a normal plane otherwise. It cut out over us and fell 100 yards from the bridge without damaging it.

Further on into the town two main squares OK and the Cathedral Abbaye aux Hommes. Abbaye aux Dames from a distance was not structurally irreparable, towers, roof etc. looked all right. Other churches pretty well destroyed including St Pierre, a most extra-ordinary late Gothic church with a Norman tower and buttresses but covered in flamboyant Renaissance motifs. North of the town better than south. Don't know what'll ever be done with it. Went into Abbaye aux Hommes. A service was just finishing with lighted candles, it is very beautiful, far better than Bayeux inside, simpler and darker with a pure Norman nave and a smaller choir.

24 July 1944

Jimmy couldn't come to Caen, so lay by his car. He said surprisingly that he hoped he would take a long time dying in order to see things as they are when mundane angles are eliminated. This war has proved that the possibility of death becomes commonplace and I don't know whether in the squalor of a field hospital I at least would have peace of mind or whether anybody ever knows over a long period definitely that they will die.

Canadian and our attack timed for 3.30 a.m. and searchlights were to produce artificial moonlight. At about two, I woke and found it light as day, then heard planes and saw we were absolutely swimming in flares all round. Put on mackintosh and bombs started, went into front room of house which looks east, good view, biggest bombing I have seen by a long way. Phosphorous flares used which burnt a long time on the ground, bombs all round the edge of our suburb, hit a Canadian gun in the field by the ACV, our mess damaged, and a few chaps wounded, a lot of ammunition went up and burnt afterwards. Not much encouraged to hear that the house four up from us had collapsed without a hit and they were digging out Canadians. After this quite soon our barrage started which is almost intolerable as we are surrounded by heavies. At 6.30 our advance seemed very slight after all this shattering din.

26 July 1944

Yesterday's attack was a complete failure – made no ground and cost a great many lives of the Canadian infantry. For the moment all idea of attacking by Canadian Corps given up. The Germans have brought in opposite us the 9 SS Division from West of the Orne and 2 Pz Division from Caumont and there is a new infantry division on its way from Pas de Calais. In fact it doesn't look very hopeful on this sector. Pretty idle day, up early and got summary finished off and went to Tac HQ before breakfast.

28 July 1944

The Americans are doing wonderfully, have taken Coutances and are threatening the road Vire-Granville. 2 Pz Div. has already switched back across the Orne and West; we are to attack in Villers-Vire direction. Found Jimmy, talked but I can't feel he is in the least glad to see me, don't know whether I am like a business-man who expects his bit of fluff to soothe his weary brow or whether in fact having known him now nine months and done everything possible to be nice to him one wouldn't reasonably expect a little more attention. He isn't easy to understand and he is moody and doesn't see I mind. I am sure he does at least disguise the fact that often he would rather not be disturbed.

At dinner sat opposite Algie [Lumley-Smith] who had been at 11 Armoured Division for a time after 131 Brigade. He had met John Barrett there who asked if he knew me, which he said he did well.

Barrett apparently took no notice and said what a monster I was and then said that the general opinion at Division was that I was a pansy but he couldn't see that, and was I? Algie, dear boy, said he'd known me 16 years and he bloody well knew I was. All this in A Mess at Corps practically gave me a fit and disturbed me greatly because I didn't think that was the opinion at 7 Armoured Division. In point of fact I never met any normal cavalry officer who used the word 'pansy'. They talk coarsely but not altogether disapprovingly of buggers, whom obviously they regard as vicious but not otherwise different to themselves, and pansies are I think in that jargon chorus boys. In the Barrett class however, the suburban, they are no doubt more unenlightened. This question does not cause me much qualm but I hate criticism.

30 July 1944

Went over and saw Jimmy, he couldn't possibly have been nicer. After lunch walked with Sandy then theoretically tea with Jimmy to which I brought my honey pot but he'd just had lunch and no brew materialised – Jimmy is priceless the way he never attempts to entertain one. Sits on the only chair himself etc – unlike Sandy who overwhelms one. Went to Corps, Monty had been there and said this was the great week of the war. Rommel has been badly wounded at Lisieux. US have made little advance today but fairly steady on their line east of Granville which penetrates the only good enemy position. News though very uncertain and towns reported alternately in our hands then German all day.

3 August 1944

Shelling during night killed two signallers in next field. Hear Corps Commander sacked, replaced by Horrocks. Imagine our general [Erskine] is fairly secure, however mopping up of large infantry pockets behind must be done and that puts a brake on the advance.

116 Division now in action round Vire; interesting to see whether enemy can get his remaining fighting divisions on US front out through Vire. Washed very late in hot sun. Horrified to hear our general also got the sack. Everyone very depressed. Presumed reason failure to get to Aunay two days ago – we were only put on to it in the afternoon and roads were blocked. Perhaps he was too self-confident in his dealings above. All very sad indeed. He made a farewell speech and asked me to write to him.

5 August 1944: Letter Home

We didn't stay with Nanny [Canadians] as there wasn't much future there. What we had done was to keep everything over here while the Americans made their breakthrough. As you realise, the whole plan of the invasion was that the British army should protect the American army, and for a long time no German tanks appeared on the American front at all. In the end two divisions which had already been fought by us moved across to them, but they never had anything like the force opposite them we had here, and it has really been most successful. Everything is going now as it should have gone in the third week of the invasion, except of course that now there are fewer reserves in the background. Today for the first time the enemy is withdrawing fast in front of us and it will be interesting to see where he will stop; to my great surprise it looks as though he may not stop on the Orne.

Monty was I suppose disappointed and our general [Erskine] returned to England yesterday, as did the Corps Commander. We were frightfully disturbed; it didn't seem the way to treat the captor of Tripoli in the middle of a battle. The new man is a guardsman called Verney, quite a different sort of man, quiet, thoughtful, assured, nice I think. There was a frightfully funny conference yesterday. He wasn't given a moment before he was ordered to fight a battle and he didn't know the country or the Division. So at the conference he more or less left it to the various commanders to say how they wanted to organise it. Each of them said in turn, 'Well,

Loony, you'll want the usual, I suppose' (meaning a regiment of guns, a troop of engineers or whatever else he controlled) and Brigadier Loony or whoever it was said, 'Yes, yes, the usual I suppose.' This went all round the circle. At the end Verney said to the only chap he knew before, 'You know, I must find out what this *usual* is.'

9 August 1944

Really hot day after mist. The Canadian attack started yesterday with 1,000 night bombers and broke through south of Caen.

After lunch went to see Jimmy, through Aunay-sur-Odon. There are bulldozed tracks through high banks of dusty rubble and rafters, just a bedstead here and there and a foul smell but no wall or sign of civilization till you reach the ruined church, a bad church but a superb ruin which no doubt will be expensively restored. But the town will never be. There are great bomb holes full of black ooze and the bulldozers climb over mountains of rubble in a cloud of dust. I took some photographs and went on up the Mount Pincon ridge, covered in trees, and found Jimmy where they'd been some days since we took Pincon. He had had a bloody time, under the ridge, mainly because liaison has been so bad and 43 Division were claiming Ondefontaine when in fact they'd only one patrol there which was destroyed. All the time, while we were down below being told to get on as Ondefontaine was free, Jimmy could see the Germans, and the infantry he was with had 350 casualties all round him from mortars trying to get on up the hill.

I don't think Jimmy was so scared as he was in Italy but I haven't seen his diary so I don't know; anyway, today he was happy. I brought some beer and we had honey and bread and then a very funny omelette. His crew are still in the throes of a big emotional crisis which is tiresome for poor Jimmy. Sandy and I went to Corps at eight o'clock and saw Bill Nolan and heard the Americans were in Alençon, but don't believe rumours about the Americans much. Back to Division and after dark through Aunay again to 11th

Hussars RHQ with some photographs which Sandy and Jimmy wanted. Aunay smells worse every minute.

11 August 1944: Letter home

It has been lovely sunny weather and for the moment we are not doing very much. For the first time round here you often get a view and this house looked out across to Mount Pincon [our objective on landing]. Every Frenchman for months has brought us information about Mount Pincon, the huge naval guns dragged up there at night and the subterranean ammunition dump, but I don't think it was anything but a big radar station.

You can imagine we envy the Americans tearing round Brittany and the Loire, into places which are not ruined. The war goes very well, the German attack, which was to have cut through to Avranches and the west coast of the peninsula, got hell from the air and failed badly and now they are in a hopeless position, pouring good money after bad with new reinforcements arriving and only one road left from Paris to supply all their divisions. If the Americans can hold Alençon, the Germans will be attacked on all sides, and must get out or fight to the death a battle already lost. Here on the British front they are slowly being driven back but fight very hard, naturally, or we should encircle them. It is tiring, unexhilarating fighting, but it pins down Germans and kills them. 'Peaceful little Vire' I last heard of in flames, the American Fire Services went in and were shelled out so I suppose it was left to burn.

13 August 1944

Form is that the enemy has had five armoured divisions and one and a half more on the way lined up to attack round Mortain; the Americans were waiting for him. Suddenly yesterday he started to pour back east. The Americans are threatening the only road back all along the line from the south and we to a less extent from the north. Unfortunately the Canadian attack has petered out; they lost 50 and the Poles 50 tanks and it is said that after that they were held up by dummy tanks.

Aunay was too much; there was a dreadful corpse in a pothole in the road and no one did anything about it, a woman's, half buried. I really couldn't face it again, and managed to find a way round. Went on over to 11th Hussars, asked myself to lunch with Jimmy, on to Corps, back to Jimmy. We talked about the religious ascetics and devotees and how far this personal effort has any value to the world, and Jimmy said that of course Christianity is the only thing which demands both devotion and activity. Do you know, it had never occurred to me. Order came for the squadron to go out immediately on patrols. I lay pondering and left very sadly.

14/15 August 1944: Letter to Jimmy

Every night I wheedle out of the General the plans of the High Command, and consequently the chances of seeing you peacefully. I am so anxious now to see you out of the battle and driving off yesterday on a perfectly clear road to Mont St Michel with Tony [Pepys] I could think of nothing else. We are all being given two nights off but the question is 1) how to get you the same 2) how to make you want to come.

Mont St Michel is better that these photographs. It is a misty castle alive in a desert of grey silver sand and silver blue sea, completely fairy book. It is very small, 150 people live on the rock, surrounded by walls and a limitless horizon. The abbey has been burnt and this has turned the Norman nave a deep red while the choir is green from the salt air, it is more beautiful than anything I ever saw, it is quite empty. Round it are the halls and grand chambers of the Dominicans and the Knights of St Michael, and sunlit walls and stone stairs and everywhere the sea. You get wonderful food – salad and omelette like a soufflé and sole and veal and any wine you want, and Bill [Nolan] says you can sleep

286

there, very well. There is in fact nothing wanting except you. Your armoured car is the only thing which shows up on my map but it is a long way off. When I was told I could have two nights off (apart from the General asking me to go to Mont St Michel with him – which I have yet to get out of) I thought I would ask Bill to be attached to B Squadron. Then I thought you would undoubtedly be furious.

15 August 1944

Listening on the air, I suddenly gather that Jimmy has lost his Dingo. I go to where RHQ was and find D Squadron and Toby and he knows nothing and of course I pretend not to be more than faintly interested and stay talking and have lunch, then to RHQ when I saw the Colonel and find that Jimmy, 'thinking of girls', lost two cars but is all right. On to B Squadron who are on a ridge near the Orne, not a very exciting view though and no Jimmy who is resting back at B echelon quite near RHQ. Flog back there and find Jimmy asleep. So sit down by him and read Aragon. After about an hour he wakes up and we lie and talk and he tells me how his armoured car ran on a mine (and he cut his nose) and it was largely Bill's fault because he'd been down the road and knew there might be mines there and never said so but hustled Jimmy on, and then he got on a narrow track and walked in front guiding his Dingo and it blew up a few yards from him and nothing hit him but a valise off the Dingo which really was a miracle. His driver was completely shaken and he had pretty well to carry him back and the wireless didn't work so no one would have known where they were if he'd been hurt. This was all the same night they first went out, two days ago. Jimmy was rested and very sweet and when I said I must go said 'Why?' I was more pleased by that than a chap should be and stayed till eight, sacrificing my dinner.

On to Corps for a brief visit and back to Division. There this morning Noel and Martin, Bro and Ralph all went off for two nights, to Mont St Michel. I saw the General at 11 p.m. and he told me he hoped we'd get ten days out of the line. At midnight orders to join Canadian army and to have the whole division concentrated on that side of the Orne tomorrow. Situation: 131 Brigade short of 600 chaps and many at rest camp by the sea, 22 Brigade unable to man large number of tanks, over 100 men sent back to England not yet replaced. I dealt with maps. 131 Brigade moved at dawn and Division HQ followed. G2 acting G1, so I went out with the General in the Queen Mary, his car. The invasion of the South of France has been announced, against negligible opposition.

19 August 1944

Our own planes strafed our troops all yesterday afternoon and it was impossible to stop them. The IO of 1/6 Queens was wounded and of 8th Hussars, Tony Newman, very badly. About midnight planes dropped flares and we were heavily bombed. I don't know who by.

Moved up to a very nice leaguer through St Pierre sur Dives which is less liberated than most places, out of corn fields into rolling bocage country. Absolute mass of prisoners began coming in, and Frenchmen of all sorts. According to the BBC the battle of Normandy is over. RAF yesterday claimed 4,000 vehicles and 250 tanks. Germans announce Abetz has left Paris and Vichy is in hands of the Maquis.

24 August 1944

We are in a nice orchard by a farm where French people came yesterday with great bouquets of dahlias and gladioli and the news that Paris is in French hands. Resistance chaps have been quite invaluable, one on each patrol very bloodthirsty.

Advancing today unopposed east from Lisieux. Roads up to the Seine reported crammed with enemy vehicles waiting to cross. Heads falling at a low level now, new very *inglese* CRA [Head Gunner] sacked an LO for saluting badly and ticked off a signals officer for

288

having no tie pin. Only the General has proved first class. Division HQ moved in triumphal progress, General says forward troops are covered in flowers and bells ringing. Locals did not know we were coming and Bosch were here last night. On road beyond Lisieux I had a long talk to two awfully nice prisoners from 9 SS Division.

Jimmy very funny about 11th Hussars' veiled language on the air. 'You know where I had breakfast the morning before last, over?' 'No, not quite sure, over.' 'Well, you see the red thing, not the big red thing but the small red thing, over.' 'You mean the red thing that goes through the mottled thing, over?' 'Yes, well you don't take that red thing but you go hard right on to the next one which goes through the white bint (St Jean le Blanc) to Shepheards (L'Hotellerie), you see that, over?' 'Well, yes you mean . . .' 'No no no, left of there . . .' Yesterday they had a report line called OVER and Sandy called Jimmy: 'B are you over OVER over?' 'Well, I'm over the blue thing so I suppose I must be over OVER over' etc.

27 August 1944: Letter Home

There isn't much this side of the Seine; most surviving Germans must now be across. Just when the *Daily Sketch* said the battle was over bags of prisoners came in and also escaped Allied airmen, French collaborators, liberators and Maquis and there were masses of captured papers and the enemy was in confusion so it was difficult to say what he was up to. I don't think he has got an awful lot back across the Seine, not enough even to hold a proper line, though no doubt he will try, instead of being sensible and dropping back on his own frontiers. We captured all the secret files of German Seventh Army. When the disastrous attack on Avranches was ordered General Hausser wrote an order of the day, 'On the successful execution of the operation which the Führer has ordered depends the decision of the war in the west and with it perhaps the decision of the war itself. I expect all corps and divisional commanders to take good care that all officers are aware of the unique significance of the whole situation.'

Here every 11th Hussar car has a Maquis on it and they have been invaluable, we have a French liaison officer in a red hat, who, like everything out of the ordinary, comes under me. We don't agree (but I have won) on the question of whether or not these chaps should be given battledress. It is quite obvious that you can't walk up and blip German soldiers over the head wearing battledress. A lot of hooligans are apt to dash around saying they are Maquis and shooting into the air after we arrive. In Brittany they hanged a lot of collaborators, but they've done very well. I had a German battalion commander given to me by them whom they ambushed a fortnight ago, he was very browned off.

28 August 1944

Looking back on the war I can see that all I have enjoyed in it, and I have enjoyed a great deal, has been through some other person, first Michael Parish, and then in the Cairo days a collection – Robin [Maugham], Billy Brooksbank, Bill Maclean, and others, then Flash, then after a lonely hiatus at Homs and an unsatisfying experiment with Toby [Horsford] – which continued in Italy and to some extent in England, the hiatus I mean – Jimmy. Jimmy is by far the most extraordinary. He is certainly the best person I have known since Michael Mosley, the goodest person that is. He has for me enormous charm. He is absolutely guileless. He has no worldly interests and very little in other people. I have always had friends who told me I was brilliant or beautiful or who laughed at me or something, Jimmy is completely passive. In the first time in my life I have had actively to try and please someone else.

30 August 1944

Saw Jimmy and gave him the St Christopher that Oswald Normanby gave me, which he will lose, and he gave me his last volume of diary. I am afraid that the first thing I looked for was what he said about me, and that was satisfying. He doesn't mention me on every page, and the two occasions I took so much to heart, Dunwich and Chateau St André, don't come in, but of the London time (he doesn't mention Flintham) he says, 'Liking him enormously, respecting his friendship more than any other male's, may be more than anybody but Mum.' I am slow to grasp facts but this is not one I need doubt and (like the end of the war) it is a very exciting one. He says too, 'He has been wonderfully candid, honest, and has an immense charm which always makes me feel happy when I am with him. I came to look forward to our Sunday lunches which became a sort of ritual, as one of the few breaths of fresh air I tasted during the general run of insincerity and the unsatisfyable restlessness that made up my life.'

Much later, after landing in France, he writes, 'Myles came down in the evening and I went back to Division with him to collect a map. It was wonderful seeing him again and we talked about the difference of loving and being in love. He said, "But really, how can anybody listen to me on love?"' It was my first night in Normandy and we sat late on a stone bridge, very cold, I remember it very well. Jimmy says, 'I think being in love is the highest expression of a human being's selfish desire for satisfaction' and 'to possess completely you must know whether the person is good or bad, lovable or not. If the former, though at first impelled by selfish drive, develops into love, that is love for the person for their sake, and there follows an outflowing of one personality into another that is the highest integration and fullest freedom. Even now it can never be self-sufficient, for no person is good or big enough to completely absorb another personality. Love with a capital L, the highest activity of human nature, can only find its true expression in love of God.'

To me the essence of the problem is that men do not properly fall in love with men, however good – what is 'properly'? Jimmy and I are much better friends now than we ever were. I have a kindliness and patience with him, and really almost unselfishness, which I have never had with other people. In fact, I love him very much. I am not in love, though the boundary is a very narrow one. I don't know whether this is luck or intuition on Jimmy's part but he manages me very well. On his side I feel now a lack of restraint and a real affection which I never felt before. I am seriously worried because I foresee that it will end with the war. It shows how important sex is. Without it I find girls silly, yet no normal chap would hesitate five minutes between dining with his best friend and the silliest girl alive, she wins every time. It is very true what he says about knowing. I suppose Jimmy knows me quite well because with him I come out of my cocoon and I never tell him anything but the truth; he never asks any questions.

I remember that first evening in Normandy. 11th Hussars were in a farm and I went there late when it was dark and I could hardly see Jimmy's face, sitting in a room with other chaps. I was excited to see him and shy, particularly because there were others there who knew me but didn't know how well I knew Jimmy, and I got Jimmy to come over to Division. But I didn't know whether he was pleased to see me, till now I read it in his diary. I think mostly I am better about expressing my feelings, it must be necessary because in a way I am sensitive and if I don't know what Jimmy is feeling, of whom I am so fond, obviously one's own feelings must be a mystery most times to others and indeed I know they are.

Going to bed tonight in the rain I thought that it was 'sober satisfaction' I felt when I had my small successes, won the Victor Ludorum at Eton or got the MC. No excitement, but in the long run both were a great satisfaction to me. I wonder why it is that the things that move me are the silliest things, vulgarly sentimental. It is not the capture of Paris but the cheering crowds, not the first hand but the *Daily Mirror* reports of heroism and goodness, which bring tears to my eyes.

3 September 1944

Victory is very tiring. Yesterday I had a twitch in one eye which worried me very much, today it is the other. I shall go about in a flutter of eyelashes and then break down completely.

Moved from near Doullens to near Lens across the Arton hills and Vimy ridge and then suddenly looked down on the plain, Bethune studded with slag heaps, a surprising sight. Heard this morning that Jimmy's friend Donald was killed. I am sorry as Jimmy was very fond of him. Generals and Corps Commanders asking for more maps but 12 Corps are pretty useless. However army delivered some, nothing like enough. Spent whole morning giving them out. In new location crowds of civilians and endless Resistance chaps. At midnight stories of Germans about 5 km away sent all the men flying over here, Germans 3,000-strong with tanks said to be shooting and seizing, probably a column escaping from the coast. This terrified Tac Corps next to us and a general stand-to was ordered. Guards are in Brussels.

5 September 1944

Moved lunchtime and crossed Belgian frontier – cheering crowds all the way. Just on the frontier all one town cried *finie la guerre* and we really thought it must be, particularly as the BBC seemed to confine itself to national anthems. It was surprising news to me but not impossible. Germany has to surrender unconditionally but its end is so very close either way. My feelings were definitely mixed. It seemed an anticlimax. I'd like to cross the German frontier, at least to capture Ghent, but preferably Berlin. This is ridiculous. I foresee a trying time after the armistice, both in Europe and at home. I have got to take the appalling decision as to what to do with my life. But I am heartily tired of the war, only in the way one gets used to everything. Its horrors are known to me and I know how to cope with them.

6 September 1944

Division moved to a small chateau at Scheldelwindeke, really the hunting box to a larger chateau belonging to the Dukes of Luxembourg. A most confusing day. The enemy, cut off along the sea, is trying hard to escape. We found 70 Division in Ghent where last night the colonel of the regiment who went in parleyed with the German general – taken blindfold to his chateau leaving tanks at the Hotel de Ville. General said he couldn't surrender to a colonel so Brigadier Mac was sent for and he of course bogged it, sending for the General at a barricade and being rude. The Germans obviously wanted to surrender but had orders not to, and nothing came of it. They pulled out during the night.

During the day we took 4,000 POW and it was difficult to deal with them. All our centre lines were cut at intervals and an LO returning at night was almost captured, his jeep was lost. I had the General's bath in the chateau. Pouring rain. We slept by the lake, a great advantage of which was that no one could see us not getting up for the stand-to which has been instituted at dawn. There are very good apples, a wood with very fine oak avenues in an eight-pointed star, an ice house with beeches growing on it, a walled kitchen garden with a moat round it, and sundry canals, with the rain, in all, too much water.

8 September 1944

11th Hussars in a very new villa which had been a German officers' brothel, but its bar had an inexhaustible supply of very good beer. Sandy there, we went on to Jimmy who was trying to find 'To be or not to be' in *Hamlet* and definitely tiddly and quite charming saying how happy he was. He has a Belgian he has picked up called Jean who is an artist he is delighted with. Sandy and I ate fried eggs and Jimmy and the others got stuck into champagne. Later Jimmy made his Gettysburg speech twice and subsided into a chair where he gently passed out in the shadow of the bar. We went on talking and drinking and I behaved shamefully and talked trivialities to Sandy while I fondled Jimmy.

9 September 1944

Found the 11th Hussars moving but Sandy very nicely arranged for Jimmy to come in to Ghent with me – also Jean the artist. We went to the Pont St Martin and on the way passed two dead civilians and broken tramlines by the cathedral. Civilians quite calm but shells disturbed our sightseeing falling by the castle which we wanted to see. The canal each side of the Pont St Martin has a broad paved front and most delightful houses, some of the stepped gable type, backed by the two churches and clock tower of the town, altogether very pleasing. Jean took us into a long building which had been a monastery. The church tower was used by us as an OP [observation post] and they told us the Germans were 600 yards away and we were just putting in an attack to drive them out of the north part of the town. The monastery is now let room by room, very collegiate, Jean's brother has a wildly Montmartre room there with copper pans hanging up and bad frescoes and lots of quotations chalked up, mostly about women and love.

Went to see cathedral. Some awful 18th-century screens completely spoil it, it is pink brick with hugely tall stone pillars, the effect is of colossal height and the roof is beyond seeing, unfortunately the choir doesn't offer a very pleasing prospect. At certain angles one was reminded of those pictures of Pieter Neefs – hatchments on the walls and the stone and brick vaulting. In the crypt very poor pictures from the museum, and as I came up the priest ran after me – Was it safe? Quite safe, I said, except for the odd shell. At that moment an odd shell hit the choir and glass poured down. I looked round for Jimmy who was sitting quietly by the door, and another hit the church. We decided there was no future in Ghent.

We got into the jeep and drove off down the main street up which carriers and a few tanks were coming. Just as we reached a cross-roads there was an almighty bang and a shell burst on it, a cloud of dust rose, against it a despatch rider slowly rolled sideways and lay still on the other side of the road about five yards in front and a woman knelt on the pavement wounded. I drove on through a thick fog of dust and out the other side, feeling bad about not staying to see about the people wounded there. Jimmy I am sure was not much scared, certainly no more than I. I see that it is that same fear of operating on one's own which I too have, more really than fear of death.

15–16 September 1944

Twenty-four hours' leave to Brussels. Dolled up in service dress and went to 11th Hussars. Sandy burying a sergeant and wouldn't come. Rooms booked at Hotel Metropole, mine a nice one looking on a square which was crowded, good bathrooms. Lunch at the *Epaule de Mouton* just off Grande Place, not allowed to serve military but people there invited us to be their guests, most wonderful lunch and lots of Bordeaux. Jimmy very gay and sweet, put on his gabardine coat, looked like something out of an opera. Found another place for dinner, steak and chips and more Bordeaux. Jimmy mad after girls.

We went back to the hotel and met everyone we didn't want to see, then sent away the jeep which was a great error and went off to the nearest night club. The ones we found weren't much and Jimmy wanted one called *Boeuf sur les Toits* which was miles away. So there was nothing for it but a tram. *Boeuf sur les T* okay if you brought a girl but not otherwise. Drank very poor champagne and Jimmy silent and furious. Told by some ass trams stopped at eleven o'clock and curfew midnight and Jimmy decided the only thing was a brothel. I brazenly demanded one in hotel and guided Jimmy and Geoffrey Churton there and fled.

Back to bed and left a note in Jimmy's keyhole to come and see me when he came in. Deafening noise in square of roaring cars and chaps shouting, spent my time getting up and putting on light and reading *Madame Bovary* and getting up and putting it out and trying to sleep. Visited Jimmy's room, note still in keyhole. Actually he had baled out of the brothel hot on my footsteps. The maddening thing was I discovered later that the night club went on till six in the morning and my idea of collecting a girl from one during the night was probably quite right. Anyway Jimmy was quite unreasonably miserable and consequently I was too, feeling it was all my fault. In fact I cried which I haven't done for eight years, but not very much. I asked Jimmy to make a bargain, that we should regard ourselves as brothers. This was a very funny idea, but we had talked about family ties being the lasting ones at dinner. Jimmy with very great lack of enthusiasm agreed. Went and had a bath and discovered I felt jolly well.

Left Brussels 11.30, lovely day, took them all back to 11th Hussars, Jimmy still moping. Told him I would stop calling him darling, which I thought pretty decent of me. Wrote to Jimmy about brother business, which I mean seriously but I don't think he can; anyway today I had no idea what he was feeling. That is the awful thing that one doesn't know what other people are thinking.

17 September 1944: Letter home

It has been a very busy time, too busy for one to realise what was going on, and when in writing I used the word victory I did so hardly expecting to be believed. It has of course been a great victory, which has carried us here, between Ghent (which we took) and Brussels. Next day we crossed the Belgian frontier where the crowds were all wildly enthusiastic throwing chrysanthemums and hard unripe pears with great vigour. The Belgians are very like the Dutch with many charming blonde children. We harboured that night by a very pretty white farm with a moat round it; the people were delighted to do my washing and afterwards we were told that if we hadn't been there it would have been burnt down as they were collaborators. We were in an orchard full of plums, and when the General had a conference, instead of listening I went round shaking the trees and feeding the brigadiers.

Since then we have had a prisoner from the Stomach division (one of the divisions in the bag is the Stomach Division from Walcheren Island, all the men have gastric ulcers and the officers all lack an eye or something). This is young Count Hugo Schön-born from Bohemia, who began by asking if he could get in touch with Lady Iris Mountbatten! Prisoners were not at that moment having an easy time and this was an artist and not strong, so I've kept him and he is still here living with my batman Walsh and wearing battledress; he is very grateful and happy. I also have four French LOs (two counts), four Belgian LOs, two or three odd Belgian officers and 11th Hussars alone have a private Maquis army. Jimmy had a prisoner the other day who on the way back in his armoured car said very lugubriously, 'To be or not to be, that is the question.'

25 September 1944

Yesterday let Division move without me and lunched with my family. It was 'Kermesse' in the village and they had sung the *Te Deum* for victory, consequently a colossal lunch. The most inter-esting thing I learnt from this family was that though the number of collaborators was very small in Belgium and they had not all the same aims; one party was fascist but national, another for unity with Germany etc. When Belgians did muck in with the Germans they behaved more outrageously than anybody. This famous camp at Beerdonck where people were tortured was largely run by Belgians. It is very interesting; no doubt licensed brutality has an appeal to others besides Germans.

The scheme for demobilisation has come out, also extra pay. The scheme is really purely age, as most people have served throughout the war. No advantage from being abroad, though it probably aged me ten years.

An incredible document has been captured from the High Com-mand of the Wehrmacht addressed to officers. Dealing first of all with 'the false interpretation of the word surrender' it says: 'In many cases the word of the Führer alone can be given in explana-tion of the apparently senseless sacrifice involved in fighting to the last man. In such cases the company commander must ensure obedience with all the means at his disposal. Usually he will himself ensure that he reaches safety in good time.'

It goes on: 'Every member of the Wehrmacht must realise that it is of paramount importance to save the Officer Corps for the reconstruction of the Fatherland. It was the German Officer Corps which almost achieved the world domination for Germany in the first assault of 1914–1918. It was this same Officer Corps that rebuilt Germany for this second attempt at world leadership. That this second attempt might also fail was foreseen . . . our complete final victory seemed until recently so assured that we can prepare again with high spirits and in good heart for a further struggle. In order to prepare for this third unavoidable trial of strength for the leadership of the world we have need of officers. Manpower we have been able to find in quantities at all times. For this reason care must constantly be taken to maintain the Officer Corps at its present strength. Nevertheless certain company commanders must at the same time be detailed to stay with their troops and in case of necessity to sacrifice themselves as well. Examples of this sort are necessary for the maintenance of the troops' morale. Division Commanders will nominate junior officers to die the hero's death.

'Reference subversion in the ranks . . . NCOs will be instructed not to proceed openly against the leaders of groups of this kind – it is more to the point to detail a man for certain special duties in the front from which experience shows he will not return. Another method of getting rid of dangerous subversive elements and of rendering them harmless is to take the following actions: the man who has been found out is informed that his family has been bombed out. He is therefore immediately sent on leave. Officers will inform the Gestapo and/or SS. The man is then arrested on his homeward journey.'

28 September 1944

A lovely sunny day after a lot of rain. We are in a village between Veghel and Uden. On the way yesterday we passed more destroyed

British transport on the road than I have seen in France, the result of the centre line being cut by tanks. The Arnhem bridgehead has been evacuated and less than 2,000 of 1st Airborne Division returned. Churchill has said he can see the war against Germany continuing into 1945. The BBC announced that the Sherwood Rangers were the first into Germany; I am very glad. This is the end of this notebook. It has ended properly I think, because rather than just a record of the battles in Normandy it has been a record of my love for Jimmy against that background. We are friends, and the limits of our friendship are determined. I have given up all my spare time, and much time I should have spent working, on pointless visits to him, and neglected seeing many people I genuinely wanted to see, and entirely given up writing letters. I have won not so much the friendship of a self-centred boy as the conviction that we understand one another. I feel that of very few people.

1 October 1944, Brabant, Holland

I can't tell you what a wretched place Holland is. All those chaps skating and old brick houses are a myth. It's quite cold enough here, they could skate if they wanted to. This is Brabant, perhaps it is better elsewhere. It is all astonishingly new. There are pine woods, about 20 years old, and poplar-lined tracks, all young trees, and in the villages every house is 20th-century and every church owes its inspiration to the genius of Kelham Hall [Nottinghamshire]. The people who went first into Eindhoven say that they did get a very great reception and it was very funny to see stolid unsmiling Dutchmen wearing paper hats and waving little flags. However, they are friendly and I am sitting in the front room of a cottage where I have my bed and the people, though speaking no known language, are very nice.

You ask about politics. Back in Normandy one saw few French people, only dazed peasants, and then as we rushed up north the Germans had been there the day before, and again one saw only the farm people and they hardly knew what was going on. In Belgium they were all too excited. Life in Brussels was pre-war with night clubs and champagne and no one was bothering much; the King seems very popular, the Queen Mother less being a German and the King's wife not at all, merely for being so. His brother, who is regent, is also very popular. The resistance in Belgium was better organised by far than in any part of France we were in, and here it is better still.

14 October 1944, Brabant

I went to lunch with the Regiment yesterday and was taken into Germany. We drove through beech woods and oak scrub and bracken all turning colour, particularly the oaks which must be Turkey oaks and were a brilliant scarlet, and came to a village with some rather nice white houses with green shutters on a hillside, and at the end of the village street some wire, a derelict tram and a sentry box. On the other side the first house flew a white flag. The Americans were at the barrier and when I began walking down the road there were shouts of 'Captain, Captain', and we were told no one was allowed down it except at night. So we don't seem to own very much of Germany in this part. I think my liking the Germans is pure prejudice as one practically never sees a nice one nowadays. The furthest my ideas for Germany have got is that it is absurd to talk of world union and at the same time of splitting Germany up.

30 October 1944, Tilburg

It was a great shock to me to hear about Uncle William and it must have been to you. It is very sad in every way.

We are in a small park in the middle of Tilburg, quite a big town which I haven't explored, but I don't think it's wildly interesting. Martin and I have done ourselves very well and got into a house overlooking the park. The people I am staying with are mad on

301

riding and have books and books of photographs showing them in top hats and her jumping very high and him very low jumps. They are awfully nice. If it was decent weather I would go riding with them. Funnily enough, I often long to ride. The Germans took all horses and all fodder; he hid two horses and had to steal from his own fodder when they were asleep! He is a big wool chap, wool and shoes seem to be the things here.

Yesterday I took my hostess out in the jeep to find milk and butter and on to see Jimmy and came upon Richard Wingfield-Digby looking rather unshaved by the side of the road, and he told me the Germans were 800 yards further on. I told my hostess she was now within seven kilometres of the enemy and she was very impressed, and we withdrew. You forget that Hildyard stands for one of a noble and generous disposition.

11 November 1944, Tilburg

'Taken off a German' means the troops who first lay hands on a prisoner take his watch and money but sometimes overlook his fountain pen which is pinched by the G3(I). There is a lot of loot to be got off prisoners and most just I think goes not to the fighting soldiers but to the wholly undeserving guards. It got so bad I made a row because they used to strip them of all the papers I wanted, and marked maps. I practically never search a prisoner but your pen came off an officer who did arrive once direct to me.

I run the interpreters branch and it is quite a job, under that heading we have French Maquis we picked up from Normandy onwards, Belgian White Brigade and friendly disposed persons, Dutch ditto, Dutch from the Dutch Brigade borrowed by me and some official ones as well. All unofficial ones are strictly forbidden and the problem is how to pay them as labourers and how to make them official without disclosing that we have them or that they are of conscription age etc. Also no one ever tells me when they get a new one and I am always discovering new ones. One pet the other day was recognised by the Bishop of Breda as a German sailor.

Hugo Schönborn, the artist, really is the prize; and Enoch, the Armenian guitar player who speaks no word of any known language and can't play either – he was also a prisoner I thought rather an asset.

I am sending de Courcy a very long letter to forward from Hugo to his Imperial Highness the Count Wamberg, Archduke Max. He has been about three weeks writing it and an English translation on which I insisted and I supposed he was asking the Archduke, whom he scarcely knows and who must be fairly old, to get in touch with his wife or something. Not at all, it is purely an expression of loyalty in wonderful courtly language and a history of his life. He has done another picture of me, better-looking but equally unrecognisable. He never gets past the first sitting as then I put him off for another month.

4 December 1944, Tilburg

Since I last wrote I have had a night in Brussels, staying with Bobbie [General] Erskine who is Chef de Mission. Jimmy and I drove down and he couldn't get permission for the night, so I was going back with him the same evening but Bobbie Erskine pressed me so hard to stay that I did and enjoyed it enormously. He is doing extremely well I think. I don't suppose he understands half of the ins and outs but he is firm and good tempered and the Belgians think a lot of him. While Belgium is a military zone and he is Eisenhower's representative, he and not the ambassador represents the Allies and he is a very big chap.

Things are not too good in Holland; as you know probably, they are about starving in Eindhoven. Unfortunately not us but the Dutch government in London promised chocolate and cigarettes with liberation and in fact they don't get bread. It is a supply problem, though I don't think we are being very sensible in not explaining the difficulties to the people. Apparently whatever the soldiers were prepared for, the Dutch government and civil affairs planned on a complete evacuation of Holland and getting Antwerp

303

and Rotterdam. These free governments seem to be hopeless pushes, and very unpopular always. Because it is a supply problem you get parts of Belgium and Holland where there is plenty of food and we have a place I sometimes dine with Jimmy where you get eggs anytime, steaks, chickens, better etc, all black market of course. But Brabant anyway is not self-supporting. It gets shelled at a quarter to six every evening and last time they hit the projector in the cinema next door and killed the operator which annoyed everybody. You will say this is most dangerous, but I go at least ten miles nearer Jerry to get there!

I gather about 70 of the SRY [Sherwood Rangers Yeomanry] are going home under the five-year scheme and it'll mean a good deal of work for Myrtie looking after them. Monty was here the other day and leave to England is starting on 1st January. I am not at all sure I *want* to come back to England. What one would like, of course, would be plenty of leave. But it would be frightfully depressing in England unless I got a good job and the only thing I'd call a good job would be one in London and I don't suppose that's so easy. When I was staying with Bobbie Erskine he told me of a brigadier in another division who had committed suicide and he added that it didn't surprise him in the least, he was a man who had no friends and war was intolerable without them – which showed insight for a major-general and is true. To come back in the normal way under this five-year plan and go to Catterick or some training camp would be frightful.

20 December 1944, Tilburg

I added in my last note that I was just off to Paris (contrary to your advice). Toby's colonel came in that day and said why on earth not go, and I was getting bored waiting for battles which never came off, so I asked permission on the spot. Generally speaking, leave is only 48 hours and more than that counts against January leave, but I got three nights and four days and a chit saying I was on duty. Michael Pitt-Rivers gave me a note to the PA to the British general in Paris which turned out to be invaluable. Toby Horsford collected me early next morning in a staff car and we got off before it was properly light. It poured with rain the whole way and Toby drove as usual very fast and I read the maps with my normal inefficiency, passing through Soissons, when I was aiming for St Quentin. Early on we kept skidding and Toby said with great emphasis, 'The one thing I can't stand is a pile up'! We were then attempting to regain the main road down the Meuse to Liège, which I'd lost, and an American truck pulled out right in front of us and we found ourselves in the ditch. We had to get a breakdown to pull us out.

In the open fields of the Somme teams of six oxen and four horses were hauling carts across the fields; it seems to get more and more countrified as you approach Paris. We were there by four o'clock, having taken eight hours, and that was good as it gave us time to find the Faubourg St Honoré in the light and there Michael's friend Sandy Hope got us official duty cards. That took us into the hotel for officers working in Paris below the rank of lieutenant colonel. We went to dinner with Sandy Hope who shared with a friend a magnificent flat in Passy. After dinner Toby went to see a girl who had been a great passion six years ago in the Haute Savoie. Sandy took me to a night club he had started called the '44' which is very good indeed.

Toby and I went next day to lunch at Maxim's and were surprised to find it was a club, however the secretary having assured himself we were bon ton, made us members. Maxim's was collaborationist and it has been ordered to carry on, and bear any loss, all profits to the Red X! The food was incredibly good, we had oysters, and the drink was perfect too. We went shopping with Toby's girl, everything was staggeringly expensive – a pullover £10, books worth 30/- about £6. Toby's girl, Mihri, had a dinner party in her house for us that night and we went dancing at the '44' till it shut, but I'm afraid I never spoke a word of French the whole time I was in Paris.

The Germans have been sending us a lot of leaflets including a very nice Christmas card which says, 'We thought you'd be home for Christmas, cheer up, console yourself with Jerry – he wishes you

305

a very merry Christmas and the best of luck in the New Year', all very gay in blue and silver. [This was the Ardennes offensive.]

22 January 1945, Tilburg

I have been really frightfully busy. It thawed and then we had heavy snow and two days of sunshine so that everything is muffled and sparkling. But I can't enjoy it much. This is to tell you that I have settled for 14th February for my leave. And also the great news that we are now all getting the five-year plan in one month so I shall certainly take it in the spring, by which time the Russians should be in Berlin anyway. Our battle has gone very well.

This is hardly a letter, but we move tomorrow. All the towns in front have been well liberated and are cold, roofless, windowless and lightless and I am less likely to write than ever. Tell Toby about 14th February, it is not so incredible to me actually, I don't feel it is so very long since I saw him.

1 March 1945, Schleswig-Holstein: Letter to Toby

My journey back went like clockwork. This in comparison with Jimmy who took eight days to get back, carrying a case of gin. After three days at Gravesend he forced himself on to a boat, was thought to be a deserter and marched off under close arrest by six coppers.

Nothing to do at all here and I have no intention of being around very much. I could certainly have stayed much longer in England, but I still think it is best to aim at April/May for my month, because I think we shall force the Rhine and the Germans will collapse quite soon, or that's how it looks at the moment. It was wonderful being with you. As I expected I did not feel that it was very long since I had seen you and I hope you didn't find me too much changed either.

I found Toby Horsford just departing in an ambulance for hospital and half dead of bronchitis, with pneumonia probably to follow, after goose-shooting by moonlight. You wear enormous waders to collect the birds off flood water, but as you can't see the canals you fall in. Their skiing was a great success, in Paris they were asked to take with them a Frenchman who looked like a tramp and was bundled in the back with the petrol and immediately got tight, he turned out however to be about the richest man in France and arranged everything for them including three women from Lyons!

So far I have managed to spend most of my time away from this rather dismal village and have been enjoying myself very much. The battles here in which we take so far only a very distant interest have gone as you can see wonderfully well and it is hard to see how the Germans will be able to defend the Rhine. However, we shall see. I gather I shall be able to take my three weeks whenever the situation here is suitable, so it depends on the Moffer, as they call the Germans locally.

24 March 1945, Schleswig-Holstein

I have never known such weather. I drove down to Brussels Friday afternoon a week ago in the pouring rain in order to give a lecture at the divisional school the next morning. Next day the sun shone and since then we have had day after day of unbelievable weather. An hour ago the gliders went over to join in the crossing of the Rhine which started last night. It sounded quite fantastic, but without the air-drop the operation would have had to be postponed (and there was always the danger the weather would change between last night when the first infantry crossed and this morning when the paratroops were dropped).

Jimmy has been offered a partnership in a good Edinburgh firm of solicitors, he has no money and wants to marry. How awful to be Major Ashwell, but do you think I should *ever* make £1,000 a year any other way? It sounds quite ludicrous to me but I realise I must grow up and be practical. [I became Honorary Secretary to the Territorial Army in Nottingham. Major Ashwell was my predecessor.]

307

Toby and I spent one night in Brussels. You are forbidden now to eat in a restaurant, but risked it; we had lobster omelette and chicken. After that we wanted to go to a nightclub and found that they all closed at eleven or even earlier and only after searching found a very moderate sort of place. Toby produced both girls, both married. I did well out of mine as I admired a picture on the wall in her house and she said 'take it', so I did. She also produced the first pink champagne I've ever drunk. [Toby came hurtling back saying he had to jump out of the window of his girl's house, her husband came back.]

Later

The battle has gone well [of the Rhine – a great failure]. We have to wait for a bridge for the tanks, there is no security so you should hear what we are doing by name. John Verney is here, we met by chance at Army where I went to a conference which began with the words, 'This is the last planned operation Second Army will make' and ended with a lunch where I talked at length with our host the head 'I' about whether to stay in Germany till one gets out of the army. John and his colonel then came and stayed the night, decided they wanted to fight with us and the General asked Monty for them next day.

Good Friday, 30 March 1945, Schleswig-Holstein: Letter to Toby

I am by the outer of two moats round a small brick house on a mound where once there must have been some kind of castle. Inside nothing worth looting except the old deeds which I have taken to safeguard them. The family were turned out, leaving food on the table. Everything has gone splendidly really and will I hope go even better. We haven't met many enemy. The day before yesterday I went to see a Brigade IO and was told he was up at a battalion so I went to find him. He wasn't there; there were some prisoners and quite a lot of shelling, so after talking to the prisoners I came home. He arrived at the battalion afterwards, and was killed by a direct hit. The same day, the troop that Jimmy gave up to become IO of his regiment went up a track, after being told by a civilian it was clear, and ran into an assault gun which wrote off the whole troop and killed their officer. Yesterday I went to see the leading squadron and the road up was under observation from an assault gun which hit a house across the road, and frightened me; otherwise little excitement, no shelling and no bombing rear of the fighting.

I got a new Jeep without a hood and it is nice like that. I stand up and whizz past all the ghastly traffic blocks looking frightfully busy and important, but I've now swapped it for a Dingo and wish at moments I hadn't. I am wearing a very smart Volksturm armband. We had Graf von Schlieffen in here last night but he wasn't a very attractive Graf so we kicked him out again; his grandpa organised the Schlieffen Line and Plan. It is nicer country than Holland – just after the Rhine there was a forest, and I noticed what I never noticed before, beech seedlings three inches high with the nut still intact at the top. It has the leaves in it and sends down a stalk and root.

I go up and see Jimmy every afternoon, he is really quite useless as an IO and my armoured brigade IO was killed almost the first day, so I have to do most of the work myself. However, it has gone well enough. It is a big job on the roads as they are jammed with traffic, the villages on them are worse almost than anything in Normandy.

Martin says that the Kindergarten here has posters decorating the walls showing bands of little Nordic infants giving the what-for to little Jews – making them run the gauntlet and pouring hot water down their trousers. Also a moral story of a handsome blond who marries a little Jewess and they are happy till baby comes, but baby has long greasy ringlets and a hooked nose and all the other children give it hell.

I have been mentioned in despatches for the period 6 June to 31 July 1944. I can't wear two oak leaves though, so it's not much use.

309

5 April 1945, Schleswig-Holstein

It is simply pouring, and today we have crossed lovely country and soon we shall be out of it again, on the North German plain which sounds deadly. This is the Teutoburger Wald and hills of Hanover. Their southern side is a wooded cliff, where we had a lot of trouble from over 2,000 officer cadets from Hanover who fought extremely hard, although they arrived under the impression they were on an exercise. Every time we think we have destroyed the German army something like this turns up.

8 April 1945, South of Bremen

I have just been for a walk through a little wood where white anemones made a show just like snowdrops, and came to a building absolutely surrounded by people – Germans looting a small factory of bicycle tyres and clothes. I told them I would shoot anyone who was there in ten minutes and they faded out. There is supposed to be a curfew all day except two hours for civilians but military government is as inefficient as ever. In general, however, the curfew does work and you see no one about except for the liberated workers – Poles, Yugoslavs, French and Russians in long peacock green overcoats and maroon-banded hats who salute all along the road. They wander about aimlessly but apparently happily and they don't loot, therefore we presume that they are reasonably well treated. The army loots. So far as food goes anyway it is splendid. Hugo my count is back. He was a success in hospital lecturing on modern art and has been most useful today, first frying me potatoes and onions and now producing a cooked duck's egg.

I don't think I've had many excitements though – the German populace is incredibly servile so far, often I drive miles and miles with no one else on the road and think how in almost any country one would expect to be murdered, one practically never hears of a sniper, every house flies a white flag. As you can see things are going very well and on the face of it there seems no reason why we shouldn't go straight on to the Elbe and finish off our part of things in no time at all. All the same I don't think the well informed expect the victory march before June. My original idea was to come back on leave at the end of this month and I think that might still be possible – the trouble is that no one ever knows how long a quiet period will last. Personally I really can't see why the whole thing can't be finished this month but I suppose supplies etc.

11 April 1945, South of Bremen: Letter to Toby

My ACV tinkles like a bell as it goes along with bottles of hock and liqueurs. We get 40 marks to the pound (50,000 in Switzerland, I see) and I got a few this morning for the parcel. Otherwise I see no reason why we should ever spend a sov. Everybody is after loot, the gentry for Mercedes Benz, shotguns and drink, the chaps for anything they can lay their hands on.

I am very well. Intelligence is not so easy as it was when we cleared up to the river – when I sat in a room with a telephone to Corps and a telephone to each brigade and never stirred and there were just two or three divisions on the front which one soon knew backwards. Nowadays Corps is 100 miles behind and I spend hours catching up with Brigades and there are no German divisions, only battle groups of the oddest chaps. They fight all right but they can't form a line, while the overrun populace shows no sign of hostility so far and in the village yesterday when the Volksturm was called out, they popped him in the cooler and handed him over when we arrived. That, though, is an exception; in general they carry on with their farming, which does very nicely thank you judging by the local larders and the stock around.

27 April 1945, Schleswig-Holstein

Monty has been here, pinning on medals in the rain. The Germans didn't really try to fight in Bremen. 'This is the way the world ends, not with a bang but a whimper.' This is the moment when in old-fashioned wars the Allies start double-crossing one another, which is interesting with Joe and ourselves about equidistant from Kiel.

We had a German officer in who left Stettin three days ago under the impression Germany and England were now allies. He came to take over a battalion here, searched everywhere for it and only found us. Another very nice one, aged 21, got within 80 miles of Cairo three years ago and ran out of petrol. He was mad to join us against Joe, mainly because they almost killed him once dressed up as Germans. Asked if he knew the Germans did the same in the Ardennes he said, 'Oh yes.' He said all good Germans would fight to the death but unfortunately there are very few good Germans.

The Surrender of Hamburg

On 29 April three envoys came into our lines to inform us that the Phoenix Rubber Factory was being turned into a hospital and to negotiate for its immunity from attack. The party included the owner of the factory, an MO and an interpreter from the Staff of Major-General Wolz, Commander of Hamburg. The question of the possible surrender was raised, and it appeared likely to be considered.

The next day the envoys were sent back with the following letter from the Commander 7 British Armoured Division, translated into German by Hugo Schönborn.

To: Major-General Wolz Kampfkommandant, Hamburg

Herr General:

1. The Reichsführer SS has already made an offer of unconditional surrender to the Western powers. This offer was made through Count Bernadotte in Stockholm.

2. Before attacking Bremen we demanded the surrender of the city. As this offer was refused, we had no alternative but to attack

with artillery and air support. Bremen fell in 24 hours, but not without much unnecessary bloodshed

3. In the name of Humanity, Herr General, we demand the surrender of Hamburg. For you as a soldier there can be no dishonour in following the example of famous German Generals such as Gen d Pz Tr Josef Harpe GOC 5 Pz Army, Genlt Fritz Bayerlein GOC LIII Corps and many others who have surrendered themselves and their Comds. From the political point of view, there can surely be no reflection on you if you follow the example of the Reichsführer SS.

4. We therefore ask you, Herr General, to send into our lines an officer empowered to negotiate the surrender. Our forward troops have been warned to expect his arrival and not to shoot at him. He will be treated according to the Geneva Convention, and returned after the parley to his own lines.

5. The population of Hamburg will not easily forget its first large-scale raid by over 1,000 high bombers. We now have at our disposal a bomber force 5–10 times greater numerically, and operating from nearby airfields. After the war, the German people must be fed: the more Hamburg's dock installations are damaged, the greater are the chances of famine in Germany.

6. If this offer is refused, we shall have no alternative but to attack Hamburg with all the forces at our disposal.

The following morning we returned to their own lines the remaining two officers of this delegation with a verbal warning that we were quite prepared to sit round Hamburg, bomb it and let the Russians do the assault. At this Herr Prof Stabsarzt and Ritter von Laun burst into tears. The two officers walked off towards Hamburg, there was a loud bang and a patrol later found they had set off a trip mine and Schumines. That night General Wolz sent his senior staff officer with the following reply to our letter:

1 May 1945, Hamburg: to Major-General Lo Lyne, Commander of the Allied Troops

Herr General:

The thoughts for which you have found so lucid an expression in your letter of 29 April 1945 have been considered by myself and by countless other responsible Commanders: not unnaturally, considering the present military and political situation.

The eventual surrender of Hamburg would have far-reaching military and political consequences for the whole of the part of northern Germany that is not yet occupied, and for Denmark. For this reason, the orders given to me to hold Hamburg to the last man can be seen to have a clear justification. But in spite of this I am prepared, together with an authorised representative of Reichsstatthalter and Gauleiter Kaufmann, to discuss with a representative empowered by GOC Second British Army to make decisions on military and political matters, the eventual surrender of Hamburg and the far-reaching consequences arising therefrom.

May I ask you to inform GOC Second British Army of these proposals and to request that a time and place for discussion be fixed.

Wolz
Major-General

It was understood that General Wolz was negotiating on his own authority and indeed against the direct orders to defend the town. His staff officer was returned to him with the message that GOC 7 Armd Div. would see General Wolz the following night if General Wolz came to offer unconditional surrender.

Late in the night of 2 May General Wolz arrived in person. His opening words were: 'The principal point is the actual time General Lyne wishes to enter Hamburg.' During the day General Wolz had been ordered by General Keitel on the telephone to surrender, on the orders of Admiral Dönitz. Further he was informed that a delegation of generals and admirals from OKW would be arriving early next morning to see the Army Group Commander.

General Wolz showed himself most anxious we make our take-over of Hamburg as easy as possible. All officials would remain at their posts until replaced. There would be no demolitions, all SS troops had already marched away. It was agreed that we should cross the FDLs at 1300 hours 3 May.

In fact, on account of technical delays, our troops crossed the city frontier at 1700 hours.

5 May 1945, Hamburg

Well, our delegations did their job. The party from OKW arrived next day and I hurried round with cigarettes taking snaps which I hope come out. The leader was a general-admiral, Dönitz's first Sea Lord, and there was a wonderful general, Chief of Staff to the C-in-C, with a monocle and wide scarlet lapels to his overcoat. They all bristled with diamond crosses and Hollywood could never have produced their arrogant young staff officers.

Hamburg was quite extraordinary. It is mostly very damaged or in complete ruins, but round the huge lake in the centre there are palatial private houses undamaged. All the civilians were ordered to stay in and did so. There were no white flags, but the Town Hall and main hotel were crowded with busy staff officers, half of them German, all being Junkers together. I took over the Wehrkreis HQ, full of staff officers controlling in theory north-west Germany, and German generals and admirals drove around getting different orders from everyone they saw and it was all very confusing and I'm glad we left.

9 May 1945, Hamburg

VE day was the most heavenly day imaginable. The sort of day really for lying in the sun and looking up into a tree. I spent it in fact driving 100 miles to see Jimmy in hospital. [He had fallen downstairs.] He has a crack three inches in his skull so it's not surprising he's had bad headaches. I hope very much it will get him back to England.

Toby [Horsford] had a wonderful bonfire that night. He had all the villagers building it all day, from road-blocks timber and small stuff on top, about 20 feet high and the Nazi flag flying on top. The Colonel lit it, there was a four-piece band, rum punch, two batteries of verey-lights firing continuously and a great deal of odd firing, the Colonel was carried around and everybody made speeches and got very drunk. We were a bit windy about setting fire to the nearest farm but everything passed off all right, till at five o'clock this morning the farm's huge thatched roof burst into flames. It was directly opposite our house and we ran out in our pyjamas. It was a furnace in no time.

I was on leave from 16 May until 3 August 1945.

No date, soon after 4 August 1945, Berlin: Letter to Toby

I am glad you liked Jimmy. He tells me he tried to impress you he was clever and failed. He was not a success at Flintham – he is extremely shy, completely self-centred, and made no effort to be one. If we continue to be friends and he comes more often they will like him all right. It is stupid of them to be anti him. Apart from yourself he is the person I am most fond of. We have been friends for two years and though I am frequently infuriated because he gives so little in return, we shall probably continue to be friends. It depends entirely on myself. So far as he is capable of liking other men Jimmy is fond of me, but would never make any effort about it. I think he is very good for me. He is entirely un-homosexual (whatever Robin may think) and if I am physically fond of him, that is as far as it goes, except that it is excellent for me to practise self-control. I continually practise it, because by nature I like people extremely and am very easily sick of them.

Jimmy and I promised one another last year to be brothers. I should have told you before, but I can't make out whether that form

316

of words has any meaning or not. There are, after all, various relationships between brothers. However good a person Jimmy may be he is not the ideal friend, but I feel moderately certain this doesn't matter, that we have a permanent relationship, which is the advantage of brothers.

I am saying all this because I like arranging things in my own mind and do it best on paper, and also because it is a good thing you should always know what I am feeling and caring about. The obvious question is why I should have chosen as a great friend someone who is not capable of great friendship. The answer is that really very few men are capable of great friendship among themselves, that their friendship rests on a community of interests, not emotions. Particularly during the war I have made friends with people like Michael [Parish], and Toby [Horsford], who are wonderfully cheering because they are alive and enthusiastic and like one's company. Even before the war when I appreciated someone like Michael Mosley, I found it easier to live on the surplus energy of someone like Robin [Maugham]. But that is not really liking people. Jimmy doesn't help my vanity or take me out of myself. But I really like him. He is young and self-centred and remote and unhappy about himself, but he is extremely intelligent, critical, sincere, and not self-seeking. It is the first time I have liked anyone without being certain they liked me, or really tried to understand anyone.

Martin, Toby and I went to a so-called cabaret the other evening, actually a sort of show, a stage and rows of seats and incredibly bad. The other two walked out, I stayed and talked to a German boy next me who had been two years in a royal Tiger battalion in Italy and walked back over the Dolomites. I had him to lunch yesterday. It is extraordinary how serious Germans are; he is 20 and would like to be at the university studying either anatomy or forestry, only the university like everything else is burnt down. I would rather like to attach him as an interpreter or something, but at the same time dependants are a ghastly bore and foreigners much worse. On the other hand after an hour with him I speak German without thinking. It would be perfectly easy to live here three months and never speak to a German except for the slaves in the mess. I would definitely like to feel I knew what was going on in Berlin, but fraternisation doesn't allow anything indoors as far as I can make out, officially, and it isn't smiled on at all. The men walk about with girls but except for a few like Jimmy who visit actresses the officers don't at all.

Jimmy went very drunk the other night and slept on too late to join his party back in the morning, so he stayed till afternoon in a flat and was invited in on the family meal. It was the only meal of the day and consisted of a cube of brown bread about three inches across and some syrup. The food position is apparently extremely bad and distressing. There are no fats available in the world and no prospect of providing the Germans with sufficient nutrition this winter – you cannot live, they say, on bread, potatoes etc, without fats. They will therefore die. I hope they will tell them that the reason they get nothing is that the surrounding countries are now using their own supplies and that Germany depended on starving every country before herself and chose to have her country fought over and stocks destroyed – i.e. that we are not doing it on purpose, but it is a terrible thing.

11 August 1945, Berlin

The position seems to be that no one meets any Germans but prostitutes and black marketeers. The Berliners live largely on barter; there are little notices offering exchanges pinned up along the main streets and there is a huge crowd always outside the Reichstag. It is forbidden to us and I haven't investigated it yet. It is rather annoying to hear of the fortunes people make though. Someone picked up an American the other day who said he had sent home $8,000 from Berlin. His activities that day had been to go to the Reichstag, be offered a Leica for a kilo of butter, drive 20 kilometres to his unit and get the butter off a mess corporal for 100 dollars, drive back and fail to find the Leica man but sell the butter for 500 dollars. Although what the Germans want from us is food and cigarettes, and what we want I suppose is money, cameras or jewellery, a German recently offered a British soldier 400 cigarettes for his wristwatch. Wristwatches are the only thing we can legitimately sell and you can get £75 for one any day from the Russians so long as it ticks. The Russians were handed pay for the last two years in Berlin and will pay anything. When we took over the British zone here we had naturally a lot to do with the Russians, but apart from the General, none of us are having anything to do with them now. I gather that contact with them has been a very considerable eye-opener to the troops, who took over barracks in an absolutely undesirable condition. Everybody says the Russians are very nice but just completely different in their standards to ourselves. The Russians one sees look extremely scruffy. It is amusing and interesting that their only criticism of ourselves has been that they don't like our battledress because there is insufficient distinction between officers and men, and that our officers are too familiar with the soldiers.

I see Micky Riviere is engaged. Toby Horsford's [engagement to Elizabeth, Michael Parish's sister] should be out soon, after a stormy passage through famille Horsford. If anybody had a right to crib I should have said it was Clem Parish. However, when the two fathers met for lunch it was Toby's who said that Toby was an unsuitable person for a nice girl to marry! Toby had eleven letters yesterday from Elizabeth, six I noticed written on the same day. He sits up all night writing back which makes staying with him quite intolerable. Otherwise I might have stayed much longer with 11th Hussars when I arrived in Berlin.

My own mess is directly opposite the house I have settled in. It is a sort of suburban street on the edge of the Grunewald with new villas of which more than half are utterly destroyed. I still cannot understand how it happened, as it is difficult to destroy scattered houses. The making habitable of houses I should think is impossible before the winter. Schools etc must come first and it is doubtful whether they will be done as there is a very great shortage of labour and materials. The position is that in the centre of the town 80 per cent of the houses are uninhabitable and in the suburbs 30 to 40 per

319

cent. The population is about 3,000,000 and increasing daily. In our zone there are about a million, and about 100,000 houses; of these 29,000 are beyond repair, 21,000 need major repairs and 20,000 minor repairs. The good houses are of course frequently seized by us as more and more HQs come in – the Control Commission whose function is mysterious is only just arriving and is said to be larger than all the troops at present in Berlin. There can be little incentive for a German to make his house watertight. They are also turned out to make room for Jews and persons released from concentration camps. Factories and things cannot work because the Russians removed all the machinery. The prevalent view is not that the Russians are deliberately setting out to prevent reconstruction but that the damage they did when they first arrived and what the Germans regard as their destructive habits and lack of discipline will nullify their declared policy. And at the same time those who however feebly and impractically do genuinely hope and occasionally work for a restoration of democracy in Germany feel that the system set up by the Russians is as little democratic as the system they overthrew.

5 September 1945, Berlin

We have been having days of the most perfect weather. Yesterday Toby and I went on a photographing tour of Berlin, clambering over ruins to take derelict guns and tanks silhouetted against Germany's most famous buildings. I not only have a camera but one the same as the one I lost, or almost, and am delighted to have it again. It was bought most shadily from a woman living in a wooden hut on an allotment by the lakes, mainly with poor Jimmy's cigarettes, he now hasn't a thing to smoke. He is going to England about the time I leave Berlin for an interview for the Sudan Civil. I hope it will come to nothing and he is beginning to learn French with the idea of going into the Diplomatic. Sounds funny to learn it from a German but it is really more sensible than starting absolutely from scratch on German.

I went to *Fidelio* last Sunday, very late by myself and got packed in the gallery. To my surprise I enjoyed it quite a lot. I didn't understand much but there were some lines about Freiheit which I hope struck home to the citizens the other days of the week. Earlier I went to the Russian film *Berlin* in order to see whether they did fight in the town or merely blew it up. It appears they fought, they scrambled very nimbly over ruins, fired large guns incessantly at point-blank range into buildings and fought in tanks, it was a little difficult to see against what. There were some quite good shots, of crowds saluting Hitler and their outstretched arms switching to the hungry clutching for Russian bread. The commentary, in German, did not give much of a hand of Great Britain and America.

6 September 1945, Berlin: Letter to Toby

We've been having wonderful weather lately which would make life pleasant anywhere, otherwise I don't think you'll miss much by not seeing Berlin. I was a good deal relieved by what you said about Chou, because Elizabeth reported to Toby that you were het up and miserable about her and I feared that having found no one else very exciting you were starting up again. I should say one's friendships are always temporary, the best one can find at the time, if I found friends so easily. But in fact I think what is true for most people is not true for me. I do not enjoy the company of people I like moderately unless they are exceptionally amusing, because as I've discovered over and over again ordinary nice people bore me in almost all circumstances; I have to like them very much. I don't think I do get bored with people I have liked, as you say you do. The trouble for me is that I react so seldom and that I am spoilt and want so much from people. Consequently I am always in danger of being lonely and bored. Which is why I love Flintham, where I am happy alone. But I am sure the only answer is to get married.

We leave Berlin in a week, and as 11th Hussars stay here and Jimmy is group 40 that is the end for the time being of our seeing much of one another. It has been of quite enormous value to me, and undone the harm which Hugh [Chisholm] and then the war did to me. That affair made me think life was emotion, I was thoroughly dejected afterwards and then with the war thought I'd made the great discovery that life was success and ambition. It certainly isn't for me. I am only happy through other people.

Jimmy has been the best possible teacher, for wartime, that love isn't all emotion, that one must think of other people, and lots of other things which I expect most people are born knowing. Jimmy was a lucky choice, he is intensely interested in himself and so helps one to get to know him, he is unemotional but not shocked at other people's feelings, he is moody and unsure of himself and seldom amused and lazy, so it is easy to be useful to him. (What you call vulnerable? He is not touchy, like me.) He is intelligent and likes to talk of abstract things. He is astonished that I like him so much and have not got bored with him. Finally he is extraordinarily honest and candid, ungrasping, humble and anxious to find truth, and he is frequently gay, foolish and drunk. I hope you will like him, since I like him so much more than the other people we know in common. His only criticism of you – or two – was that he thought you didn't like *him*, secondly you were very serious! I think Robin [Maugham] is mad about this seducing business, he is still under a banshee from me for doing it to Jimmy when he was drunk. Considering we are old friends he couldn't have done anything more likely to antagonise me, which seems unnecessary.

We had a holiday for VJ day, but as every day is a holiday for me I didn't notice it and we were never quite sure which day it was. I'm afraid it passed over our heads.

16 September 1945, Itzehoe: Letter to Toby

We are in Schleswig-Holstein and it is raining and really if I was staying here it would be terrible but my parachute is securely in place. I have arranged to be back in England for Toby and Elizabeth's wedding on 3rd October but now there is an invitation to a party in Nottingham on 29th September for the chaps who were captured in Crete and I feel I should go to that. I think I have organised myself very well, to leave here for good in ten days, come to England over my interview for this secretaryship which will be 9th or 11th October, possibly stay over Stephen Mitchell's wedding on 17th October – but probably not, and return to the SRY. I am demobilised sometime after 10th November and while I am with my regiment I shall go to Berlin and try to see Jimmy off to Vienna and look round there.

Daddy doesn't think I shall get this secretaryship and I haven't really very good qualifications. I hoped to hold it for a year and have the strength of mind to chuck it before I had to sign on for five years. If I don't, I think I shall go to an agricultural school and see how I stick that. Do you think that's a good idea? Anyway I shall be glad to get away from this push. Itzehoe is hell anyway, little red brick villas on the edge of a small town, over an hour from Hamburg. There are some big plantations outside worth exploring, pleasant last evening when it was sunny and I found Brueghelesque scenes, burghers from the city working in the fields, women and children digging up pine-tree roots and piling them in long skeleton-like carts, boys running down hill pulling a kite with long paper streamers into the air. But back in the mess and I am glad of my parachute.

I don't think I have any news I didn't send to Flintham yesterday. I shall be seeing you extremely soon.

I did go to the Sherwood Rangers at Hanover. I worked on the Regimental History *and left in November for demobilisation. The* History *was finished by Martin Lindsay and published under his name.*

A NOTE ON THE TYPE

The text of this book is set in Linotype Sabon, named after the type founder, Jacques Sabon. It was designed by Jan Tschichold and jointly developed by Linotype, Monotype and Stempel, in response to a need for a typeface to be available in identical form for mechanical hot metal composition and hand composition using foundry type.

Tschichold based his design for Sabon roman on a font engraved by Garamond, and Sabon italic on a font by Granjon. It was first used in 1966 and has proved an enduring modern classic.